THE IRAQ WAR

THE IRAQ WAR

A MILITARY HISTORY

Williamson Murray

Robert H. Scales, Jr.

THE BELKNAP PRESS OF
HARVARD UNIVERSITY PRESS
Cambridge, Massachusetts, and London, England

2003

Library of Congress Cataloging-in-Publication Data
Murray, Williamson.
The Iraq war : a military history / Williamson Murray, Robert H. Scales, Jr.
p. cm.
Includes index.
ISBN 0-674-01280-1 (alk. paper)
1. Iraq War, 2003. 2. United States—Armed
Forces—History—20th century. I. Scales, Robert H., 1944– II. Title.

DS79.724.U6M874 2003
956.7044'24'0973.—dc22
2003056668

For Lesley Mary Smith and Diana Maria Scales
Ladies of unsurpassed beauty and intelligence

CONTENTS

PROLOGUE

The Gulf War, 1991

Battles are won by slaughter and maneuver. The greater the general, the more he contributes in maneuver, the less he demands in slaughter.

Winston Churchill, The World Crisis, 1923

Shortly before 3 a.m. on the morning of January 17, 1991, an American F-117 Nighthawk soared across the skies of the brightly lit city of Baghdad. The stealth aircraft flew too high for Iraqis below to see, and it was undetected by the probing pulses of Iraqi radars. In air defense centers throughout the country, tired technicians peered through clouds of cigarette smoke at empty radar screens. They heard nothing overhead—just the steady background hum of air conditioners. Yet they knew that twenty minutes earlier American helicopters had attacked two radar sites on the border with Saudi Arabia. Both had ceased transmitting. And twelve minutes after that, at 2:51, the Nukhayb Intercept Operations Center controlling air defense over western Iraq had also ceased activity. Surely the anticipated Coalition attack on Iraq had begun. Yet nothing appeared on their screens.

Then, at exactly 3:00, all hell broke loose over Baghdad. A violent explosion rocked the city's main communications center, housed in a structure the Americans called the AT&T building. Instantly Iraq's communications with the outside world went down. When CNN's live television feed from Baghdad died, a huge cheer went up from American planners in Riyadh: the end of the CNN feed was a sure sign that bombs from the F-117 had hit their target.

At almost the same moment, 2,000-pound laser-guided bombs from other Nighthawks hit command posts throughout Iraq. Within the next five minutes, the air force headquarters, the Air Defense Operating Center, the presidential palace, the AT&T Building (a second time), and the Salman Pak Intercept Operations Center felt the destructive force of the Coalition's coordinated air attacks. Meanwhile, Tomahawk cruise missiles launched from surface ships and submarines in the Red Sea and the Persian Gulf struck softer targets. Flying extremely low at subsonic speed, Tomahawks penetrated Baghdad's central electrical transformer stations and exploded, throwing out carbon-filament wires that shorted out systems. Instantly, the electrical grid throughout much of the country failed. Backup generators took over in air defense centers not yet under attack. Still the radar screens showed nothing.

By now the technicians were powering-up their radars, desperately searching for the invisible aircraft and ground-hugging missiles that were smashing the air defense system throughout the length and breadth of Iraq. And suddenly, there it was on the screen, the massive attack the Iraqis expected: two great formations of aircraft pointed directly at Baghdad. The first was moving into the country from the west, off carriers in the Red Sea; the second was from the south, out of bases in Saudi Arabia.

What the radar controllers could not know was that the force approaching Baghdad was not the fleet of fighter bombers they imagined. It was two large formations of aircraft carrying electronic suppression "packages." The western group consisted of three navy EA-6B Prowlers—aircraft whose mission was to jam Iraq's radar, forcing operators to run at full power. Like switching from parking lights to headlights, going to full power would illuminate radar installations for detection by the electronic intelligence gear of accompanying aircraft. Flying alongside the jammers were F/A-18 Hornets carrying HARMs (high-speed anti-radiation missiles). The HARMs could either attack predesignated targets or follow the radar signal to its source, destroying the installation. Just to make sure the air fleet looked even more like an attack force, four A-6 Intruder aircraft dropped twenty-five TALDs (tactical air-launched decoys) to fill the screens on the ground with radar returns.

In the south, twelve air force F-4G Wild Weasels, accompanied by EF-111 electronic jammers and a number of BQM-74 drones, also fired HARMs at active radar sites. All this aerial activity evoked precisely the response its planners had hoped for: Iraqi radars were now running at full power, beaming their exact location to the aircraft and missiles overhead. The navy fired forty-five HARMs at preselected surface-to-air missile and radar sites and six more at targets of opportunity. The Wild Weasels launched twenty-two HARMs at operating sites.

Meanwhile, another wave of Nighthawks, again flying unseen and undisturbed by the action below, attacked Sector and Intercept Operations Centers controlling the air defense system, other command and control centers, and leadership targets. Ten out of sixteen laser-guided bombs (LGBs) from these F-117s hit their coordinates with one-meter accuracy.

What made the situation so confusing to the Iraqis—at least to those who survived—was the fact that the first attacks had come out of an apparently empty sky, followed by a massive attack that fired missiles at radar and SAM sites rather than dropping bombs. Then later, again with no warning, LGBs started to rain down on the city. Sometime during the early morning hours of January 17, Iraq's integrated air defense system, supposedly built with the most advanced Soviet and French technologies, collapsed. Iraq would remain blind and vulnerable to Coalition air attacks for the remainder of the war.

Before bombs began to fall on Baghdad, Saddam Hussein, Iraq's self-proclaimed expert on all things military, had predicted that stealth aircraft would "be seen by a shepherd in the desert as well as by Iraqi technology, and [the Americans] will see how their stealth falls just like . . . any [other] aggressor aircraft."[1] His prediction entirely missed the mark. During Operation Desert Storm, F-117s flew approximately 1,300 sorties and scored direct hits on 1,600 high-value targets in Iraq; they executed the great bulk of Coalition strikes against targets in downtown Baghdad. No Nighthawks were lost during the war. But in the Iraq of 1991, those punished for being wrong did not include the nation's leader. Saddam issued his usual vote of confidence in his subordinates by ordering that the commanders of both the air force and the air defense system be shot.

73 EASTING

Their horses are swifter than leopards, more fierce than the evening wolves; their horsemen press proudly on. Yea, their horsemen come from afar; they shall fly like an eagle swift to devour.

HABAKKUK 1:8, seventh century BC

Forty days later, on February 26, the American ground offensive was moving through the deserts to the west and south of the Euphrates. On the northern tip of the Coalition's armored wedge was the 2nd Armored Cavalry Regiment, with its 125 M1A1 Abrams tanks in front, followed by its Bradley armored personnel carriers. The regiment was under the command of Colonel Donald Holder, one of the army's intellectuals who was also a fine muddy-boots soldier. The army had designed its cavalry regiments to move ahead of the main divisions, seeking the enemy so that the heavy divisions could destroy him. And that was precisely what the 2nd Armored Cavalry Regiment was doing as evening approached.

In command of Eagle Troop (E Troop), 2nd Squadron, was a tough young captain, H. R. McMaster. Outspoken, enthusiastic, a natural leader, the sandy-haired McMaster had only recently taken over the troop. A graduate of West Point, he would become the epitome of a soldier-scholar, earning his doctorate in history from the University of North Carolina and publishing a well-received book on the culpability of America's military leaders in bringing on the Vietnam War. But for now McMaster was a gung-ho commander who believed in leading from the front. In the run-up to the ground war, he had honed his troop—135 soldiers, equipped with nine M1A1s and thirteen Bradley scout vehicles—to the point where they were prepared to react almost instantaneously to the presence of the enemy.

From the first, McMaster made it clear that his troop was not going to shun combat but to seek it. The company's aim would be to engage the enemy aggressively and tenaciously from first contact. There would be no waiting for reinforcements. McMaster's tanks with their sabot rounds of depleted uranium were loaded and ready to fire at the enemy line. But over the course of the day a ferocious *shamal* threw everything it had at the opposing forces—rain squalls, heavy winds, and pelting sand. Only infrared sights were able to pierce the gloom. The Iraqis, who possessed few thermal sights, were blinded by the weather, and the noise of the lashing rain and impacting sand drowned out the sound of approaching vehicles.

At 4 p.m. as they passed a group of houses on their left, Eagle

Troop came under machine-gun fire from a small group of dug-in Iraqis. McMaster wheeled his giant Abrams tanks around and, with support from the Bradleys, blasted the Iraqi position. Swinging back into formation, McMaster and his troop crested an unmarked ridge line at location 73 Easting. At that moment, McMaster's gunner shouted a warning of "contact." Arrayed in front of the troop was a fully deployed Iraqi armored brigade, some tanks glowing brilliantly in U.S. thermal sights, others with less of a signature because their engines were off.

McMaster counted eight Iraqi tanks in his immediate vicinity, all dug in behind berms and waiting for the Americans to cross the ridge line and drop into their sights. But the *shamal* had obscured the presence of the Americans. Without hesitation Eagle Troop attacked: "Fire, fire sabot" was now heard again and again, as tank commanders drove their seventy-ton monsters forward at speeds of up to twenty miles per hour. Eagle Troop's nine M1A1s moved methodically through Iraq's first line of defense, firing over sixty sabot rounds with their main guns, the sabot rounds blasting their way through the berms and then through the tanks on the other side. The Bradleys trained their wire-guided antitank missiles (TOWs) and chain guns against the armored personnel carriers and tanks of the enemy. Within three minutes the Americans had broken through the front line, and the Iraqi brigade had died in its tracks. A mile beyond lay the second line, and this too Eagle Troop took on and methodically destroyed.

By 4:18 McMaster, his tanks, and the Bradleys were past the entire Iraqi brigade's position, having covered six kilometers. Behind them lay a swath of wreckage: at least thirty-nine burning tanks, their ammunition and fuel spilling out over the desert and exploding in flashes, along with forty to fifty armored personnel carriers and an equal number of trucks. Nearly 500 Iraqis lay dead or wounded on the desert floor. The entire battle had taken barely twelve minutes.

With nothing but open desert before him, McMaster now took account of his own troop and its losses: "Battle stations, give me a combat power report." To his astonishment, not one of his soldiers had been killed or wounded in the engagement. Some equipment stowed on the outside of the Abrams and Bradleys had been shot up by Iraqi fire, but all the vehicles were fully prepared to continue the fight.

At that moment Eagle Troop halted. On its flank, Ghost Troop, which had seen little fighting, reached its position along the line of 73 Easting. Over the next four to five hours both troops would come under intense attack as the Iraqis desperately attempted to prevent the 2nd Armored Cavalry Regiment from cutting off their escape. Badly led, with no ability to fight as a team and now vulnerable to air attack as the intensity of the wind and rain decreased, the Iraqis died by the hundreds, if not thousands. The ground traversed by the American cavalrymen had become a vast killing zone. Nearly 150 Iraqi tanks had been lost in this action alone. Altogether, the 2nd Armored Cavalry Regiment's tanks and armored personnel carriers fired over 300 sabot rounds and TOW missiles. One entire brigade of the Republican Guard's Tawalkana Division and much of Iraq's 12th Armored Division died during that disastrous battle.

TACTICAL VICTORY, OPERATIONAL FAILURE

Kind-hearted people might of course think there was some ingenious way to disarm or defeat an enemy without too much bloodshed, and might imagine this is the true goal of the art of war. Pleasant as it sounds, it is a fallacy that must be exposed: war is such a dangerous business that the mistakes which come from kindness are the very worst.

CARL VON CLAUSEWITZ, *On War,* nineteenth century

These two clashes of arms—the air attack on Baghdad and the ground offensive in the desert—have, together, become a metaphor for the overwhelming American triumph in the 1991 Gulf conflict. It was a triumph built not only on the superiority of American technology but on military organizations that trained long and hard at the business of war. By contrast, their opponents neither trained hard nor prepared themselves intellectually for the harshness of the battlefield. Yet, as an early history of that conflict proclaimed, it was, for the Coalition, a "triumph without victory." When the shooting ended, Saddam Hussein's regime, one of the most vicious tyrannies of modern times, remained in power. And his survival allowed him eventually to claim to his own people and to the rest of the Arab world that Iraq, not the United States, had won the war. In societies where reality is often incomprehensible, such claims reverberated as the truth.

Meanwhile, Americans across the political spectrum were astonished at how little the war had cost and how decisive their victory appeared. President George Herbert Walker Bush even went so far as to suggest that America and its military could now put the dark memory of Vietnam behind them. Yet in retrospect, no matter how impressive the battlefield victories might have appeared, for a variety of reasons the United States failed to win the peace.

Perhaps the most important reason was the inability of the American military, U.S. intelligence organizations, and the nation's political leadership to understand the nature of the regime they confronted. From the first, American leaders calculated that Iraq possessed a first-rate military, "battle-hardened," according to "experts," by the war the Iraqis had waged against Iran for eight long and terrible years, beginning in 1980. Most strategists calculated that Saddam's dictatorship itself was the weak link in Iraq's defense. Decapitate the military, they said, and the political regime will quickly collapse.

Such estimates were sadly wrong. There was nothing effective or efficient about the Iraqi military, except its ability to kill its own people. Nevertheless, in the prewar period the American military expended massive efforts to transport 500,000 soldiers, marines, and airmen to the Gulf in a huge build-up. Their miscalculation of Iraqi strength led them to put off their offensive from November 1990 to January 1991. And it led them to mount an air campaign that lasted thirty-eight days—enough time for Saddam, had he been smart, to pull his forces out of Kuwait long before the Coalition's ground offensive began and then to claim that his army had remained undefeated by troops too cowardly to attack face to face.

Even after the Coalition's decisive show of force, faulty assumptions from the past continued to drive America's strategic policy. General Norman Schwarzkopf, commander-in-chief of the Coalition forces, saw no reason not to allow Iraqi commanders to resume flying their helicopters, given that the nation's bridges had been destroyed. Meanwhile, President Bush was urging Iraqi citizens to rise up and overthrow Saddam's regime. Dissidents, particularly the Shia in the south and the Kurds in the north, seeing the wreckage of defeat, raised the standard of rebellion. In Basra, a regular army tank officer led the first assault on the Baath Party. Unfortunately, the rebels received no aid from the American administration, which dithered about possible Iranian influence in the south and worried about making a long-term commitment to the region.

But Saddam and his Baath Party did not dither. Instead, they promptly turned the "elite" Republican Guard divisions against the rebels. Some units of the guard had been destroyed by advancing Coalition ground forces, but most, though bloodied by air attacks, remained capable of responding to internal threats. Moreover, at the end of the conflict the guard divisions were advantageously placed to respond to the most dangerous rebellion, that of the Shia in southern Iraq.

Saddam retained power after the war in large measure because the mechanisms for internal control, both of the Iraqi government and the Baath Party, remained intact. During the night of February 12, American planners of the air campaign had targeted a number of intelligence, secret police, and political sites in an effort to destabilize the regime. One of the targets was the Al Firdos Bunker, a backup command post for intelligence services. Unfortunately, it also happened to be an air raid shelter for families of the regime's ruling elite (there were no air raid shelters for the great majority of the population). An F-117 attack devastated the bunker and killed everyone inside. Iraqi television and CNN (now back on line) immediately beamed the carnage around the world. The global and domestic backlash caused U.S. leaders to declare targets within Baghdad off limits. For all intents and purposes, the effort to destabilize the regime virtually ended on the night it began.

With their political infrastructure in place, their military forces close at hand, and a ruthless determination to remain in power, Saddam and his henchmen turned to the business of restoring control over the rest of Iraq. What followed was a bloodbath, extreme even by Iraqi standards. Tanks, armored personnel carriers, and attack helicopters overwhelmed the ill-equipped masses of disaffected citizens. In the north the Americans eventually stepped in to protect the Kurds and stop the slaughter, but not before thousands of men, women, and children were killed. In the south, there would be no help for the Shia. Memories of the American hostages held for 444 days by the Ayatollah Khomeini and his Shiite supporters continued to haunt American policy makers. They feared that support for the Shiite uprising in Iraq would lead to a resurgence of Iranian influence and power in the region. By mid-April Saddam's brutal regime had extinguished the flame of rebellion, though the stench of the bloating dead wafted over the destruction for weeks.

While the performance of U.S. forces on the tactical level had been exemplary and new technologies impressive, at the operational level the campaign was not well orchestrated. Its biggest failure was the lack of an overarching sense of joint cooperation between ground and air forces. The air campaign was conducted by a first-rate airman, General Chuck Horner, who consistently placed the overall objectives above parochial thinking. Schwarzkopf had empowered Horner, as the joint air component commander, to design and implement the air campaign, despite the navy's desire to return to the dysfunctional system of separate aerial command and control that both services had used in Vietnam. Much of the success the air campaign enjoyed resulted from Horner's sophisticated thinking, as well as that of his planning staff, the infamous group known as Black Hole. Nevertheless, the air plan had weaknesses. The aerial assault was an exercise in overkill and lasted far too long. Moreover, some of the planners believed that an air campaign by itself could dispense with the need for a costly ground campaign. Proponents of the go-it-alone aerial strategy missed one critical fact: in a Middle East that entirely equated victory with military success on the ground, reliance solely on an air campaign would have guaranteed Saddam a political victory.

The ground campaign exhibited equally striking operational weaknesses, concealed only by tactical successes on the battlefield and Iraqi ineptitude. Neither before nor during the conduct of the campaign did senior commanders react quickly to changing situations. When the Iraqis launched Scud missiles from the western desert aimed at Israel and Saudi Arabia, Schwarzkopf responded by throwing some of his most capable aircraft, including F-15Es, at the problem. When civilian leaders in the Pentagon suggested that the 101st Airborne Division with its helicopter assets would be an ideal force to attack the missile-launching area and end the danger of retaliation from Israel, General Colin Powell, then chairman of the Joint Chiefs of Staff, and Schwarzkopf obdurately refused to listen—such a change might upset "the plan."

One looks in vain for "jointness" in the planning for the Gulf War's ground campaign. Marine operations moved too far too fast, in effect propelling the Iraqis out of Kuwait before the drive from the west could close the trap door on the fleeing enemy. In a rare burst of adaptivity, Schwarzkopf responded to this miscalculation by decreeing that the hammer blow which V Corps was to administer through the deserts of western Iraq must move a day early. Unfortunately, Lieutenant General Frederick Franks, commander of V Corps, who received the order early in the morning, could not get his troops under way until late in the afternoon. He maneuvered according to his plan, but not fast enough for Schwarzkopf. After the war ended, Schwarzkopf would blame such mistakes on Franks, when in fact he himself had assumed the mantle of orchestrating the ground campaign and was therefore entirely responsible for the failures.

The drive to surround the Iraqis and destroy the Republican Guard would undoubtedly have led to the fall of the Baathist regime, had it succeeded. It did not, because army and marine forces failed to close the door at the Rumaila oil fields. Then strategists in Washington decided to halt the ground war after just 100 hours. Schwarzkopf raised no objection; yet it was clear even to reporters in Riyadh that American forces had not blocked the Republican Guard's avenue of retreat to Basra. After the war, some insiders claimed that the 100-hour decision had been made because of bad press, when images of the "highway of death" leading out of Kuwait were published. In fact, those photographs were unavailable to the media until early March, after the war was already over.

To be sure, in a Clausewitzian world dominated by friction, uncertainty, ambiguity, and chance, mistakes will inevitably occur. And in fact the Gulf War represented the first time in forty years that the U.S. military had conducted a successful campaign at the operational level. Military activities in Vietnam had invariably occurred at the divisional level (rarely) and below (mostly) and had almost entirely been concerned with tactics. In the Gulf War, U.S. military leaders confronted complex operational problems that their organizations had not faced since the Korean Conflict. Nevertheless, missteps at the operational level ensured that the Coalition's brilliant tactical performance on the battlefield would not achieve the kind of strategic and political victory that could have toppled Saddam and his regime.

The sequel to the Gulf War was a different story, as the following chapters will show. The second Iraq War displayed a combination of tactical and operational virtuosity that obliterated the Baathist regime. On the simplest level, the war that broke out on March 19, 2003, resulted from the failure of the United States' policy makers to seize the victory its armed forces had so decisively won in the winter of 1991. Yet, human life is rarely simple, and the value of history lies in its ability to tease out the complexities and constraints confronting policy makers and military strategists alike.

To understand the origins of the second war fought by Coalition forces against Iraq, one must understand not only the immediate precursor events but the nature of the regimes involved, the calculations of military and political leaders on both sides, and the impact of unfolding events on their thinking. In the case of Iraq, some of these factors will never be known, since much, if not all, of its decision making took place in the impenetrable mind of Saddam Hussein. Other factors will inevitably be distorted, either as memory fails or as participants actively warp the record to improve their appearance before the bar of history. The historian's job, fraught with obstacles though it may be, is to make some sense of what is always an ambiguous, incomplete, and sometimes contradictory record.

The nature of Saddam Hussein's Iraq and the response of America's leaders to what they regarded as its potential for aggression set this war in motion. To understand these interactions, we will examine the region's history and geography, the origins of the Baath Party, America's reaction to the rise of Saddam Hussein, and the course of events from spring 1991 to the outbreak of war in March 2003. In the years leading up to war, as always, the incalculables of history—friction and chance—drove policy makers, diplomats, and generals alike toward an uncertain future.

1

The Origins of War

Of audacious character and untiring physique, secretive about
himself and ever ready to incriminate others, a blend of arro-
gance and servility, he concealed behind a carefully modest exterior an unbounded lust for power. Sometimes this impelled him
to lavish excesses, but more often to incessant work. And that is
as damaging as excess when the throne is the aim.

TACITUS, *The Annals of Imperial Rome,*
describing the Praetorian prefect Sejanus, first century BC

On July 18, 1979, just five days into his new presi-
dency, Saddam Hussein called a meeting of over
three hundred Baath Party senior leaders. Wearing his military uni-
form and calmly smoking a Cuban cigar, Saddam listened as one of
his henchmen announced the discovery of "a painful and atrocious
plot" to overthrow the regime and its new leader.[1] The president then
stepped to the rostrum to reveal the details and to invite the plot's in-

stigator, Muhyi Abd al-Hussein Mashhadi, who had just returned from a grim visit to one of the Baathist torture chambers, to reveal the details. Promised his life, Mashhadi confirmed all.

In a cloud of cigar smoke, Saddam returned to the podium, this time with a list of the plotters. As an assistant read each name, guards escorted the unfortunate party member out of the hall. Fear spread throughout the audience; some started to weep. All wondered whether their name too was on the list. When the show was over, Saddam's thugs had taken away sixty-six senior party members. Then, in a final gesture to indicate the new regime's direction, Saddam asked the surviving delegates to volunteer to serve on the firing squads. Barely two weeks later, many of these functionaries would participate in the executions of their fellow Baathists. Mashhadi himself would be shot as an Israeli spy. As with those who "plotted" against Stalin in the late 1930s, there would be no mercy.

In a society steeped in blood feuds, Saddam's move to involve a substantial number of senior leaders in the executions of their comrades was a stroke of genius. The message was clear: no one would be trusted in the new regime; no one could feel secure. All, no matter how high or low their position, knew that arrest and torture could be their fate at any moment. After Saddam's premier performance, no one dared to question openly the ideas of the nation's president. Even within the confines of their own families, Iraqis feared that Saddam's agents might be listening; they seemed to be everywhere and nowhere. Dissent and initiative within the government quickly disappeared. As enormous monuments, statues, and portraits went up in public squares, portraying Saddam as the Great Uncle of Iraq's people, the main political attribute of the Republic of Iraq became mind-numbing fear.

In five thousand years of hosting empires, the fertile valley between the Tigris and Euphrates rivers has endured many tyrannical regimes.

Sumerians, Chaldeans, Hittites, Assyrians, Babylonians, Medes, Persians, Macedonian Greeks, Seleucid Greeks, Romans, Parthians, Arabs, Mongols, Ottoman Turks, and the British have all passed through and left their mark, for good or ill. Some, like the Assyrians, have come "like a wolf on the fold"; others have stayed long enough to build more than they destroyed.

Between the seventh and thirteenth centuries, at a time when few in Europe could read, much less write, Baghdad was at the center of a cosmopolitan culture renowned for learning and the arts. But in 1258 the Mongols stormed the city from the east and killed the caliph by rolling him in a carpet and then trampling him under the hooves of their horses. Across the region, they pillaged, raped, and slaughtered with a ruthlessness rarely seen in history. The society of the time was not capable of totaling its losses, but somewhere near three quarters of a million died in the year of the first Mongol invasion. Many of the complex irrigation canals on which agriculture had depended since the dawn of civilization lay in ruins.

A century later, under Tamerlane, the Mongols returned. Unlike most other conquerors, including even the fearsome Assyrians, the Mongols left no monuments or temples to their gods, only memories of horrifying brutality. At Tikrit on the upper Tigris they constructed a pyramid of skulls to mark their passing. Few escaped their fury. What little was left of the irrigation system soon collapsed, and the region degenerated into a backwater, its people ravaged by disease, malnutrition, and outright starvation, its productive base barely at subsistence level for its meager inhabitants.

The Ottoman Turks fell heir to this now-blighted terrain, and for the most part ignored it. As Europeans expanded their empires in the sixteenth century, the ancient Mesopotamian Valley held little interest for the conquerors, pirates, and trading companies that dominated the Atlantic and the Mediterranean. North and South America, India, the

East Indies, and the Caribbean all offered a better return for risking one's life.

The twentieth century finally brought change, not all of it welcome. In the early years, a war with Italy over Libya, followed by conflict in the Balkans, placed the Ottoman Empire under direct assault. Humiliating defeats thrust new leaders to the fore, but the "young Turks" proved no more competent than their predecessors in forestalling the empire's decay. In 1914 the Turks sided with Germany in the war that broke out among the great powers. They immediately came under attack from the British, whose initial missteps thoroughly disproved the idea that muddling through is an effective way to wage war.

In 1915 the British launched an assault on the Dardanelles to open up a route to Russia. The naval attack failed first; then a badly planned landing on the Gallipoli Peninsula left thousands of British, Australian, and New Zealand soldiers dead. In the east, as Britain's Indian Army invaded the Ottoman Empire through Basra, one of the planners thought it reasonable to take a crane along to unload the army's supplies. However, the crane was loaded on board ship first, with the supplies piled on top. The ensuing campaign reflected this kind of ineptitude throughout. In 1915 the British advanced on Baghdad and suffered a crushing defeat at the hands of Ottoman troops near Ctesiphon, the ancient capital of Parthia, taken briefly early in the second century AD by Roman legions under the emperor Trajan.

In 1916 a more coherent and effective assault on Ottoman forces in the Tigris-Euphrates Valley led the British to victory. By spring 1917 Baghdad had fallen. From Egypt, British troops under General Edmund Allenby invaded what was then called Palestine—present-day Israel and Jordan. Slowly the Ottoman armies crumbled. By 1918 Jerusalem and Damascus had fallen to British and Anzac troops after sustained fighting. In October, no longer able to bear the strain of war, the Turks conceded defeat.

What to do with the spoils of the Ottoman Empire was only one of a number of intractable problems confronting the victorious powers at the end of that most dismal conflict. While the actual fighting was going on, two minor functionaries in the British and French governments had negotiated the Sykes-Picot Agreement to divide the empire between their nations. But the respective governments and various other representatives had also promised portions of the region to the Zionists for a homeland and to the locals if they would revolt. Some Arabs, under that magnificent mythmaker Lawrence of Arabia, finally did rebel, though their contribution was relatively small in comparison with the pretensions of their later claims.

In the end, British and French diplomats divided up the areas falling to Allied armies in much the same higgledy-piggledy fashion they had divided Africa during the nineteenth century. The French received the territory that today forms Lebanon and Syria. The British received Palestine as well as the three Ottoman provinces of Basra, Baghdad, and Mosul, which they merged into modern-day Iraq.

Other than rich farmland in the valley, Iraq had few natural resources—except oil. And it had oil in abundance: the greatest reserves of any nation after Saudi Arabia, and the easiest and cheapest petroleum deposits to extract anywhere in the world. Initially, Britain's acquisition of Iraq had little to do with oil. At the time, the British aimed at acquiring territory that could extend the raj's security. But they also acted from simple greed: if they had failed to take control of the area, the French would undoubtedly have seized it.

The land occupied by the British looked good on a map; it was geographically cohesive. To the west and south lay one of the world's great deserts—a flat, featureless expanse inhospitable to human life except for a few Bedouins. Scorching heat in summer, sudden deluges and terrible sandstorms in winter, and virtually no standing water at any time made for a desolate and empty landscape. Northeastern Iraq, with peaks rising above 10,000 feet and rainfall more plentiful, was inhabited largely by Kurds, whose tenuous connection to Arab culture was Islam. In the south, the rivers converged in a region of swamps and irrigation canals, home to a people known as Marsh Arabs whose cultural roots reached back millennia. Between these extremes of desert, mountains, and swamps lay the fertile Mesopotamian Valley. Like the Nile delta, it owed its richness and productivity to alluvial floods, which replenished the land with new soil from the Anatolian plateau. The majority of Iraq's townspeople and farmers lived within this relatively confined area, as they had for thousands of years.

Political and religious cohesion was another matter. The cross-currents of invasion had left a population as disparate as that of the Balkans in terms of ethnicity, religion, and tribal loyalty. The Arabs around Basra in the southeast practiced the Shii form of Islam, while the Arabs centered around Baghdad were largely Sunni. Most of the Bedouin tribes were also Sunni but were regarded as ignorant robbers by the more sedentary peasants and urban-dwellers. In the north, the Kurds were Sunni, too, but they were not Arabs, and their culture was quite different from that of their neighbors to the south. Throughout the Tigris-Euphrates Valley, especially in the north, survivors of other ethnic groups as well as the remnants of fallen empires were scattered about. Within the Kurdish and Arab areas, in communal groupings, lived Assyrian Christians, Chaldean Christians, Persians (Iranians), Turcoman Muslims, and Jews—the last consisting mostly of descendants of survivors of the Babylonian captivity.

Out of this conglomeration of conflicting interests, the British attempted to unify their mandate from the League of Nations. The local population immediately rebelled, not so much because they believed the occupiers had broken a promise to give the Arabs freedom but because their new rulers were Christians. The outcome was never in doubt, but the British suffered 2,269 casualties in persuading various groups that they would not tolerate rebellion. In the decade during which the British controlled Iraq directly, they brought only a modicum of order to a deeply divided region. At times Royal Air Force fighter aircraft were sufficient to intimidate marauding tribes galloping out of the deserts to the south. For most of the time, an uneasy peace held.

To knit Iraq's three disparate provinces together, the British placed on Iraq's new throne a Hashemite desert chieftain who had followed T. E. Lawrence in his guerrilla war against the Ottomans. Third son of the sharif of Mecca, Faisal had hoped the rebellion would lead to a pan-Arab state. Now king, he supported his fellow Sunni Arabs in dominating the new territorial entity called Iraq.

The basic political problem of the infant state lay in the fact that the Sunni represented a minority of Iraq's people, and, like Faisal, they were deeply suspicious of the large Shiite population in the south. A major reason why the British had included the Kurds in Iraq's territory—a move with which Faisal was in full accord—was to increase the proportion of Sunnis in the country. Faisal's regime proceeded to expel many of the Iranian clerics who exercised influence over the Shia and in effect to disenfranchise Iraq's most populous ethnic group.

In 1932 the League of Nations ratified Iraq's independence, although the British kept control of several air bases and determined the nation's foreign policy. With a veneer of democratic institutions overlaid on a thoroughly tribal society, the state maintained a tenuous balance between the deeply antagonistic but leaderless Shia in the south, the rebellious Kurds in the north, and the British-anointed Sunnis in the center.

BAATH IDEOLOGY AND THE TYRANNY OF SADDAM HUSSEIN

The measure of a regime of terror is the victims of its peace, not the casualties of its wars.

SAMIR AL-KHALIL (Kanan Makiya), *Republic of Fear,* 1989

During the Hashemite monarchy, the history of Iraq began to merge with wider currents in the Arab world. Two young Syrian intellectuals, Michel Aflaq and Salah al-Din al-Bitar, who met while students in Paris in 1929, would critically influence the course of events. Both were from Damascus, the former Greek Orthodox in his faith, the latter a Sunni Muslim, and both were fanatical believers in a future Arab nation. What Aflaq and al-Bitar took back to Damascus in 1941 was an amalgamation of idiosyncratic but exceedingly dangerous ideas about how to reform the Arab world—ideas that would give birth to the Baathist Party in Syria and later in Iraq.

In the early 1930s, as the Great Depression corroded sureties that had undergirded the West for nearly a century, radicalism in Europe's universities and among the continent's intellectuals spread widely. The writings of Marx and Nietzsche were influential, as were Lenin's vitriolic attacks on European imperialism. The ongoing experiment in the Soviet Union suggested that an ideologically driven totalitarian regime could accomplish great things in reforming a less advanced society. Germany's recovery from the Depression and the Third Reich's diplomatic and military triumphs provided yet another example of how easily a motivated authoritarian nation might overturn the existing international order.

Unlike nationalists such as Ho Chi Minh, Vo Nguyen Giap, and Pol Pot, also educated in the French system, Aflaq and al-Bitar explicitly rejected the Marxist component so attractive to French intellectuals. Aflaq's turning away from Marxism was part of his attempt to reject everything about the Western intellectual tradition: "The philosophies and teachings that come from the West invade the Arab mind and steal his loyalty before they rob him of his land and skies. We want a unified nationalist programme of education that derives its roots from the peculiarities of the Arab nation, the spirit of its past, and the needs of its future. It should preserve loyalty to the Arab homeland and the Arab cause without sharing in this venture any other homeland or cause."[2] Yet in the end, influences from the West would permeate the Baathist message, despite Aflaq's disclaimers.

Among these influences were Fascism and its insidious, even more dangerous derivative, Nazism. Baath ideology was deeply antisemitic well before the state of Israel became a reality in 1948. The idea of the "leader" held a place of importance in Aflaq's writings that Adolf Hitler would have found congenial. But neither Aflaq nor al-Bitar possessed the political skill of a Hitler or Mussolini. What they provided instead was an ideological framework that allowed Arab intellectuals and members of the middle classes to respond to challenges posed by the West's irruption on the Middle Eastern scene.

After the Second World War ended, Baathist ideology proved more attractive than Marxism in both Syria and Iraq because it was not tainted by connections to the Soviet Union—an outsider to the region and, to many Arabs, as Western as the colonial powers. On the other hand, Baathism did not retreat into a religious fundamentalism that rejected what the West had to offer in science and technology. Islam played surprisingly little role in Baath ideology. Like the Communists, the Baathists could appeal to modern interests but at the same time also claim to represent a return to a glorious Arab past. Thus, they could reject the corrupt colonial regimes ruling the Middle East into the early 1950s without throwing into the dustbin of history the awakening dreams of Arab nationalism. In effect, Baathism set about to create a new myth on which a pan-Arab nation, which had never existed, could rest.[3]

At the root of Baath ideology was a ruthlessness modeled on Nazi and Communist totalitarianism. The greater one's love for the nation and its principles, the more necessary it was to be cruel to the nation's people when the occasion arose. A good Baathist must "engender fierce hatred until death towards those persons who represent a contrary idea. It is worthless for members of the movement to content themselves with combating opponent ideas by saying: why bother with persons . . . The antagonistic idea does not exist by itself; it is embodied in persons who must perish, so that it too may perish."[4]

Unlike earlier Arab nationalists, the Baathists were careful observers of the political structure of the Communist Party. They were also exceptional organizers. Party discipline, a conspiratorial atmosphere, and dreams of an Arab nation proved an intoxicating brew for activists bewildered by the challenge of Western influence and power. Drawing on the secretiveness and suspiciousness of its native clans, the Baath Party built political organizations in both Syria and Iraq that survived the inevitable purges, persecutions, and upheavals of the postwar years. In the end, they proved more resilient, popular, and adaptable than their Communist opponents.

In 1958 a group of officers led by General Abd al-Karim Qassem overthrew the Hashemite monarchy and proclaimed the Republic of Iraq. The coup participants and their supporters slaughtered the young king (Faisal's grandson), his family, and most of his ministers in an orgy of violence. The next five years were a period of turmoil. The main political support for the new regime came from the Communists, while much of the opposition came from the Baathists. A young Baath Party activist, Saddam Hussein by name, led an assassination attempt against Qassem that failed, even though the would-be assassins riddled the president's car with bullets. Qassem survived, but so too did Saddam.

In 1963 the revolutionary mayhem in Iraq reached such a level that a small group of officers, most of them Baath sympathizers, overthrew Qassem's government. Again blood ran in the streets. The victorious Baath Party, concerned about rumors that Qassem had survived, displayed the dead president's body on television, focusing the camera on his gruesome wounds. As the rebels set about establishing a new regime, mass arrests, torture, and executions occurred throughout Iraq. But the usurpers moved too fast. The party was not yet politically strong enough to suppress dissent, nor had its Communist opponents been discredited sufficiently. The result was a counter-coup that nearly destroyed the Baath as a force in Iraqi politics. Arrests by those now in power decimated the party's ranks but never quite put it out of business. Baathism survived because it was the only serious political alternative to Communism.

In this maelstrom of political violence during the 1960s, Saddam Hussein found his niche. Born fatherless to a peasant mother near the remote town of Tikrit, he gained what passed for an education in the local primary school and later in Baghdad. His uncle, a fervent admirer of Hitler and Nazi antisemitism, served as a father-figure to the young man. Combining a violent streak with a taste for intrigue, Saddam provided the emerging Baath Party with a political operative whose street smarts and ruthlessness fit the requirements of the times.

In June 1967 a third major war between the state of Israel and its Arab neighbors erupted. The Six-Day War saw Israel's modern military destroy the armies and air forces of Egypt, Syria, and Jordan in operations on three different fronts in less than a week. Not for the last time the world was exposed to images of dispirited Arab soldiers, abandoned by their officers, surrendering *en masse*. For most in the Arab world, the defeat was inexplicable—a shattering humiliation at the hands of a minority group their ancestors had despised for thirteen centuries. The Iraqi Army participated in the Six-Day War only peripherally; a few of its units arrived on the Syrian front during the last days of fighting and hardly engaged in combat. Nevertheless, the shock in Iraq was visceral, as it was throughout the Arab world. Iraq's current political and military leaders were thoroughly discredited.

The Baathists were ready and waiting. In July 1968, with enthusiastic support from much of the officer corps, the party regained power. This time, its leaders moved slowly and deliberately. A thorough purge eliminated most of the party's overt opponents, but limits were imposed. Torture was employed, but not egregiously at first. The party consolidated its power, moved its supporters into key positions in the bureaucracy, and built up a political structure to ensure a popular following. Leading the regime was Ahmad Hassan al-Bakr, a fellow Tikriti clansman to whom Saddam had attached himself.

The hanging of fourteen "spies"—including nine Iraqi Jews—in January 1969 in downtown Baghdad's Liberation Square suggested the *modus operandi* of the new government. A national holiday was declared to celebrate this "victory," and for those unable to attend the execution, Iraqi television broadcast the events. The Baathist minister of guidance declaimed: "Great People of Iraq! The Iraq of today shall no more tolerate any traitor, spy, agent or fifth columnist! You foundling Israel, you imperialist Americans, and you Zionists, hear me! We will discover all your dirty tricks! We will punish your agents! We will hang all your spies, even if there are thousands of them! . . . Great Iraqi people! This is only the beginning! The great immortal squares of Iraq shall be filled up with the corpses of traitors and spies! Just wait!"[5]

Saddam now served as chief administrative assistant to al-Bakr and head of the secret police—a position within the Baath Party analogous to Stalin's position among the Bolsheviks in the early 1920s. A voracious reader of biographies of the Soviet dictator, Saddam saw in Stalin a model of how megalomania, narcissism, and paranoia could thrust a determined leader to the pinnacle of power. Perhaps only in his taste for directly torturing his victims was Saddam different from Stalin. Yet, most senior party leaders minimized Saddam's importance to the party as well as his intelligence. They regarded him as simply a paper-pushing bureaucrat with a handy predilection for brutality. It was a mistake all eventually regretted. Part of this denigration undoubtedly occurred because Saddam spoke with a Tikriti accent; his hometown was not one of the more cosmopolitan localities in Iraq. Saddam marked those who held such attitudes and bided his time.

Saddam's political position, combined with his diligence, allowed him to place his agents and followers in crucial offices throughout the bureaucracy. Slowly but steadily the tentacles of Saddam's influence reached into every corner of Iraq. Three separate secret police organizations—the Amn (internal security), the Estikhbarat (military intelligence), and the Mukhabarat (Baathist Party intelligence)—kept track of Iraqis at home and abroad. By the late 1970s al-Bakr had become a figurehead and in 1979, on the anniversary of the coup, Saddam persuaded him to step down. The theatrical purge of July 18 established a tone of terror for the new regime.

What set the new president off from most of his fellow Baathists was his focus on control of Iraq rather than on revolution to unify the pan-Arab world. Saddam's emphasis was on what Stalin called "socialism in one nation." For much of the 1970s he seemed to be in a position to make Iraq a major player on the international scene. Throughout the decade and into the early 1980s, oil prices soared at an all-time high. Vast construction projects dotted the Iraqi landscape. Saddam could buy whatever arms he desired on foreign markets. The French were even willing to sell him the technology to make nuclear weapons, and in these transactions the French premier and later president, Jacques Chirac, would play an enthusiastic role.

In January 1980 Saddam revealed his goals in the international arena: "We want our country to achieve its proper weight based on our estimation that Iraq is as great as China, as great as the Soviet Union, and as great as the United States."[6] This was an extraordinary claim. Even with its oil deposits, Iraq had neither the wealth nor—at barely twenty million people—the population to make a play for world domination. Yet Saddam's actions over the coming decade would underline exactly how serious he was in staking this claim.

INVASIONS OF IRAN AND KUWAIT

Our opinion of the Gods and our knowledge of men lead us to conclude that it is a general and necessary law of nature to rule whatever one can. This is not a law we made ourselves, nor were we the first to act upon it when it was made. We found it already in existence, and we shall leave it to exist forever among those who come after us.

THUCYDIDES, *History of the Peloponnesian War,*
spoken by the Athenian negotiators at Melos, fifth century BC

In September 1980, as Iran struggled with revolutionary upheavals, Saddam ordered his army to invade his neighbor to the east. By the time the Iran-Iraq war finally ended eight years later, somewhere between half a million and a million Iraqis and Iranians had died. Iraq's massive holdings of foreign exchange had turned into huge debts, in effect bankrupting the state. Moreover, the precipitous drop in oil prices in the mid-1980s left the Iraqis with little hope of recovering the financial clout they had once enjoyed.

Iraq and the United States were now on a collision course—one driven by Saddam's ambitions and abetted by the United States' economic interests in this oil-rich region. In the decades before 1980, the two nations had had virtually no contact. The United States had been content to allow the British to play a leading role in Iraq during the period of the Hashemite monarchy. Even after Qassem's nationalist regime overthrew the king in 1958, Iraq was ignored by most American policy makers—including those somewhat familiar with this remote part of the world. In the coup-prone 1960s, the U.S. Central Intelligence Agency provided some support to the Baathists in their struggle against the Communists. But the stunning Israeli victory in 1967 and the Arabs' tendency to blame their defeat on America's political and military support of Israel ended the tenuous connections between the two nations. In 1968 Iraq broke off relations with the United States.

As America's military and economic influence in the world drifted ever lower in the 1970s, U.S. policy makers staked much of their political capital on Iran and the shah's regime. For most of the decade the United States lavished its most modern weapons on this ally—a policy that hardly endeared it to the Iraqis, always suspicious of their neighbor's intentions. And then in 1979 came the Iranian revolution, the fall of the shah, and the replacement of his pro-American government with Ayatollah Khomeini's ferociously anti-American Islamic republic. The hostage-taking at the U.S. embassy by Khomeini's followers caused many Americans to sympathize with Iraq's invasion of Iran in September 1980. But the antisemitism of Saddam's regime, its anti-imperialist stance, and its terrorist leanings did little to improve relations with the United States.

As the Iran-Iraq war dragged on, however, and as it appeared that the Iranian fundamentalists might win, Iraq seemed to be the lesser of two evils to many American policy makers. The Ayatollah outclassed even Osama bin Laden in his vituperative attacks on the West. At one time he claimed that "holy war means the conquest of all non-Moslem territories . . . It will . . . be the duty of all able-bodied men to volunteer for this war of conquest whose final goal is to make Koranic law supreme from one end of the earth to the other."[7] Diplomatic relations between Iraq and the United States were reestablished in 1984.

Washington began supplying Iraq with satellite intelligence but few weapons and little ammunition; other Western nations and the Soviets willingly filled those gaps. Meanwhile, all of the Western powers, in the most shameful fashion, averted their eyes from Iraq's use of chemical weapons not only against Iranian soldiers—contrary to all international conventions—but against its own citizens, the Kurds in the north.

With the ending of the Iran-Iraq War in 1988, a number of American politicians hoped for more stable relations with Iraq. The new administration of George H. W. Bush courted Iraqi business, while wheat sales played well in the midwest. Even following the Israeli strike against the Osiraq reactor in 1981, few in U.S. intelligence agencies had picked up on Saddam's renewed efforts to build nuclear weapons using 1950s technology. The day of reckoning came in July 1990, as Iraqi troops moved into Kuwait in an almost bloodless military occupation. After a few days of hand-wringing, the Americans reacted in a manner that seemed, at least to those who did not understand their urges and moods, entirely out of character. They sought confrontation—political, economic, and if necessary military—to force the Iraqis to surrender Kuwait.

In retrospect, the U.S. government could have done little diplomatically to persuade Saddam to back off from his aggression. He calculated, mistakenly, that the United States had neither the military means nor the mental toughness to risk war. He idly dismissed stealth technology and, even more dangerously (like Stalin in 1941), failed to appreciate the operational skills of his opponent. He had no inkling of the enormous superiority of the Coalition's air power—after all, did not Iraq possess a modern air defense system that integrated sophisticated French and Soviet technologies? If war came, Saddam believed that his army, which had fought off Iran for eight long years, was capable of inflicting losses on the American military that its people would not tolerate. As he commented to one interviewer, the Americans had proved in Vietnam that they could not endure heavy casualties without losing their will. Saddam's actions throughout the crisis leading up to Operation Desert Storm suggest that he never really believed that President Bush would risk war.

Ironically, a number of experts in the United States, many within the services themselves, shared Saddam's misconceptions. They calculated that Iraq possessed highly effective fighting forces, especially its battle-tested army. American casualties would exceed 10,000 in the event of a ground war, they estimated. Confronted with such numbers, the U.S. military took six months to deploy a mountain of ammunition and supplies and over half a million personnel to drive the Iraqis out of Kuwait. When war finally came, American forces deconstructed Iraq's air defense system in a matter of hours and then waged a relentless air campaign against the nation's military and economic infrastructure over the course of the next month. When the ground offensive commenced thirty-eight days later, Coalition forces liberated Kuwait in short order.

In the afterglow of the 100-hour ground war in the Gulf, America's political and military leaders basked in what appeared to be an extraordinary success. Certainly in comparison with the gloomy prognostications of the prewar period, the military victory seemed miraculous. Yet, American leaders remained unclear about their goals for postwar Iraq. They had failed to destroy Saddam's Republican Guard divisions, which immediately set about slaughtering Shiite rebels in the south, and they were uncertain about Saddam's potential to threaten his neighbors and America's allies in the future. Both before and after the war, U.S. leaders—politicians, military experts, and intelligence analysts—made the mistake of consistently underestimating the political strength of the Baathist regime. Saddam's political system, with its ruthless controls, was able to absorb the most terrible of battlefield defeats, as long as the instruments of tyranny remained in place.

For his part, Saddam was no more capable than the Americans of understanding his opponent or the lesson the United States had administered in January and February of 1991. Once Saddam and his crew had dispensed with the business of murdering their fellow countrymen in the south, they turned to the problem of restoring Iraq's position in the Middle East. To them, the United States' failure to consummate its victory must have seemed inexplicable. What possible explanation could there be? The most obvious, from an Iraqi point of view, was that the Americans had been unwilling, despite their technological superiority, to close with the Iraqi army on its home territory and finish off the job. In Saddam's state, where bearers of bad news soon found themselves before firing squads—if they were lucky—it became increasingly easy to portray the disaster of 1991 as a victory, at least to the captive people of Iraq. The nation's leadership had stood up to the military might of the United States and survived. A delighted dictator promoted his officers and generals and passed out decorations to the survivors.

CONTAINMENT

The Iraqi case has a great deal to teach us about what happens to an outlaw state that is not overthrown when it consistently breaches international norms but is subjected to a combined regime of sanctions and unbridled tyranny: it corrodes and rots, devastating and impoverishing the vast majority of the population, without necessarily becoming any easier to revolt against or overthrow from the inside.

KANAN MAKIYA, "How Saddam Held On to Power,"
The Iraq War Reader, 2003

In the period between the two Iraq wars, Saddam pursued a foreign policy of confrontation, directly with regard to postwar sanctions imposed on Iraq by the United Nations and indirectly with regard to the

United States. Here, he was encouraged by the wavering course followed by President Bush and his successor, William Jefferson Clinton.

With the failure of Iraqis to rise up and overthrow their dictator, the Bush administration attempted to follow a policy of containment. On the one hand, such a policy involved sanctions to prevent Iraq from rebuilding its military infrastructure and to isolate the nation economically from the rest of the world. Sanctions were never completely successful. A substantial black market funneled oil out of Iraq through Jordan and Syria, while Western goods seeped back in. But food shipments and medical supplies did not trickle down to the Iraqi people. Thus, sanctions served to exacerbate the pain of war without loosening in the slightest Saddam's iron grip.

In addition to sanctions, containment also involved arms inspections focused on weapons of mass destruction. After the war, UNSCOM (United Nations Special Commission) attempted to apply the tough criteria of the Soviet-American arms control arena rather than the weaker certifications of the Non-Proliferation Treaty with which Iraq had complied prior to 1991. UNSCOM's was not an easy road. In a June 1991 incident, agents of the Mukhabarat fired live ammunition directly over the heads of inspectors. Despite consistent and general Iraqi dissimulation and unwillingness to cooperate, UNSCOM inspectors stumbled on elaborate efforts to build an Arab nuclear weapon as well as major programs in chemical and biological weapons. At times the Iraqis complied with the U.N. demand to destroy such materials; at other times they obfuscated and lied. These discoveries underlined how inadequate Western and U.S. intelligence had been in unraveling clandestine Iraqi nuclear programs in the period before the Gulf War.

In lobbying for Arab support just prior to the 1991 conflict, President Bush had assured Coalition partners that the United States would remove its forces from the Gulf once Kuwait was liberated. The Americans lived up to that promise with the withdrawal of their ground troops. However, the air force left residual equipment and personnel behind on bases in Saudi Arabia, partially to ensure Iraq's compliance with the terms of the armistice. Unfortunately, that decision allowed Osama bin Laden to claim that the United States was now in permanent occupation of the holiest sites in the Muslim world—a claim that would reverberate on September 11, 2001, with devastating force.

For Saddam, the central question was how to overturn the sanctions and escape UNSCOM's smothering embrace, both of which were inhibiting Iraq's rearmament. In a series of seemingly contradictory moves, Saddam tested the United States again and again, sometimes over little matters, sometimes over major matters of policy. This confrontational stance guaranteed that the United Nations would not lift political and economic sanctions. Saddam's instinct for conflict, buttressed by sycophants in his entourage, undoubtedly led him to take this tack, but a lack of American resolve was probably a contributing factor. A policy of containment hardly sent a clear message that the Iraqis were playing a dangerous game.

Just how dangerous was suggested in Clinton's first year as president. During a visit by former president Bush to the Middle East, the Kuwaitis discovered that Iraq had set in motion an assassination attempt targeting Bush with a car bomb. The Clinton administration responded by firing off a number of cruise missiles against the headquarters of the Iraqi intelligence agency responsible for the plan. But the attack was launched at night, because the administration feared killing civilians, even those who were members of Saddam's secret police. The only people who died were janitors, and the perpetrators escaped. This weak response no doubt further confirmed Saddam's view that the United States was capable of making only symbolic gestures.

Like so many well-meaning Americans, the new U.S. president could not grasp the nightmarish intentions of a tyrant like Saddam Hussein, and the guidance provided by his recently appointed foreign policy team was weak. Knowing little about U.S. military institutions and having no hands-on experience in foreign affairs, Clinton was poorly prepared to deal with the complex issues of war and peace.

The debacle in Somalia in early 1993, where the death of eighteen American soldiers was sufficient to cause the withdrawal of the United States from the Horn of Africa, further confirmed Saddam in his willingness to take risks. The extent to which he now underestimated the United States is suggested by an incident in October of that year. A substantial contingent of the Republican Guard rolled south from central Iraq toward Kuwait, in an apparent attempt to overturn the results of the Gulf War. Even Clinton could not abide such a sudden and drastic reversal. Immediately, substantial numbers of American soldiers and marines deployed to Kuwait, aircraft carriers moved out to the Middle East, and air force squadrons converged on the area. Saddam withdrew, perhaps on the advice of generals who, whatever their slavish loyalty to the regime, had no desire to face the Americans on another battlefield. With the Iraqis in retreat, Clinton refrained from taking direct retaliatory actions, and the Republican Guards returned to their barracks unharmed.

The saddest aspect of these cat-and-mouse games was Saddam's rejection of the U.N.'s proposal to trade oil for food and medical supplies. As the Iraqi population steadily sank into desperate poverty, he held out for the lifting of all economic and political sanctions. Saddam's rationale for standing firm was twofold. First, such a program of exchange would allow the United Nations to interfere in Iraq's internal affairs, and that was intolerable. Second, before too much longer the U.N. would likely end sanctions altogether, to prevent thousands of Iraqis from starving; and if it did not, to nearly all in the Islamic world and many in the West these deaths would not be his fault.

In 1996, inexplicably, Saddam finally yielded. The U.N. then permitted Iraq to sell nearly one billion dollars' worth of oil per month on the open market. Humanitarian aid flowed toward Iraq, but most of it was siphoned into the bank accounts of leading Baath loyalists, foremost among them Saddam's sons, Qusay and Uday. Very little humanitarian aid trickled down to average Iraqis. Moreover, U.N. workers were under constant harassment by the regime's thugs, and at times their lives were directly threatened. In 1994 Saddam went so far as to offer $10,000 to any Iraqi who killed a U.N. relief worker in northern Iraq. In July 2000, when gunmen dispatched from Baghdad began taking shots at U.N. personnel in southern Iraq, the United Nations pulled its agricultural teams out of the region.

Meanwhile, substantial amounts of cash earned through black market shipments of oil went straight into Saddam's coffers. Most of these funds were used to build or refurbish palaces for his entourage rather than to purchase arms for defense from external attack. But then again, Saddam did not expect the United States to ever actually attack him.

Compliance with UNSCOM's inspection efforts was the one sure way to get the sanctions lifted, but throughout the 1990s Saddam went to great lengths to impair UNSCOM's activities. A number of factors drove Saddam down this road. First, UNSCOM's inspectors proved far too effective in uncovering Iraq's programs to develop weapons of mass destruction, especially nuclear programs. The Iraqis were forced to dismantle them one at a time. Second, the inspections were providing a bird's-eye view of how badly the war had damaged Iraq's infrastructure and how deeply sanctions were biting into Iraq's military and political stability. For a regime based on secrecy, such transparency was unacceptable.

The Kabuki dance between UNSCOM inspectors and truculent Iraqis continued year after year. Saddam would push matters to the brink of war, only to back down under U.S. and British pressure.

In 1999 the situation finally came to a head. After a series of confrontations, the Iraqis barred UNSCOM inspectors from Baath Party headquarters. On December 16 the Clinton administration replied with Operation Desert Fox—a series of cruise missile and fighter bomber strikes aimed primarily at the Republican Guard. This operation was launched on the day the House of Representatives voted articles of impeachment against Clinton for lying to a grand jury in the Monica Lewinsky affair. Whatever the actual connection between those two events might or might not have been, Saddam certainly thought he saw a connection, and it confirmed his belief that America—now embroiled in scandal—was incapable of taking tougher actions than distant bombardment. No matter how skillfully delivered or how brilliant the target selection, air attacks were simply not going to bring the Baath Party down. Moreover, by these attacks the United States had rendered the possibility of further weapons inspections moot.

In the mid-1990s Saddam began to take direct action against the no-fly zones enforced by the United States and Britain over northern and southern Iraq. Despite considerable efforts of the Iraqis to shoot down one of the offending planes with a lucky hit from a surface-to-air missile, Coalition aircraft continued to fly with impunity over much of Iraq. When the Iraqis invariably missed their target, the aircraft under attack would fire back and destroy the offending missile and radar sites. Saddam began to place his missile batteries and radars inside schools and monuments or on top of archeological sites, inviting the world's sole superpower to play a game of chicken.

By the turn of the millennium Saddam was convinced that the end of sanctions was in sight. At the United Nations, questions were being asked about the purpose of enforcing the no-fly zones. To what end were sanctions continued—except the starvation of innocent Iraqis? Although the collapse of sanctions would inevitably lead to Iraq's regaining a measure of its power in the Gulf, Saddam was not willing to help the process along even one inch through self-effacing compromise. Defiant as usual, he offered rewards of $10,000 to the family of every suicide bomber in the Arab world who attacked the state of Israel. Some experts on Iraq wondered what he would be capable of doing if the sanctions were lifted and Iraq were again in control of its petroleum fortune. But most refused to address the implications of Iraq's past track record for the future, if sanctions should go away.

In January 2001 George W. Bush and his team of advisers took office, following a narrow election victory and unseemly squabbling on both sides over the counting of ballots in Florida. Could the incoming administration marshal the will of the nation to tackle the Iraqi challenge head on, or would the president go down the road of evasion and avoidance that Bill Clinton and Bush's own father had followed in dealing with Saddam? This was the difficult question the new administration asked itself. As it turned out, the president did not have to come up with a response. The question was answered for him by others.

A CLASH OF CIVILIZATIONS

Spartans, in the course of my life I have taken part in many wars, and I see among you many people of the same age as I am. They and I have had experience, and so are not likely to share in what may be a general enthusiasm for war, nor to think that war is a good thing or a safe thing.

THUCYDIDES, *History of the Peloponnesian War*, fifth century BC

On September 11, 2001, the fanatical operatives of Osama bin Laden flew jetliners into three symbols of American power: the twin towers of the World Trade Center and the Pentagon. A fourth jet, targeted for either the White House or the Capitol, crashed in Pennsylvania as passengers struggled heroically to take back control of the aircraft. At this point, the game changed. For the first time since the War of 1812, the citizens and symbols of the United States of America had come under sustained attack on American territory. There was little to link the Iraqis to these events, while much connected the Taliban in Afghanistan to Osama bin Laden's Al Qaeda terrorist network, not least of all the fact that its leadership was harbored there.

September 11 forced Americans to reevaluate their understanding of the external world. History had not ended with the fall of the Soviet Union in 1989. A "clash of civilizations" between portions of the Islamic world and the West now seemed very real. That clash had little to do with poverty; the suicide pilots had come from the Arab middle classes and had enjoyed many material privileges. Nor was the Islamic world reacting to the aggressions of the crusader West, as former president Clinton suggested in October 2002. During thirteen centuries of relations between Christianity and Islam, most of the time Islam has been the aggressor. The central problem lay in the fact that history was asking the Islamic world to adjust to modernity in barely eighty years—a condition that the West had taken well over five centuries to create.

Without the events of September 11, George W. Bush, like his predecessors, would not have garnered the will to conduct a war against Iraq. And the American electorate would not have supported it. It is even less conceivable that Tony Blair would have been willing to participate in such an endeavor. The road from September 11, 2001, to March 19, 2003, will emerge in greater detail in the memoirs of those who participated in the debates and in the documentary evidence that eventually will be released into the public domain. But the skeleton of what happened is already available in outline.

The pressing problem confronting the United States in the aftermath of September 11 was what actions to take to combat terrorism around the world. Firing off cruise missiles against uncertain targets, such as terrorist training camps in Afghanistan, would hardly address the threats raised by Al Qaeda's murderous attack. The problem of tailoring a response was particularly difficult because the terrorists responsible represented neither a government nor a state. Rather, they owed their allegiance to an individual and his extremist beliefs. Granted, bin Laden and many of his chief lieutenants were harbored by the failed state of Afghanistan, whose Taliban rulers had hardly any friends in the world. But it was a difficult place to reach, and the fact that its warriors had fought the Soviet Union to a standstill in the 1980s gave the administration pause.

Not surprisingly, many in the West despaired. The attacks by Islamist fanatics were all America's fault, they said, and military intervention in Afghanistan would lead to another Vietnam quagmire. At the other extreme, some argued that the United States should respond immediately with an all-out invasion of Afghanistan. More prudent counsel in the Bush administration took a middle course. Using a skillful combination of diplomacy, special operations forces, and precision capabilities to attack the Taliban's supporters, together with a liberal use of cash and weapons to buy the cooperation of Afghan tribesmen, the United States overthrew the Taliban regime in short order. The Al Qaeda network was severely damaged, though the operation failed to catch or kill bin Laden. Still, the performance of U.S. forces in Operation Enduring Freedom, as the Afghanistan conflict was called, underlined the military capabilities the United States could project when it had the will to do so. What was not so clear was whether American leaders were prepared to follow through and establish a more equitable government in Afghanistan from the wreckage of twenty-five years of war.

In summer 2002, the Bush administration began to assemble a coalition to deal with Saddam Hussein once and for all. For American leaders and those states willing to participate, the most compelling argument for the use of force against Iraq was the potential threat of weapons of mass destruction. Before the Gulf War in 1991, the international community had possessed incontrovertible evidence that Iraq had embarked on massive programs aimed at developing biological and chemical weapons. After the end of that war, UNSCOM inspections uncovered solid evidence that Iraq was close to possessing a nuclear device when it invaded Kuwait. The Gulf War's air campaign and the inspections that followed set Iraq's nuclear program back substantially—that much was known—but no one, including intelligence agencies, could be sure how far. The extent of Saddam's biological and chemical weapons program was also unknown. Weighing heavily on the Bush administration was the fact that Saddam had already shown a willingness to use chemical and biological weapons against his internal and external enemies: Kurdish citizens and Iranian soldiers. Moreover, Saddam had stated in innumerable speeches that he would not hesitate to use weapons of mass destruction (WMD) against Israel, if the opportunity arose. Most threatening, perhaps, was the prospect that, as a rogue state, Iraq seemed capable of passing nuclear or biological devices to terrorists to use against the United States.

The intelligence regarding Saddam's WMD program in the period immediately before the launching of military operations was ambiguous—as intelligence always is in an uncertain and unpredictable world. Intelligence analysts were likely misled by a predisposition to interpret the bits and pieces of information that filtered out from Iraq in accordance with Iraq's past behavior, and in a way that would obscure their own previous failures. After all, prior to the Gulf War, Iraq had one of the most ambitious programs in the world to develop nuclear weapons, and yet the American intelligence community had failed to discover it. In late 2002, Saddam's penchant for secrecy did his regime an enormous disservice. By providing such grudging and inadequate support for Hans Blix's U.N. weapons inspectors, Saddam signaled that he had something dangerous to hide. This behavior cleared the road for Bush and Blair to launch a preemptive invasion, ostensibly to prevent the use of those presumed weapons, even without U.N. support.

The intelligence community was not the only group predisposed to believe that a WMD program was under way in Iraq. The military was persuaded as well. The stringent protection measures that the Coalition enforced on their troops is strong evidence that military leaders themselves expected chemical or biological attack.

A major factor for the Bush administration in the summer of 2002 was the disarray of international sanctions against Iraq. Clearly, the United Nations was not going to abide the continuation of sanctions for much longer, and a number of opportunistic nations were already drumming up business for their products, which Iraq would have the money to buy from its enormous petroleum sales. Saddam had already signed a huge contract at unfavorable terms with French construction firms to revamp his antiquated oil infrastructure. The long-range prospect of rearmament must have worried policy makers in Washington even more than fears that the Iraqis actually possessed and would use weapons of mass destruction in the near term. As MacGregor Knox, Stevenson Professor of International History at the London School of Economics, pointed out in June 2003: "'Regime change' in Iraq seemed imperative not because Saddam necessarily still had weapons of mass destruction—although the Coalition, judging by the rubber suits the troops initially wore, genuinely feared that he did—but because his continuance in power and his oil wealth guaranteed that he *would* have them again if he survived."[8]

Moreover, there was also an undertow of feeling in Washington that the foreign policy of the Clinton administration had projected an image of the United States as a paper tiger, unwilling to use force even when its citizens and their vital interests were at stake. To many detractors and enemies around the globe, the United States appeared incapable of risking the lives of its troops to defeat a rogue state like Iraq. In the post–September 11 world, as the Bush administration understood, an international reputation for weakness could prove to be extremely dangerous. The destruction of Saddam's regime in a short, swift military campaign offered the chance to warn others that the United States' interests could be threatened only at terrible cost to the aggressors.

Policy makers in the Bush administration probably hoped to establish as strong a coalition as the one the president's father had put together in 1991. That desire contributed to the decision to go through the difficult processes of diplomacy in the United Nations. The result was a serious deterioration in U.S. relations with Germany and France. The German antiwar reaction should not have surprised American observers. The deeply ingrained pacifism of German society today represents the success of U.S. efforts after World War II to alter the mindset that had made the Reich such a disaster for Europe and the world in the first half of the twentieth century.

French attitudes were also consistent with that nation's past performance in doing business with Saddam. It was the French who justified their decision in the early 1980s to supply Iraq with technology to build a nuclear weapon by arguing that the Israelis already possessed one. With the lifting of sanctions, huge profits would be made in Iraq, should Saddam survive to reward his friends, and French businesses were already in the queue. Ironically, the obduracy of Chirac's position in early 2003 that no evidence, no matter how compelling, could convince France to support a war against Iraq played a major role in swinging British public opinion behind the Blair government in its support of the Americans.

Britain's decision to align itself with the United States reflected a number of concerns. One was the worry that Iraq would use WMD on its neighbors and enemies, and, more important, that it would return seriously to the business of producing these weapons once it was free from trade restrictions. But a more subtle motive underlay Blair's strong support of the United States. For the past six decades British governments had performed a delicate balancing act between deeper participation in the affairs of the Continent and maintenance of the special relationship with the United States. As a senior British general suggested to the authors, a failure to support the American initiative in Iraq would inevitably have upset that balance, and Britain would have fallen into just the sort of entanglement with Europe that it had been careful to avoid.

By early January 2003 the date for war had been pinned to the wall. American and British military power was flowing with increasing speed to the Gulf. The United States aimed to make an example out of Saddam's regime, for better or worse. Ironically, only Saddam and his followers appeared to miss the warning signs of the gathering storm. They might have wriggled out at the last moment by wholehearted cooperation with the weapons inspectors. They did not. Consequently, the United States was able to serve up Saddam's regime as a salient warning to those who would dare to attack America's vital interests anywhere on the globe. But in Iraq, as history has repeatedly shown, victory always seems to entail more than just military success.

2

The Opposing Sides

War is not an exercise of the will directed at inanimate matter, as is the case with the mechanical arts, or at matter which is animate but passive and yielding, as is the case with the human mind and emotions in the fine arts. In war the will is directed at an animate object that *reacts.*

CARL VON CLAUSEWITZ, *On War,* nineteenth century

Thirty years after Vietnam, most Americans find it difficult to remember the sad state of U.S. military institutions following their humiliating experience in Southeast Asia. By the end of 1972 the bedraggled remains of the conscript forces, dispatched in 1965 to "pay any price, bear any burden," had returned to garrisons in the United States, Korea, and Europe. The new all-volunteer army consisted of disillusioned, often bitter soldiers equipped with weapons that bordered on the obsolete. A drug culture reigned in the barracks such that officers and NCOs dared enter only if fully armed.

The American people, especially the upper and middle classes, sickened by the slaughter in Vietnam, looked with disdain on their nation's defense forces. Polls in the early 1970s indicated that barely 50 percent of citizens thought their country should defend Canada if that nation were attacked. Only the U.S. nuclear deterrent and the Soviet-Chinese stand-off prevented the Communist powers from moving directly against America's vital interests. Yet, out of that grim situation eventually emerged a new, all-volunteer, technologically sophisticated military, which within two decades would prove itself on the battlefields of the Middle East and elsewhere. The story of that dramatic comeback is one of the greatest in American military history.

It began when a new generation of military leaders came to power in the late 1970s, men who had watched their superiors butcher the war in Vietnam. The first step was to restore discipline by weeding out the drug addicts, the poorly educated, and the lazy. The next steps involved the reinvention of the military as a serious profession—one that demanded intellectual as well as physical prowess. For officers, the latter challenge required serious focus on the complex tasks involved in articulating violence on the battlefield. The publication in 1976 of a brilliant translation of Carl von Clausewitz's *On War*, originally written in the 1820s and considered by most military historians as the most perceptive theoretical treatise on war ever written, provided an intellectual rationale for rethinking the profession of arms in the United States.

Changing the U.S. military was neither easy nor swift. The most difficult change, but also the most profound, occurred in the leadership's reconception of the nature of war. In the late 1970s one of the army's most respected senior generals, Donn Starry, began to develop a concept of operations that he and the army would later term

"AirLand Battle." Starry's epiphany occurred when he served as a corps commander in Germany and confronted the real threat of a massive Soviet offensive through the Fulda Gap—the prominent terrain corridor that runs from former East Germany toward Frankfurt in the west. It was not so much the first wave of invaders that worried him as succeeding waves of follow-on forces. In developing his concept of AirLand Battle, Starry's aim was two-fold: to hold and defeat the initial Soviet onslaught while at the same time attacking and substantially disrupting movement of the Red Army's reserves deep behind the front line.

Around the same time, a number of military thinkers, influenced by German and Soviet terminology, began examining what the military today terms the operational level of war—the maneuver of large formations and firepower at the corps level and above. Such operations may include specific missions, such as the landing of an expeditionary force in Normandy, or they may be generic, as in the conduct of amphibious assaults throughout the Pacific. Operations over vast distances and extended periods, called campaigns, involve armies, fleets, and air forces with personnel numbering in the tens of thousands. But operations may also include the activities of smaller forces for shorter periods of time. By the mid-1980s, a new second-year intensive program at the army's Command and General Staff College at Fort Leavenworth emphasized the study of past campaigns as a means of understanding operational planning in the future. It reinforced the trend toward a more thoughtful approach to the study of war.

By 1986 these intellectual developments culminated in the appearance of a new edition of the army's basic manual on how to conduct complex military operations, *Field Manual 100-5*. The concepts in that manual represented a revolution in how the army thought about and prepared itself for war. The new emphasis was on maneuver, deception, exploitation, and decentralized leadership. The latter was particularly important, because if army units were to move rapidly, then junior officers and NCOs would have to make decisions on the spot to take advantage of changing situations and opportunities. Within this new doctrinal framework, junior leaders would not have time to wait for orders. *FM 100-5* was followed by an equally revolutionary statement of change in the Marine Corps' basic doctrinal manual. Its *Fleet Manual 1: Warfighting* articulated principles similar to those in *FM 100-5*.

All of this intellectual ferment would have amounted to little had the American people and their representatives refused to appropriate funds for military resources and equipment. The Soviet invasion of Afghanistan in December 1979, along with the disastrous failure of U.S. military forces to free embassy personnel held hostage in Iran, finally awoke the nation to the harsh reality that the external world was indeed a dangerous place—a world where the Soviet Union and others posed a direct threat and where military power mattered. The result was that defense budgets began to rise in the last years of the Carter administration. With the election of Ronald Reagan in November 1980, the floodgates of military spending opened wide.

THE REBIRTH OF AMERICAN MILITARY POWER

The end for which a soldier is recruited, clothed, armed, and trained, the whole object of his sleeping, eating, drinking, and marching, is simply that he should fight at the right place and at the right time.

CARL VON CLAUSEWITZ, *On War,* nineteenth century

In the 1970s, along with the reintroduction of ancient verities that had stood the test of time—training, discipline, and professionalism—came an unprecedented and growing wave of technological change. These innovations had begun to transform the U.S. military in the last year of America's participation in the Vietnam War. In 1972, first in Operation Linebacker I, the aerial offensive that halted the North Vietnamese advance against South Vietnam in the spring, and then in Linebacker II, the final massive aerial assault on the heartland of the North Vietnamese in December, the U.S. Air Force dropped over 27,000 laser-guided bombs against various targets. While primitive by today's standards, these first LGBs improved accuracy by an order of magnitude over the conventional bombs that pilots had been dropping since World War II with "a wish and a prayer."

To take just one example: from 1965 to 1968, in Operation Rolling Thunder, American fighter bombers had flown hundreds of sorties to destroy the great railroad bridge at Thanh Hoa, all without success and with considerable losses to the crews flying the mission. (The North Vietnamese had been able to destroy the bridge's predecessor in the early 1950s only by crashing two French ammunition trains in the middle.) The new bridge, finished in 1964, had been designed to survive heavy attacks, because the only rail route south from Hanoi passed over it. On May 13, 1972, a strike package of fourteen F-4 Phantom fighter bombers, armed with 2,000 and 3,000-pound LGBs, dropped the bridge on the second try.

During the Ford and Carter administrations, defense budgets were sparse. Nevertheless, great strides were made in designing new weapons systems, including the first steps toward developing a stealth aircraft. By the late 1970s, research was far enough along for Secretary of Defense Harold Brown to announce that a stealth bomber was in the works. Other simpler but truly modern weapons systems were past the prototype phase, and some were in the first stages of production. The F-15 and F-16 would soon revolutionize America's air-to-air capabilities; the former, with its advanced radar and air-to-air Sidewinder missiles (both upgraded over the past two decades), has outperformed every fighter it has ever faced. In the 1980s in the Falklands, the Sidewinder on British Harrier jumpjets proved itself against the Argentineans, and in the Middle East the Israelis employed it on their F-15s against the Syrians, as America's allies ran up impressive scores against top-of-the line French and Soviet equipment.

In the late 1970s the army was on the brink of fielding the Abrams tank and the Bradley Infantry Fighting Vehicle. The Abrams—the first armored fighting vehicle designed with an emphasis on crew protection—would become the most formidable tank in the world. Its upgraded 120mm main gun, firing depleted uranium rounds, combined with state-of-the-art acquisition and sighting technologies, can destroy enemy tanks at ranges upwards of 4,000 yards with first-round precision. Meanwhile, the navy was re-equipping its squadrons with the F-14 Tomcat fighter, whose radar system could reach out over 200 miles and track multiple targets. Massive Nimitz-class aircraft carriers were making up an increasingly large portion of America's maritime power at the decade's end.

But perhaps the paradigm shift in American military technology owes its greatest debt to the explosion in computer capacity in the late 1970s and early 1980s. The miniaturization of computers was a direct result of the Cold War competition with the Soviets to land the first man on the moon. By the late 1970s this revolution had moved from the space race to the arms race, as U.S. companies geared up to design, develop, and produce electronically advanced weapons systems.

In 1981, under the new Reagan administration, the United States initiated a drastic program of rearmament. Pay raises and allowances for college benefits made the all-volunteer military an attractive option for high school graduates from the working and lower-middle classes, at a time when college tuitions were rising astronomically. Reagan's defense budgets also provided for instrumented training ranges at Fort Irwin for the army, at Twenty-Nine Palms for the marine corps, and in the deserts west of Las Vegas for the air force. At those installations, trigger pullers and commanders alike could hone their skills against real "aggressor forces," which in most respects were far better trained than the actual forces of the Soviet Union. The entire regimen of training, from entrance into basic training to massive exercises at instrumented training ranges, became more complex, realistic, demanding, and unforgiving.

The U.S. invasion of the tiny Caribbean island of Grenada in fall 1983 revealed that, despite improvements in the capabilities of the individual services, they had not yet reached the ability to work together cooperatively. Army radios could not talk to air force or marine radios. One army company commander had to use his AT&T credit card to call the operations center at Fort Bragg in North Carolina to relay a crucial message to aircraft overhead. Joint command and control for the operation barely existed, as each of the services fought its own individual campaign. Recognizing these difficulties, Congress stepped in to correct a situation that neither the civilian leadership in the Pentagon nor the services were willing to address.

The Goldwater-Nichols Act, passed in 1986, forced a far higher degree of cooperation on the service bureaucracies and gave regional commanders-in-chief (now called combatant commanders) greater authority. The chairman of the joint chiefs of staff became much more than the "first among equals" in his relationship with the service chiefs. And perhaps most important, Congress decreed that officers must have a tour on a joint staff in order to be eligible for promotion to flag or general officer rank.

In the nearly two decades since Goldwater-Nichols passed, the operations conducted by the American military have displayed an increasing ability to fight jointly, rather than as separate entities. The changeover is not yet complete, and in its underpinnings of doctrine and its intellectual depth the concept of joint operations remains immature. On the other hand, a completely joint force, such as the one that Canada has attempted to create, is not necessarily desirable—it could even lead to disaster. The perspective and culture that each of the services brings to the table have been molded by the unique environments in which airmen, sailors, soldiers, and marines work, train, and fight. Truly joint operations that are militarily effective demand capabilities developed under very different conditions before they are joined together.

To most American officers working at integrating new technologies, methods of thinking, and training regimens into their services during the 1980s, a slow but steady evolution appeared under way. But from the point of view of the Soviets, the American advances seemed revolutionary—and their own system could not match them. Stealth, precision weaponry, and command and control technologies threatened the massive conventional forces that the Soviet military had bankrupted their nation to create. In effect, the new precision weapons were making tactical nuclear weapons obsolete; the U.S. military could achieve the same results that would have required the use of tactical nuclear weapons in the 1970s and before.

A number of factors contributed to the collapse of the Soviet empire in 1989, and the new paradigm of war created by the U.S. military was not the least of these. But the sudden and largely unexpected end of the Cold War confronted the American military with a startling new situation: what use were military forces created to fight the Soviet Union, now that the Soviet Union no longer existed? The question of what was going to happen to America's great military edifice in a world where the United States was the sole superpower was of crucial concern to professional officers.

It was answered almost immediately by two international crises. In the first one, President George H. W. Bush ordered the U.S. armed forces to overthrow the government of Panama, arrest its dictator, Manuel Noriega, and create the conditions for a stable democratic government. Although Noriega had been in the pay of the U.S. army and the CIA for more than thirty years, he had also been working as a double agent for the Communists. In that role he had turned over highly classified material to Cuba, facilitating the sale of restricted U.S. technologies to the Soviet bloc, and he had also sold arms to Cuban-backed guerrillas in Latin America—all in addition to pocketing millions of dollars from drug trafficking.

In December 1989 the American military executed the first part of the president's orders in exemplary fashion, by carrying out a complex, many-faceted operation, called Just Cause, which brought down the Panamanian government and its police forces in a matter of hours. Ground, sea, and air forces arrived at night, striking and capturing targets across Panama. Special operations forces, led by the 75th Ranger Regiment, parachuted onto the Rio Hato, Torrijos, and Tocumen airfields to open the door for follow-on forces from the 82nd Airborne Division. The marines seized the key Bridge of the Americas to isolate the west bank of the canal, while navy SEALs attacked over the beach to capture Patilla airfield and disable Panamanian patrol boats. Airborne, mechanized, and light infantry task forces from within Panama moved out quickly on the ground to seize the Panamanian Defense Forces Headquarters, the Commandancia, and other facilities. Firepower, also delivered from strategic distances, balanced maneuver. Two F-117s, flying from Nellis Air Force Base in Nevada, each dropped 2,000-pound LGBs near the infantry barracks at Rio Hato to distract the Panamanians just before the rangers parachuted from 500 feet onto the airfield. The most effective firepower system proved to be the AC-130 gunships, which circled continuously over friendly troops, destroying enemy vehicles and reinforcements.

In many respects, Operation Just Cause gave U.S. commanders a first tantalizing glimpse of how an invasion of Iraq might progress. Maneuver in Panama was nonlinear and focused on control of the whole operational area rather than on the sequential capture of key terrain and high ground characteristic of more traditional forms of maneuver. In this campaign, the American military also had to explain its actions to the public—literally, as it was fighting—because over fifty members of the media were already on the ground when the operation began. Street fighting in Panama City raised the disconcerting prospect of urban warfare in Third World countries—a nasty foretaste of what the U.S. military would run into in Somalia in 1993. From a military point of view, Just Cause represented an enormous success, perhaps more prophetic of future U.S. combat operations than Desert Storm would be a year later.

The second half of the mission—capture of Noriega himself—proved more difficult to accomplish. Television images of U.S. troops playing exceedingly loud rock music in front of the Vatican's embassy in Panama City to drive Noriega from his refuge and force him to surrender did not exactly represent a triumph of foresight. Moreover, a general lack of preparation to assume civil authority once the Panamanian government had fallen resulted in widespread looting and lawlessness that tarnished some of the military success. The army in particular confronted the challenge of providing thousands of Panamanians with food, shelter, and protection for months after the shooting had stopped.

No sooner had the military finished mopping up after its successful strike against Panama than a second international crisis arose—the Iraqi invasion of Kuwait. This situation raised a number of interesting strategic as well as operational issues that war planners had not faced in Panama. Foremost was the reluctance of American military leaders to use force against Iraq at all. They hesitated for a number of reasons. The most obvious was a consistent proclivity on the part of U.S. intelligence agencies and military leaders themselves to overestimate Iraq's military capabilities. This continued even after the crushing Battle of Kafji in early February 1991 revealed the weaknesses of Saddam's ground forces. Undoubtedly, the nightmare of Vietnam played its part as well. But the most influential reason behind the U.S. reluctance to use military force was the Powell doctrine, propagated by General Colin Powell, chairman of the joint chiefs of staff during the Gulf War. That doctrine—which demanded national unanimity, mobilization of the full might of the American military, overwhelming force, clear objectives, and other restrictions—set such prohibitive conditions on the use of American military power that, had they been applied to the nation's previous conflicts, it is doubtful the United States would ever have fought a war at any time in its history. But Bush and his other advisers had no faith that sanctions or international pressure would work, although they did give Saddam plenty of time during the build-up to pull out of Kuwait. Thus, U.S. forces deployed to Kuwait and Saudi Arabia for the showdown that came on January 17.

The conduct of war in the Gulf was hamstrung by a lack of synergy between the air and ground forces. By the time General Norman Schwarzkopf, with Powell's concurrence, saw fit to launch ground forces, Saddam's troops had already torched oil wells and dumped millions of gallons of crude into the Persian Gulf as they withdrew from Kuwait. Had Saddam withdrawn two weeks earlier, he might have walked away with a strategic victory in the war, because his army would have been undefeated in the field. By the time the dust finally settled, even the Palestinians, with their memorable record for backing the wrong horse, had to admit the defeat of Saddam, one of their greatest heroes. This did not prevent Saddam from claiming victory to his own people, however—a claim which many Iraqis may not have believed but which they could dispute only at the risk of life and limb.

American servicemen and women celebrated victory, but President

Bush's diplomatic and military successes in Iraq did not translate into victory at the polls. In November 1992, with economic recession lingering as Americans went out to vote, William Jefferson Clinton was elected president on a platform emphasizing economic revitalization and downplaying foreign policy and armed forces in a globalized, wired world.

During the election campaign, as Yugoslavia splintered into warring nationalities, Powell prevented the use of force to halt the spread of ethnic violence. In retrospect, a decisive reaction from America's or NATO's naval forces to the shelling of Dubrovnik by the Serbs in December 1992 might have prevented the atrocities that were to follow. But neither the Europeans nor Bush, now a lame-duck president, was willing to take such intrusive action, while U.S. military leaders certainly felt no desire to involve their forces in the Balkan quagmire.

Thus, almost from the first days of his tenure in office, a struggle ensued over Clinton's vision of a military that would make major efforts at political stabilization and nation building in the Third World—and in some cases even in the Second World—and attitudes within the services and joint staff that America's military conducted only big operations. In Clinton's first year, the disaster in Somalia only enlarged this gap. On the Horn of Africa, the fundamentally flawed policies of the United Nations, to which the United States had contributed substantially, resulted in the death of eighteen Americans at the hands of Aideed's mobs. For the most part, the generals rejected Clinton's desire for the military to play a major role in peace-keeping operations—an ironic stance, given that such a role would represent an argument for larger defense budgets and more manpower.

Then, in early 1994, one of the bloodiest and most gruesome genocides in the twentieth century took place in Rwanda—a civil war between the Tutsis and the Hutus encouraged and abetted by the policies of the French. Clinton chose to stand aside, fully backed by his military advisers. Only the most egregious actions by the Serbs in the late 1990s eventually forced the hand of America and its European allies in the Balkans.

While the United States, which has continued to spend more resources on defense than any other nation, confronted the vexing problem of what to do with its military forces, vast changes were taking place in the capabilities of the services. By the 1990s the computer revolution had reached warp speed and was having an enormous impact in communications (synchronous and asynchronous), data collection, information procuring, intelligence gathering, and speed of calculation. The Global Positioning System, which had been of limited use in 1991 in helping Coalition ground forces find their way around Iraq's deserts, was an integral part of a number of weapons systems by 2003. These ranged from cruise missiles to JDAMs (joint direct attack munitions)—bombs guided largely by GPS rather than by laser designators. With such technology onboard, U.S. bombers could now hit targets with pinpoint accuracy in any weather condition.

A downside to military developments in the 1990s was the Vietnam War generation's retirement from the officer corps. While Vietnam-era leaders never rejected technology as an important component in war, through painful exposure to its limitations they also understood—in a way civilians could not—that uncertainty, ambiguity, chance, and friction are dominant factors in the conduct of war. The retirement of those officers brought forward a new generation enthusiastic about the possibilities of technological change for its own sake. Some went so far as to claim that technology would remove the fog of war entirely from the battlefield. Others suggested that the pervasiveness of reconnaissance systems and the accuracy of precision munitions would allow the American military to destroy any mobile target in the world. To some it seemed that the dreams of the air pioneer and advocate General Billy Mitchell had come true. The United States no longer needed ground or naval forces but could fight its wars at a distance, primarily from the air. While such claims never dominated the thinking of the U.S. military, they exercised an influence over budgets and debates as a new century approached.

The post-9/11 war in Afghanistan tested these propositions. It was waged almost entirely by special operations forces (SOF) heavily supported by air power, both of which provided combat support for the fighters of the Northern Alliance. By using laser designators and GPS devices, SOF advisers were able to call in devastating air strikes on the Taliban's ill-trained and undisciplined warriors. Technology proved a huge boon to these exceedingly well-trained allied forces. Significantly, the U.S. special forces were drawn from the army, navy, and air force and worked in seamless cooperation. In the Gulf War a decade earlier, Schwarzkopf had hardly used special ops at all, but now they were the major focus of efforts to run Al Qaeda to ground. In addition to conventional air power, initially supplied largely by the navy and marine corps, unmanned aerial vehicles (UAVs) brought tactical intelligence to a new level in Afghanistan. Conventional ground forces moved in as follow-on forces, after much of the country had been liberated from the Taliban.

Two major lessons emerged from Operation Enduring Freedom. The first was that ground forces in some form are necessary for both military and political reasons. For much of the world, victory and defeat is a simple calculation of who has boots *on the ground* at the end of a conflict. The second lesson, equally clear, was that friction and uncertainty, at times intensified by the confusion that technology can bring in its wake, would continue to dominate the battlefields of the future, as it had battlefields of the past. In the fire fight on Takur Ghar Mountain over the night of March 3–4, 2002, for example, seven American special forces troopers died (one from the navy, one from the air force, and five from the army) because of miscommunications, miscalculations, and mistakes—all of which have characterized war since the dawn of history.

If anything, the most modern technologies can at times exacerbate those frictions. As a special forces soldier noted about the fight that night: "The U.S. military is fielding some outstanding technologies to support its missions. Many of these technologies saw their first combat use during operations in Afghanistan. The preponderance of the equipment and systems worked exactly as advertised. Although . . . the latest technology helped in achieving battlefield dominance, there were instances where over-confidence actually made matters worse."[1]

COALITION GROUND FORCES

For [the Romans] do not begin to use their weapons first in time of war, nor do they then put their hands first into motion, having been idle in times of peace; but as if their weapons were part of themselves, they never have any truce from warlike exercises . . . nor would he be mistaken that would call their exercises unbloody battles, and their battles bloody exercises.

FLAVIUS JOSEPHUS, *The Great Roman-Jewish War,* first century AD

By the start of the twenty-first century the military forces of the United States were undergoing significant changes in organization. Some theorists were characterizing these changes as a "revolution in military affairs." Whatever one's views on that claim might be, without doubt U.S. military forces fought the Iraq War of 2003 in a substantially different way than they had the Gulf War in 1991. What was different and what remained the same?

In organizational form, much did not change between the two wars. In overall command of military operations was U.S. Central Command (Centcom), headed by General Tommy Franks, a thirty-four-year army (and Vietnam) veteran. As with Schwarzkopf in the Gulf War, Franks had both air and naval component commanders as deputies. But because he was simultaneously responsible for the war in Afghanistan, Franks had the Third Army Commander, Lieutenant General David McKiernan, serve as the ground component commander in Iraq, whereas Schwarzkopf had taken on this job himself. McKiernan coordinated the army's V Corps drive through the desert to the west of the Euphrates and the I Marine Expeditionary Force's drive through Iraq's heartland between the Tigris and the Euphrates River, both on their way to Baghdad.

As the Combined Force Land Component Commander (CFLCC) McKiernan proved to be an inspired choice. Not only did he possess an instinct for operational issues, but he had served as the chief of plans for NATO's Allied Rapid Reaction Corps (the ARRC, "ark"), the majority of whose officers were British. The ARRC had played a major role in planning NATO's move into Kosovo in the late 1990s. McKiernan's chief deputy at AARC had been Colonel Albert Whitley, British Army. When McKiernan took over as the land component commander for the upcoming Iraq campaign, not only was he assigned a number of the brightest planners from the army and the marine corps but he also received Whitley, now a major general, as the British representative to Third Army headquarters for planning the war. And, not surprisingly, Whitley found himself as a special adviser to McKiernan, where he fit in smoothly with his old boss's style and proved invaluable as a conduit for British concerns as they began their hurried deployment to the Gulf.

McKiernan enjoyed a respectful rapport with his subordinates and, unlike some generals, he was willing to listen to them. British officers referred to him simply as General Dave. But he also possessed a reputation as a warfighter who had consistently, throughout his career, demanded realistic, hard training from the units under his command.

One of his officers described him in the following terms: "A consummate professional, very nonpolitical, absolutely handles stress well—never panics, always looks for options. Always preaches looking at the big picture—higher mission, adjacent units. Generally looks for about four things: How can I hurt the enemy [now], how can he hurt me, how will I be able to hurt him [in the future], how will he be able to hurt me. Doesn't like to be briefed by power point, likes to be briefed off a map." In addition, McKiernan forced his staff to look beyond the normal stovepipe functions and consider the larger operational issues involved in destroying the Iraqis *en masse.*

As an operational level commander, McKiernan had to decide how far to carry the armored drive through the desert, where to hit the Euphrates, when to cross that river, when and how long to stop for rest and refit before resuming the advance, how to coordinate and orchestrate I MEF's advance with that of V Corps to the advantage of both, and how to conduct the siege and assault on Baghdad. Above all, he had to think through how his opponent might react to American moves and how the Iraqis might attempt to derail the Coalition's military operations. McKiernan had to work through these possibilities in a virtual battle space that did not yet exist and which future actions by U.S. forces as well as the Iraqis might determine would never exist—all the while concerning himself with immediate events occurring in real time on the ground.

McKiernan was especially helped by a first-class staff. Here the army's vice chief of staff, General Jack Keane, played a crucial role by hand-picking some of the army's best officers to serve as the chief executors for CFLCC. Moreover, since Third Army had now transformed into a joint headquarters, the marines provided one of their most thoughtful and perceptive officers, Major General Rusty Blackman, as McKiernan's chief of staff. Respected throughout the corps for his quick wit as well as his penetrating mind, Blackman, a Cornell graduate, had served as a general officer, as the head of Marine Corps University, and as commander of the 2nd Marine Division at Camp Lejeune.

The size of the Coalition ground forces in the Iraq War was substantially smaller than those in 1991, but their organizational structure was much the same. Ground forces were parceled out among corps or, in the case of marines, in marine expeditionary forces (MEFs), divisions (containing approximately 20,000 men and women each), brigades (regiments for the marines and containing upwards of 4,000 individuals), battalions (approximately 800), companies (approximately 200), and platoons (approximately 60). Army forces were concentrated under V Corps, commanded by Lieutenant General William Wallace. He controlled approximately three divisions. Thanks to the radically increased lethality of modern technology, today's corps would equate in terms of firepower and reach to the army-sized structures of the Cold War.

V Corps' lead element in the invasion of Iraq was the 3rd Mechanized Infantry Division. During the first week of combat, V Corps received the 101st Airborne Division and a brigade of the 82nd Airborne. The fighting capabilities of the 101st rested on the mobility of its infantry units and the killing power of helicopters. Finally, as the war wound down, the 4th Infantry Division, originally scheduled to move through Turkey, began arriving in Kuwait after its equipment had made the trip from the Mediterranean and its troops had flown in from Texas.

Moving up from the south to the west of the Euphrates and then turning northeast to attack Baghdad, V Corps thus controlled the equivalent of at least two full divisions and parts of a third, with a fourth on the way if needed. The corps also brought to the fight additional engineer and supply units. It could attach them to its divisions and other units under its command, depending on the mission. At times V Corps had nearly 2,500 trucks moving along the highways west of the Euphrates to provide fuel, ammunition, and food to the divisions as they rolled northward through Iraq.

Each of the divisions and other units in V Corps brought unique and complementary capabilities to the theater. The 3rd Mechanized Infantry Division was the heaviest unit in the drive on Baghdad. The backbone of the division consisted of approximately 270 Abrams tanks that provided enormous direct firepower. Approximately 200 Bradley fighting vehicles, armed with 25mm chain guns, offered additional fire support as well as mechanized infantry support. The 3rd backed up its spearheads with Apache tank-killer helicopters and its division artillery—a brigade-sized unit that could bring direct and indirect firepower down on any Iraqi resistance.

The 4th Infantry Division was similar in organization and mission to the 3rd Infantry Division. If the Turks had cooperated with the U.S. plan to move it through Turkey, the division would have plowed through northern Iraq, undoubtedly "liberating" Saddam's hometown of Tikrit on its way to Baghdad. Of all the army's formations, the 4th Mechanized Division possessed the most up-to-date equipment. It was a fully digitized formation: its commanders could track the movements of its vehicles on the battlefield, thus reducing fratricide, while providing a coherent and up-to-the-minute picture of what was happening on the ground. The fact that on March 19 the division had barely begun to move its troops and equipment to Kuwait undoubtedly misled Saddam and his advisers into believing they still had time before an American attack, if ever they believed in their dreamworld of palaces and power that war would occur at all.

The 101st Airborne Division could not have been more different in organization. Instead of Abrams tanks and Bradleys, the division's lethal power and maneuverability came from its helicopter force. Apache helicopters with their laser-guided or radar-guided Hellfire missiles provided the means to destroy tanks, vehicles, and other targets, either moving or stationary. Close combat soldiers mounted aboard Black Hawk transport helicopters could move hundreds of miles to strike deep within enemy territory. Aerial maneuver allowed soldiers to disrupt the enemy's flow of supplies, reinforcements, and especially his command and control. Such attacks involved not only direct firepower with the accurate and deadly Hellfire but the movement of raiding parties and strike forces to seize key pieces of terrain or to reinforce or resupply units operating beyond the front lines.

The army also brought lighter airborne forces to the fight. A brigade of the 82nd Airborne Division, famed for its performance in World War II under James Gavin and Matthew Ridgeway, served as backup to the 101st, providing security to bases and supply routes. Battalion-sized units of the 82nd were also used in combination with Abrams tanks and Bradleys to form task forces to deal with Iraqi fighters in towns and cities on the road to Baghdad. A marked feature of the Iraq War was the ability of soldiers and marines to form ad hoc formations—what the Germans called *Kampfgruppen* in World War II—to deal with particular challenges. That ability reflected not only the extraordinarily high state of combat training but the doctrinal flexibility of American commanders. In the north, 82nd Airborne's sister formation, the 173rd Airborne Brigade, executed a combat drop into northern Iraq, where it supported Kurdish fighters and their special operations advisers in taking Kirkuk and Mosul. In addition, marines from the 26th Marine Expeditionary Unit (MEU) would fly in to bolster the forces in the north. The northern effort of paratroopers, marines, special forces, and Kurdish Peshmerga guerillas would all come under the command of a special forces general.

While V Corps was driving up the desert roads to the west of the Euphrates, I MEF (the marine equivalent to V Corps) crossed the Euphrates, drove up through the heartland of Iraq, and eventually crossed the Tigris River to attack Saddam's capital from the east. While the marines have three standing marine expeditionary forces (MEFs) with a division and aircraft wing as major subordinate components, they rarely get to train or deploy as corps—or division-level—entities. The basic ground combat element is the division, but the marines most frequently deploy as smaller combined arms packages called marine expeditionary units (MEUs), built around a battalion landing team composed of a reinforced rifle battalion and supporting aviation and combat support assets. Each MEF sources these MEUs in a continuous cycle of forward deployments to potential crisis spots. These deployment rotations include a robust training cycle but are geared toward MEU-level tasks, not at the theater or operational level of war. When a major contingency arises, the marines are capable of deploying and employing an MEF in division-size formations, as they did successfully in both the Gulf and Iraq wars.

In the latter conflict, Lieutenant General James Conway, commander of I MEF, had under his control the 1st Marine Division, Task Force Tarawa (a force that represented more combat power than a brigade but less than a division), the 3rd Marine Aircraft Wing, and the British 1st Armoured Division. Big, bluff, well-read, and well-educated, Jim Conway represented all that was best about the new United States Marine Corps, which General Al Gray as the commandant had built up in the late 1980s. Conway had held a number of infantry commands and served as the head of the Marine Corps Basic School in the mid-1990s. To the British, he came across as a character that John Wayne could have played; he earned their deepest respect for the moral support and friendship he offered their officers and soldiers alike. A number of British officers considered his address to the 7th Armoured Brigade just before the war began to be one of the most inspiring speeches they had ever heard. By the end of the war, relations between the marines and the British fighting men recalled to mind the finest hours of the Grand Alliance between the Anglo-American powers during World War II, a combination that brought Nazi Germany to its knees.

The 1st Marine Division consisted of three infantry regiments and one artillery regiment (each similar to an army brigade in size), supported by its own helicopter and close air support aircraft. Each of the infantry regiments consisted of three infantry battalions. The division commander, Major General James Mattis, also possessed two battalions of Abrams tanks which he attached at various times to his regiments. While a marine division may lack the armored punch of an army heavy division, it does possess considerable direct firepower support from marine aircraft, in this case the 3rd Marine Aircraft Wing's Cobra attack helicopters, Harrier jumpjets, and F/A-18 Hornet tactical fighters. The marines deploy their amtracks (short for "amphibious tractors," that is, amphibious armored personnel carriers) and light armored vehicles directly with their infantry. In the same way, the marines use their Abrams tanks more as an infantry support weapon than does the army.

Moreover, because the marines are so consistently organized and deployed in small MEU packages, they tend to parcel out armored vehicles at a lower level than is the case with the army. This has its advantages as well as disadvantages. The marine organization never provided Conway with a force massive enough to smash its way into the Iraqi capital. Unlike the army's 3rd Infantry Division, the lighter marine force faced the prospect of fighting a much tougher enemy with less direct combat power than did army forces. But here the Marine Aircraft Wing, trained directly with marine ground forces, provided responsive and effective air support.

Conway's ad hoc formation, Task Force Tarawa, combined an infantry regiment and two MEUs under its control. Larger than a bri-

gade but smaller than a division, this task force commanded five infantry battalions and two Abrams companies along with a number of
light armored vehicles and amtracs. Here again the U.S. military put
together the equivalent of a *Kampfgruppe,* which appears nowhere in
written doctrine but which met the tactical requirements and the
means at hand. Tarawa provided Conway and his marines with a second force of considerable maneuverability and combat power.

Throughout the campaign, advancing ground forces had significant
support from Coalition air forces. But the 3rd Marine Aircraft Wing
was particularly important to the forward advance of the marines,
since it was an integral part of I MEF to provide direct support. Consequently, strike aircraft were almost always on call for emergency situations and targets of opportunity. Pilots of all three of the air wing's
combat aircraft—the F/A-18 Hornet, the Harrier, and the Cobra attack helicopter—had specifically trained to support marine ground
units in combat. But also important, all their pilots had attended the
Marine Corps' four-month Basic School for officers, which had given
them a taste of what an infantryman's life was like. Equally crucial was
the fact that the marines assigned three aviators directly to each battalion to provide advice to the grunts on the ground and guidance to
their fellow aviators overhead as to where help was needed. Thus, marine air was particularly accurate and helpful to the marines engaged
in fire fights with the Iraqis.

The ground forces could also rely on support from their own integral artillery units, capable of providing instantaneous and continuous
support fires under most weather conditions. On March 25–26, when
a great sandstorm blew across Iraq from the west, artillery had to carry
much of the burden of fire support. Tube artillery and the Multiple
Launch Rocket System (MLRS) blanketed Iraqi positions with little
danger of collateral damage. During one intense artillery barrage,

Gunnery Sergeant Will Villalobos of the 1st Marine Division commented on the number of shells in the air: "It's like being an air traffic controller in Los Angeles!"[2]

The British provided a full division, the 1st Armoured Division, to the Coalition's military operations. The initial war plan had scheduled the British to participate in operations in the north, but when it became apparent at the end of December that they would not be allowed into Turkey, they began a desperate sixty-day effort to deploy a division-sized force out to the Gulf in time for G-Day (when the ground offensive would begin). It had taken the British over twenty weeks to move a division to the Gulf in 1991; for this war, they did it in ten weeks. Because of the time constraints, they were not able to get a second armored brigade there and had to substitute the lighter 16th Air Assault Brigade.

The British 1st Armoured Division (with approximately 25,000 soldiers) was not a regular division in the American sense. Rather, it was cobbled together ad hoc from a number of disparate formations. But as the British had proved in both the Falklands and the Gulf Wars, they are particularly good at such ad hocery. The division consisted of three brigades: the 7th Armoured, nicknamed the Desert Rats after the World War II formation of desert fame, the 16th Air Assault, and the 3rd Commando. The first was similar in its hitting power to a brigade of the 3rd Infantry Division. Its main battle tank was the Challenger II, similar to the Abrams but with far better mileage owing to its diesel engine. Luckily, the British had sent a number of Challenger IIs to their exercise Saif Sareea in Oman in 2002, where they discovered that their tanks needed a major desertization program to survive in this environment. The British completed a rush modification program on the tanks, which was completed in Kuwait on March 16, three days before the war began.

The 16th Air Assault Brigade's organization and purpose were similar to that of one of the brigades of the 101st Airborne, with its helicopter assets and elements of a parachute regiment. The 3rd Commando Brigade consisted of the 40th and 42nd Commandos of the Royal Marines, who were trained primarily for an amphibious role similar to that of the U.S. Marine Corps. It also contained a number of army units, such as artillery and signalers. These three very different brigades in the British division worked together in outstanding fashion to dominate southern Iraq, so that the American forces driving toward Baghdad could disregard their southern flank and attack directly through the middle of the country. The British cleaned up the area around Basra, destroying substantial Iraqi forces as they did so, and eventually laid siege to and captured the city. They also acted as a reserve force in the event that I MEF ran into difficulty.

At the beginning of the war, the 15th MEU was assigned to the British to make the opening breakthrough and capture the bridges leading to Umm Qasar, before moving on to work under Task Force Tarawa. This represented almost unprecedented international cooperation under actual combat conditions—a U.S. tactical unit subordinated to a British division which was in turn subordinated to an American MEF headquarters. Throughout the Iraq War the level of cooperation between I MEF and the British 1st Armoured Division was exemplary, furthered to a great extent by similarities in doctrine and a consistent willingness to delegate responsibility to subordinates—in other words, a decentralized approach to command and control of units similar to the style used by the Wehrmacht in World War II.

Long before March 19, Australian, British, and U.S. special forces were operating in Iraq's western deserts, where they shut down entirely the possibility that Iraqis might fire Scud missiles at Israel. They also began interdiction operations against Iraqi supply lines to Syria. In overall command of the efforts in the western desert was Special

Operations Task Force 20. Its assigned units included the U.S. 5th Special Forces Group, the British SAS (Special Air Service), and the Australian SAS. In addition, a ranger regiment, minus one battalion, made up by a battalion from the 82nd, provided additional fighting power. Altogether the special forces in the desert numbered slightly more than 4,000 men. They also possessed a few Abrams tanks and HIMARS (truck-mounted MLRS) which allowed the SOF operators to call in artillery support from distances over 40 kilometers to back up their raids and interdiction efforts.

In the north, special forces succeeded in mobilizing the Kurds, destroying an Al Qaeda nest, and capturing Kirkuk and Mosul. The American 10th Special Forces Group was responsible for the north, while a special forces general was in overall command of all Coalition forces in the area, including the 173rd Airborne Brigade and eventually the 26th MEU. In addition, C-17s flew in a number of Abrams tanks, Bradleys, and M113 armored personnel carriers to support operations. In the end, the effort in the north kept the Iraqis off balance and prevented them from setting fire to the oilfields around Kirkuk.

In the south, special forces played a major role in preventing Iraqi soldiers from destroying the nation's oil fields. That only nine of the 1,057 oil wells in that area were torched suggests how well SOFs were able to mesh their efforts with conventional forces. The Australians were especially notable in this regard. By the end of the war, Australian SAS had not only helped control the western desert but had also captured Iraq's Al Asad air base, along with over fifty undamaged MiG fighters.

As in Afghanistan, special ops proved capable not only of carrying out deadly small-unit operations but of influencing the wider aspects of the campaign by distracting the enemy and disrupting infrastructure deep inside his own country. One of the major take-aways from the war was the unprecedented degree of cooperation between special forces and conventional ground forces, and the benefits each received from that cooperation.

COALITION NAVAL AND AIR FORCES

But remember, please, the law by which we live
We are not built to comprehend a lie
We can neither love nor pity nor forgive
If you make a slip in handling us you die!

RUDYARD KIPLING, "The Secret of the Machines," 1911

Because of Iraq's geography, one might think that naval forces would have played a relatively small role in the campaign. In fact, they contributed significantly to the Coalition's victory. With only momentary exceptions, the United States and Great Britain have controlled the world's oceans over the past three centuries. This overwhelming and uncontested naval supremacy allowed the Americans and British to deploy their military power unimpeded across the sea over vast distances to the Middle Eastern theater and then to choose the timing of the campaign.

Beyond the crucial importance of maintaining sea supremacy, the U.S. Navy and the Royal Navy also brought immense firepower to support the offensive. Many British and American submarines, as well as American surface ships, carried Tomahawk cruise missiles, and by the end of the war nearly 800 of these precision cruise missiles had bombarded strategic targets throughout Iraq. Unlike the Tomahawks of 1991, most of these missiles used GPS rather than terrain-following radar to hit their targets, making them less likely to miss.

Even more important to the Coalition's effort were the four carrier battle groups the U.S. Navy brought to the theater (with a fifth, the *Kitty Hawk,* arriving from Japan as the war was being fought). At the heart of four of these battle groups were the great nuclear-powered Nimitz class carriers, each weighing over 90,000 tons. They were capable of sustained speeds in excess of thirty knots and were crewed by 5,600 sailors. The air wing of each carrier consisted of between seventy and eighty aircraft, divided among fighter squadrons (mostly F-14s), strike squadrons (mostly F/A-18C/Ds, but with a first squadron of the more advanced F/A-18E/Fs deployed), electronic countermeasure aircraft, and early warning aircraft. Two of these battle groups, the *USS Harry S. Truman* and the *USS Theodore Roosevelt,* deployed in the Mediterranean and struck targets in Iraq from the west. The *USS Abraham Lincoln* and the *USS Constellation* deployed in the Persian Gulf and hit Iraq from the south. The navy also provided a crucial link in theater ballistic missile defense. For example, early in the war the *USS Higgins,* located just off the Al-Faw Peninsula, picked up the launch of an Iraqi Scud. U.S. Air Force sensors, now alerted, confirmed the launch; both indicators were immediately passed to an army Patriot missile battery, which killed the missile. At the same time, air force and marine fighter aircraft received the launch coordinates and attacked the launching site.

While the ships themselves were little different from the carriers deployed in 1991, the aircraft flying off their decks had undergone a sea change in technological capability. Virtually all carrier aircraft were now capable of precision attack with laser-guided or GPS-guided munitions. By contrast, during the Gulf War none of the navy's aircraft launched from carriers had been capable of precision strikes. Similarly, the majority of aircraft attacking from land bases carried precision weapons; during the Gulf War, only 7 percent of munitions dropped on the Iraqis from land-based aircraft were precision bombs (mostly laser-guided). When it is all added up, at least 65 percent of the weapons dropped by Coalition aircraft were precision weapons, the majority guided by GPS. Moreover, most fighter bombers and bombers were capable of delivering several such weapons at once. The result was a significant change in basic capabilities. In previous wars, the measure of effectiveness was the number of sorties necessary to destroy a single target; in this war, the measure of effectiveness was the number of targets a single sortie could destroy.

Because in this war the ground offensive began at the same time as the air campaign rather than thirty-eight days later, the air campaign has received far less media attention than did the air effort in 1991. There was, of course, the spectacular footage of the massive attacks on the Iraqi government's infrastructure, but the reporters and cameramen in Baghdad could offer little insight into the purpose and context of these missions. Moreover, the air campaign was competing with hundreds of TV and newsprint stories from reporters embedded in ground units. Yet the importance of the air campaign should not be underestimated. It distracted the Iraqi regime's political and military leadership from events on the ground, as the army and marines gathered steam in their drives toward Baghdad. Air attacks also had a devastating impact on the combat capabilities of Iraqi ground forces, both through interdiction strikes at rear areas and through close air support to Coalition units in direct contact with the enemy.

In charge of the overall Coalition air campaign was the joint force air component commander (JFACC), Lieutenant General Buzz Moseley, USAF, whose main headquarters was located at Prince Sultan air base in Saudi Arabia. While the Saudis did not allow the use of their air bases for Coalition aircraft flying combat missions, they did make a substantial contribution to the war by allowing the use of their extensive command and control facilities. Aircraft flying out of Saudi air bases mounted substantial aerial tanker operations for refueling the enormous numbers of Coalition fighter aircraft flying north, day and night, to attack targets in Iraq. The importance of that tanking effort is suggested by the fact that through April 11, Coalition tanker air-

craft—British as well as American—had flown 7,525 sorties and delivered over 46 million gallons of fuel to extend the range of Coalition
aircraft.

At the start of planning for the war against Iraq, some air force leaders argued strongly for a sustained air campaign that would begin
well before the ground campaign. But the more that Centcom's and
McKiernan's planners looked at the political and strategic context
of the upcoming war, the less they liked the idea of an independent
air campaign. To begin with, such a campaign would have allowed
Saddam substantial time to gather support from the international
community—not to mention the Arab world—to end the conflict before the Baath regime had fallen. Second, an independent air campaign would have allowed Saddam time to torch the oil fields and
cause an environmental disaster by pumping oil into the northern
Gulf. Finally, an independent air campaign would have allowed
Saddam time to prepare his military forces to defend their country.
A number of senior air force officers, failing to understand the war's
political and strategic context, persisted in their belief that air power
could go it alone. But Franks and his superiors refused to follow
such a strategically and politically reckless course of action and over-
ruled them. The threat of weapons of mass destruction, which Coalition military leaders took seriously from their intelligence sources, was
also a factor in deciding to start the air and ground campaigns concurrently. The huge build-up of troops in Kuwait provided a tempting
target for strikes which only dispersion could mitigate—thus, the decision to disperse forward by invading Iraq.

The air component commander had a number of critical tasks: to
break the will of the Iraqi regime and people (through "shock and
awe"), destroy the Iraqi military's ability to control the movement of
its ground forces, prevent or otherwise impede Iraqi efforts to employ
weapons of mass destruction, and provide close air support for Coali-

tion ground forces. The campaign also rested on a new approach to air war, one that had begun to emerge in the Gulf War. This campaign would focus on precision attacks that would seek to destroy the will-power of the enemy, rather than embarking on systematic destruction of every possible target planners could identify. Air planners under-stood that the focus of aerial strikes should be the psychological as much as the physical constitution of the enemy. They chose targets whose destruction would achieve the greatest psychological effect, as opposed to the maximum possible physical damage, which would carry with it the potential of collateral damage and unnecessary civil-ian casualties.

Nevertheless, the air plan had weaknesses. Like many others, air-men underestimated the political control that the Baath Party exer-cised over Iraq's population. Thus, the impressive fireworks display of the "shock and awe" portion of the air campaign appears to have done little to weaken Saddam's grip on Iraq's population. Moreover, one might ask what effect was envisioned in the massive bombing of empty ministries and party headquarters—all long since abandoned by bureaucrats. The attacks on those buildings destroyed much of the documentary evidence on which a full-scale examination of Saddam's crimes would have to depend. History itself was the loser.

To execute such a complex campaign, air planners had to coordi-nate thousands of sorties each day and night, many of which origi-nated from bases outside the theater, as well as cruise missile strikes from navy ships. The coordination problem alone represented a con-siderable challenge: it meant ensuring adequate aerial tanker support for air force, navy, marine, RAF, and Australian sorties, deciding on which weapons system and bombs were most suitable for each of the targets, and minimizing the potential for midair crashes among the numerous aircraft in the sky at any given moment. All of this had to be done with maximum flexibility so that sorties in the air could be rerouted to fleeting targets of opportunity (such as intelligence that Saddam Hussein was in a certain place) or to provide immediate firepower to Coalition troops in contact with the enemy on the ground.

The strike aircraft that the air component commander folded into his air campaign plan came from a number of sources. The most remarkable was the much maligned B-2 stealth bomber. Flying out of the United States and the island of Diego Garcia, B-2s carried sixteen 2,000-pound JDAMs, guided by GPS designators. The B-1s could carry twenty-four JDAMs, each bomb capable of being targeted individually, while the seemingly ageless B-52 fired off air-launched cruise missiles. Flying out of land bases scattered throughout the Gulf, air force F-15Es (Strike Eagles) and F-16s, marine F/A-18Cs and Ds (Hornets), British Tornadoes, and Australian Hornets flew air-to-ground missions that supported attacks on Iraq's political and military infrastructure. These aircraft also supported ground forces.

The main air support for V Corps' soldiers in contact with the enemy came from air force A-10 Warthogs—an apt name for one of the ugliest combat aircraft ever designed—with some able help at times from RAF Harriers. The Warthog had been designed to fly close air support missions in the 1970s and as a result was capable of sustaining considerable damage and surviving. In one case, the daughter of a San Jose councilman, Captain Kim Campbell, flew her A-10 back to Kuwait on manual controls after it had been thoroughly shot up in the skies over Baghdad and its hydraulic systems had failed. Her father told a reporter after her safe return: "It's been a roller coaster day. Most days, pride wins; some of the time fear wins. Today the pride is still winning."[3] The marines of I MEF received much of their close air support from their air wing's Cobras, Harriers, and Hornets. Those assets, particularly the Cobra attack helicopters, also supported the

British efforts in the fighting around Basra. All in all, close air support of troops engaged in combat proved to be a devastating asset.

THE IRAQI MILITARY

The fundamental problem was the Italian general staff tradition: Custoza, Lissa, Adua, Caporetto. On those occasions the [Italian] military, as yet uncontaminated by contact with Fascism, distinguished itself by the absence of the study, planning, and attention to detail that characterized the Germans, and by a tendency to intrigue and confusion of responsibilities among senior officers . . . The [army's] deficiencies in armament, doctrine, organization, staff work, and leadership were mutually reinforcing.

MACGREGOR KNOX, *Mussolini Unleashed,* 1982

As with most despots throughout history, Saddam's political sway and ultimately his legitimacy as ruler rested on the organs of power: the army and the police. Yet, on the eve of the Iraq War his army was ill-disciplined, disorganized, and poorly trained—no match for its Coalition opponents. The roots of Iraq's woefully dysfunctional military culture, with its focus on politics and policing rather than professionalism, can be traced back to the earliest years of the nation's history.

In 1932 when the British recognized Iraq as an independent nation with its own army, they retained several air bases and control over Iraq's foreign policy. In 1933, while King Faisal was out of the country, the prime minister, Rashid Ali, used the army to carry out the first of what was to become a depressingly long list of atrocities against Iraq's minorities, this one perpetrated against the Assyrian community. The army's "victory" was celebrated in Mosul by triumphal arches "decorated with melons stained with blood and with daggers stuck in them."[4] Emboldened by that success and the prestige it had garnered, the officer corps launched no less than six coups in the period between 1936 and 1941. The last of these, in April 1941, drove supporters of Britain out of the country.

The coup leaders then made overtures to join the Third Reich, and the Germans were delighted to extend help to the rebels. In May a small number of Luftwaffe aircraft, including Bf 109s and He 111s, showed up in northern Iraq. The Iraqi revolt could not have come at a worse time for Britain: British forces were in headlong retreat not only in Greece but in Libya, while Crete was about to fall to German paratroopers. The commander of British forces in the Middle East, General Archibald Wavell—worried over the strength of Iraqi forces and the weakness of his own—recommended to authorities in London that no action be undertaken against the coup.

Winston Churchill would have none of it. He fired Wavell and ordered that a hodge-podge of forces move from Palestine and Trans-Jordan (present-day Jordan) across the deserts of Iraq to attack Baghdad. While the British were collecting their troops, the Iraqis besieged the main British air base but failed to dislodge the defending RAF. A brigade-strength force of British troops and the Arab Legion then crossed the desert, entered the Fertile Crescent, and thoroughly thrashed the Iraqi army in front of Baghdad. Churchill's comment on the result was as usual pithy and apt:

> If anyone had predicted two months ago when Iraq was
> in revolt and our people were hanging on by their eyelids
> at Habbaniya [the RAF base] and our ambassador was
> imprisoned in his embassy at Baghdad, and when all
> Syria and Iraq began to be overrun by German tourists,
> and were in the hands of forces controlled indirectly, but
> nonetheless powerfully by German authority—if anyone

had predicted that we should already by the middle of July, have cleaned up all of the Levant [Syria as well as Iraq], such a prophet would have been considered most imprudent.[5]

The collapse of the Iraqi army before a British brigade so humiliated the Iraqi military that it played little role in politics for the next seventeen years.

Then, in 1958, army officers launched their savage, brutal, and bloody coup, which was followed by a period of intense instability. By 1968, when the Baathists consolidated their power, a pall of intimidation and terror descended on the military as well as on civilians. By 1979 Saddam Hussein—now firmly in control—took steps to ensure that the army would never again prove a threat to Baathist power. Rather than choosing the "best and the brightest" to lead Iraq's military, Saddam promoted political hacks and regime loyalists with no training or experience. Faceless bureaucrats took over the army, which had no place for bearers of bad news, much less those who disagreed with Saddam's domestic and foreign policies. All Saddam required or tolerated were officers who could be counted on to murder as many thousands of Iraq's own citizens as the regime required. But as Saddam soon discovered, like Stalin in 1941 and the Argentineans in 1982, military organizations that spend their time killing the defenseless are rarely effective in battle.

On September 22, 1980, the Iraqi military began what Saddam and its leaders thought would be a *blitzkrieg* against Iran, similar to the 1967 Israeli victory in the Six-Day War—at most a two-week campaign. In less than a week it was clear the Iraqis had bitten off quite a bit more. Their advance, slow and painful, eventually led to the capture of Khorramshahr, barely inside the Iranian frontier. There it stopped. Saddam took vengeance on his generals by having a number of them shot. In 1982 when an interviewer for the German magazine *Stern* asked Saddam whether it was true that he had had three hundred generals shot, the dictator's response was simply: "No. However, two divisional commanders and the commander of a mechanized unit were executed. This is something normal in all wars."[6]

With the advance into Iran hopelessly stalled, a bloody war of attrition ensued. Iraq's initial surprise aerial attack on Iranian air bases (an attempt to replicate the 1967 Israeli strike against Egyptian air bases) failed dismally. What was left of Iran's air force, which had been almost entirely trained by Americans in the 1970s, soon gained the upper hand. Saddam was forced to disperse his aircraft to neighboring Arab states to prevent them from being destroyed entirely.

Conditions on the ground also deteriorated badly, from Iraq's point of view. A series of ill-planned and poorly executed Iranian offensives launched by ferociously motivated religious zealots in spring 1981 managed to rock the Iraqi army back on its heels. However, the religious revolutionaries now leading Iran failed to integrate these masses into what was left of the shah's professional army. But hordes of religious fanatics, including teenage boys carrying gold keys to heaven made in Taiwan, presented the Iraqis with their worst nightmare. By the end of 1982 these Iranians, at great loss to themselves, had driven the Iraqis out of all the territory Saddam's troops had conquered at such dire cost in 1981.

The stalemate of the next three years turned into a bloodbath for both sides. With no effective leaders at any level, the revolutionary youth of Iran died by the tens of thousands; not only were they cannon fodder for the superior weaponry Iraq had purchased abroad but they were also victims of the chemical warfare waged by Saddam's troops. Nevertheless, by 1986 the Iranians had slugged their way into Iraqi territory and were threatening Basra. Saddam had to promote a number of his more competent military commanders, who still continued to die in helicopter crashes and other unexplained accidents.

The conflict ended after large numbers of Scud missiles were fired at cities on both sides, killing thousands; but these civilian deaths were a mere drop compared with the numbers of combatants dying on the battlefield.

The war finally stumbled to a conclusion in 1988, when a series of carefully planned Iraqi attacks conducted by Saddam's newly enlarged Republican Guard regained the territory lost over the past four years—again at terrible loss of life. Saddam's "victory" was trumpeted by both Iraqi propaganda and Western intelligence agencies (which should have known better) as an indication of Iraq's military effectiveness. In fact, the victory, such as it was, came against an opponent who had learned little on the battlefield and whose army was finally beginning to lose its religious fervor. The losses to both sides were horrendous. One of the lower figures for the war puts the combined dead at 367,000, with over three quarters of a million wounded.

At war's end, Iraq lay exhausted, its foreign currency reserves gone, its economy propped up by loans from other Arab states, the price of oil through the floor, and the Iraqi population desperate for peace. But Saddam still had his dream: that Iraq would become a major player on the world stage, equivalent to China or the Soviet Union. He would achieve this not through rebuilding but through another piece of aggression, this time against another of Iraq's neighbors, Kuwait. The crisis he precipitated in the summer of 1990 was predictably based on an underestimation of U.S. will and an inflated sense of Iraq's own military resources.

Appearances deceive. Like Patroclus in Achilles' armor, the Iraqis were dressed in the accouterments of a modern military but possessed none of the training, discipline, professional education, initiative, and trust that modern military organizations require. The results in retrospect were not surprising. The Gulf War was a disastrous military defeat for Saddam Hussein.

In the aftermath of the Gulf War, the Iraqi military was considerably weaker than it had been when Saddam invaded Kuwait. It was strong enough to put down rebellions in the south and north of Iraq, although guerrilla war waged by the Marsh Arabs in the Euphrates delta continued well into the nineties. Only by draining the swamps to the southeast of Basra, thus ending a way of life that had lasted since the dawn of recorded history, was Saddam able to end this insurrection. A comparison of the numbers of tanks and other military equipment before and after Kuwait suggest the extent to which Iraqi military power had deteriorated. Main battle tanks decreased in number from 5,100 to 2,000; armored personnel carriers from 6,800 to 1,800; self-propelled artillery from 500 to 150 pieces; and towed artillery from 3,000 to 1,900.[9] The Iraqi air force had degenerated to such a miserable state by 2003 that it could not get a single sortie into the air against the aerial onslaught that began on March 19.

Moreover, even the most modern equipment the Iraqis possessed in 1990 had become seriously obsolete by 2003. With hardly any funding for maintenance, much less upgrades, Iraq's soldiers could have survived on a modern battlefield only by hard and realistic training. They got neither. Instead, brutal discipline and an atmosphere of dismal suspicion ensured that no one, including the most senior commanders, displayed any initiative. Slogans and banners proclaiming undying loyalty to Saddam and the Baath Party seemed to equate, in Saddam's mind, with serious preparation for war.

However great his military defeat in 1991, Saddam refused to countenance reform of his military institutions. The army's focus remained on politics and policing, with distrust and suspicion the watchwords. As before the war, the regime allowed no military units, including the Republican Guard, to enter the environs of Baghdad. To their astonishment, American commanders would discover that the Iraqis had made no serious preparations to defend their capital; the much-trumpeted worry that the Battle for Baghdad would become the Stalingrad of the twenty-first century turned out to be one more mirage. But the greatest weakness created by Saddam's ferocious tyranny was that no one, including his closest associates, either dared to contradict the leader or to be the bearer of bad tidings. Thus, Iraq's military leaders and institutions were incapable of adapting to a battle space in which their opponents moved with lightning speed and frightening lethality.

Whatever military strength the regime still retained was largely concentrated in the Republican Guard, organized into six divisions comprising a total of 50,000–60,000 soldiers. But even the Republican Guard was having problems with desertions before the war. Three of its divisions—the Adnan Mechanized Division, the Baghdad Infantry Division, and the Abed Infantry Division—were located in the north under I Corps. II Corps controlled three divisions in the central and southern portions of Iraq. Medina Armored Division was located near Baghdad to protect the capital against an attempted coup. Finally, there were two Republican Guard divisions in the south, the Nebuchadnezzar Infantry Division and the Hammurabi Mechanized Division.

The Republican Guard divisions, which some experts before the Gulf War had compared to Hitler's Waffen SS, did receive more modern equipment, higher pay, and better food, and this helped ensure their loyalty. But over the course of the 1990s, their equipment slowly deteriorated, not so much through overuse as through poor maintenance and a lack of spare parts, and there were no French or Soviet experts to provide advice or technological assistance. There is no evidence that the Republican Guard trained either hard or long. Its officers and generals were picked entirely on the basis of loyalty to the regime and not on any criteria of military effectiveness. In the coming struggle, the resistance of these units would at times prove ferocious; but when they fought, they died in place, inflicting hardly any casualties on their attackers.

The protection of the capital city, Baghdad, lay largely in the hands of the Special Republican Guard. This force consisted of three relatively well-equipped brigades whose express mission was to defend the regime against any attempted coup. Its troop strength of approximately 15,000 soldiers was under the command of Saddam's youngest son, Qusay. The Special Republican Guard handled many of the regime's most distasteful tasks. For the most part, this force was deeply loyal to the regime but largely on the same basis that Al Capone's "torpedoes" had loyally served their Mafia chieftain—there was loot to be shared. It was not a serious military force prepared and trained for combat.

The regular army was even less well prepared for war. Its best equipment was obsolete, and its worst was junk. Its units fought only as long as the Baathist controls remained in place. Otherwise, army units either surrendered or, when possible, melted back into the population. On paper, the army consisted of seventeen divisions assigned to five corps. Two corps in the north contained six infantry and two mechanized divisions. The one corps in central Iraq, stationed on the Iranian frontier, had one armored and two infantry divisions. And finally in the south the Iraqis had stationed six divisions: two armored, one mechanized, and three infantry. The exact size of the regular army was uncertain even to the Iraqis, since conscripted soldiers, mostly Shia, deserted in droves almost as fast as Baathist thugs rounded them up. Saddam's worry about the loyalty of his officers is understandable, given that over forty Iraqi generals defected during the past decade. The dictator cashiered 150 more and had a number of others shot for plotting against the regime.

In the run-up to the war, the regime got the bright idea to recruit irregulars, in most cases Baath Party loyalists and believers. In addition, a number of religious and other fanatics from Arab lands journeyed to Iraq to participate in Saddam's defense. Many sought martyrdom, others the opportunity to kill Americans. Saddam's eldest son, Uday, folded these disparate elements into an organization he named the fedayeen in honor of Palestinian suicide bombers. The idea for these units may well have come from seeing the movie *Black Hawk Down;* Uday was known to be a great fan of Hollywood movies and collected videos by the hundreds. Whatever the inspiration for the fedayeen, their military effectiveness proved to be considerably less than that of Aideed's armed mobs in Somalia.

THE WEST'S INTANGIBLE ADVANTAGE

Personal bravery of a single individual alone is not decisive on the day of battle, but rather bravery of the corps, and the latter rests on the good opinion and the confidence that each individual places in the corps to which he belongs.

COLMAR VON DER GOLTZ, nineteenth-century German general

In retrospect, the Iraqis were in a hopeless position before the first shot was fired. The military forces of the United States and the United Kingdom operated according to a professional military ethos that it had taken the West five centuries to develop. The technologies that those forces deployed were frighteningly effective in their lethality and precision, but the chief factor in the victory that occurred in spring 2003 was a combination of training, discipline, and mental preparation at every level that Coalition forces brought to the battlefield.

Thus, a number of obvious factors help explain the success of Coalition arms: technological superiority, complete air supremacy, the incompetence of Saddam and his military commanders when confronted with an external enemy, and, not least, the unwillingness of most Iraqis to fight and die for a regime they feared and despised in equal measure. But the most important reason for the Coalition's victory lies in the secret of Western military effectiveness first discovered by the Romans and then rediscovered by the Europeans in the seventeenth century: the disciplining of young men into combat formations characterized by cohesion, interdependency, and trust in one another and in commanding officers. The result is a military unit that is obedient and responsive not only to its commanders but to civil authorities as well. Of all the revolutions that have taken place in Western warfare, this was undoubtedly the most important, for on those disciplined formations—disciplined in both a civil and a military sense—the Western state was created. In that sense, the ground formations that drove through ill-disciplined armed mobs of Iraqis were the direct lineal descendants of Roman legionnaires and the pike men and musketeers of Gustavus Adolphus's Swedish armies.

Discipline is much more than screaming at soldiers on parade grounds. It is a matter of training individuals to pay attention to the details. One of the army's foremost theorists commented on this during the Iraq War: "*Training and discipline* matter. One of the more telling but very likely less noticed features of the countless TV clips showing Coalition ground troops in action was the way in which the troops carried their personal weapons. Almost without exception, trigger fingers were in the 'safe' position, extended along but outside trigger guards. Every properly instructed shooter is taught that rule. Far fewer routinely observe it. That troops in mortal danger practice it so consistently testifies to extraordinary self-discipline, the sort that only careful and rigorous training can induce."[7]

Since World War I the modern battlefield has increasingly isolated the soldier and marine as well as his combat leaders. Thus, the initiative of individuals and junior leaders has become an important component of success, because it allows the soldier or marine to take advantage of fleeting opportunities. From the outset of their military careers, the British and American soldiers and marines who fought in

Iraq had received an intensive and effective regimen of combat training that instilled in them not only the discipline to obey orders under extraordinarily difficult and dangerous situations but also the willingness to take the initiative and act on their own in the absence of orders. That combination of discipline and initiative allowed Coalition soldiers and marines to fight as teams and to do the grim business their nation paid them to do. The Coalition victory in Iraq had little to do with any advantage American and British soldiers may have enjoyed in bravery over their Iraqi opponents. It had everything to do with their cohesion and discipline on the battlefield. The Iraqi military, however brave individuals might have been—and many were extraordinarily brave—had none of these qualities.

That difference was something Saddam's military with its Baathist stooges at the top could not begin to comprehend. What is astonishing is that virtually none of the senior Iraqi leadership, especially Saddam, appears to have recognized the danger they were confronting as the Americans and British began deploying to the Middle East. The corruption of absolute power within his own realm ensured that Saddam would not understand the forces gathering outside its borders. Iraqi resistance would prove short-lived and largely ineffective, and the Iraqis would quickly throw away what few advantages they actually possessed.

3

The Ground Campaign in Southern Iraq

Let me begin by saying this will be a campaign unlike any other in history, a campaign characterized by shock, by surprise, by the employment of precise munitions on a scale never seen, and by the application of overwhelming force.

General Tommy Franks, Centcom daily briefing, March 22, 2003

On Thursday, March 20, Major General Buford "Buff" Blount, commanding the "Rock of the Marne" 3rd Infantry Division, ordered his soldiers to rest. He knew that heat, blowing sand, and the monotony of desert terrain, mixed with the fear of facing a violent death, would inevitably conspire to wear away the attention of even the most fit and well-prepared soldier. Combat units are capable of fighting continuously for approximately seventy-two hours until the combined effects of fear and fatigue sap

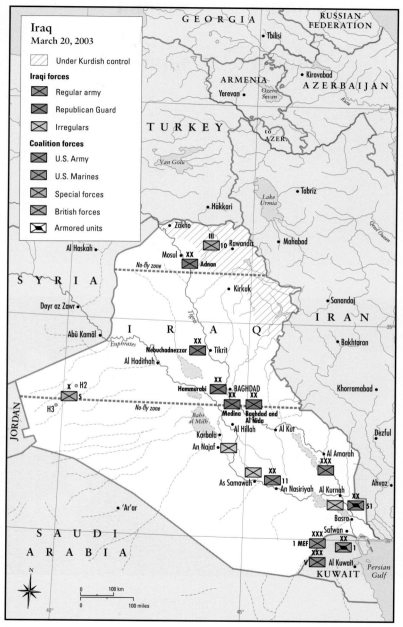

Iraq
March 20, 2003

Under Kurdish control

Iraqi forces
Regular army
Republican Guard
Irregulars

Coalition forces
U.S. Army
U.S. Marines
Special forces
British forces
Armored units

GEORGIA

RUSSIAN FEDERATION

• Tbilisi

ARMENIA
Yerevan •

• Kirovabad

AZERBAIJAN

Ozera Sevan

Kura

TURKEY

TO AZER.

Van Gölü

Lake Urmia

• Tabriz

• Hakkari

Qezel Owzan

• Zākho

III
10 • Rawanduz

• Mahabad

Al Haskah •

Mosul • XX
Adnan

No-fly zone

• Kirkuk

• Sanandaj

IRAN

SYRIA

Dayr az Zawr •

Tigris

Abū Kamāl •

Euphrates

I   R   A   Q

XX
Nebuchadnezzar • Tikrit

Al Hadithah •

• Bakhtaran

X ⊙ H2
H3 ⊙   5

XX
Hammurabi

XX
XX   XX
BAGHDAD

Medina   Baghdad and
Al Nida

• Khorramabad

No-fly zone

Bahr al Milh

• Al Hillah   • Al Kut

• Dezful

Karbala •

An Najaf •

XX

• Al Amarah

XXX

• 'Ar'ar

XX
As Samawah •   11
An Nasiriyah

Al Kurnah •

XX
51

• Ahvaz

Basra •

Safwan •

XXX
1 MEF

XX
1

XXX
V   Al Kuwait

Persian Gulf

KUWAIT

SAUDI

ARABIA

N

0   100 km
0   100 miles

Cartographica Ltd

Scott Peterson/Getty Images

Mirrorpix/Getty Images

Top: Iraqi irregulars—firefighters, police, and Baathist bureaucrats—run in step in early March 2003, as part of Saddam's propaganda effort to intimidate the United States. Bottom: Fedayeen stand at attention in Baghdad. Shrouds proclaim their willingness to martyr themselves in the fight against the Americans.

Top: Iraqi troops demonstrate in Baghdad on March 15. Their lack of discipline and training would become apparent in the days ahead. Bottom: Respected by American marine and British commanders alike, General David McKiernan orchestrates Franks' land battle from his headquarters in Kuwait, March 21.

General Tommy Franks shakes hands with soldiers from the 101st Airborne. His skill in building a team among all services and Coalition partners was an essential ingredient in victory during the conventional phase of the war.

Top: The army's left wing advances along a rough and dusty route through the desert west of the Euphrates at the beginning of the ground campaign. Bottom: Soldiers from the 3rd Infantry Division share a meal-ready-to-eat (MRE) with Chris Tomlinson, embedded reporter from the Associated Press.

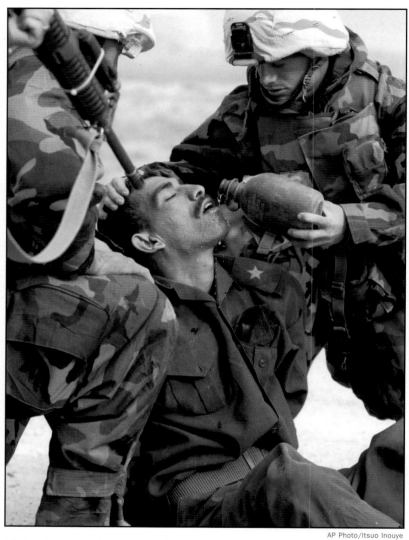

Marines from the 15th Marine Expeditionary Unit provide an Iraqi POW with water immediately after his capture in the first hour of the war.

Top: Marines from India Company, 3rd Battalion, 7th Regiment, storm the headquarters of the Iraqi 51st Infantry Division near Az Bayer on March 21. Bottom: Any excuse for a card game—members of the 15th MEU play under a gas alert. U.S. marines and soldiers wore WMD protective gear on many occasions during the drive toward Baghdad.

Mirrorpix/Getty Images

Top left: As Baghdad explodes under nighttime aerial bombardment on March 21, the lights remain on. Aircraft spared the electric plants because of Coalition hopes that the regime would collapse early in the war, under pressure from heavy bombing. Bottom: Saddam's supporters set fire to oil-filled trenches around Baghdad on March 22, but dense smoke fails to obscure targets for precision bombs and missiles guided by GPS. Top right: The stealth capability of the B-2 bomber allowed it to strike deep into Iraq without fear of detection.

Top: An M1A1 Abrams tank rolls through Iraqi territory south of An Najaf on March 23. In two Gulf wars, the Abrams destroyed thousands of Soviet-made armored vehicles without losing a single crewman to enemy tank fire. Bottom: The mild, courteous manner of Major General "Buff" Blount, commander of the 3rd Infantry Division, masks a tenacious fighter and gifted combat leader. Bottom right: Iraqis walk past the Apache Longbow helicopter that went down during an attack on the Medina Division, March 22. In subsequent engagements, Apaches would destroy hundreds of enemy vehicles without loss.

With a series of helicopter-borne firepower attacks and airborne insertions deep inside Iraq, Major General David Petraeus, commander of the 101st Airborne Division, would write a new chapter in the history of aerial maneuver.

Top: Marines from Charlie Company, 1st Tank Battalion, refuel their Abrams in a timeless ritual near Jalibah air base on March 24. Bottom: On the same day, marines from Charlie Company, 1st Battalion, 2nd Regiment, Task Force Tarawa, form a firing line during fierce fighting near An Nasiriyah.

Top: Marines from Task Force Tarawa clear buildings in An Nasiriyah around "Ambush Alley," a dangerous but critical route along Highway 7 leading north to Al Kut. Bottom: Lieutenant General James Conway and Major General James Mattis discuss the next movement for the 1st Marine Division.

Top: A 155mm Paladin howitzer from the 3rd Infantry Division's artillery fires in support of the armored advance. Bottom: Lieutenant General Scott Wallace, the army's most accomplished trainer, puts his experience to good use in coordinationg all the forces of V Corps during the march to Baghdad.

Top: Marines from 3rd Battalion, 7th Regiment, encounter an ambush on Highway 1 in the middle of the *shamal* on March 26. Bottom: A light 105mm howitzer from the 101st Airborne Division provides cover fire for infantry in contact with the enemy. While the *shamal* limited close air support, artillery was unaffected by the weather.

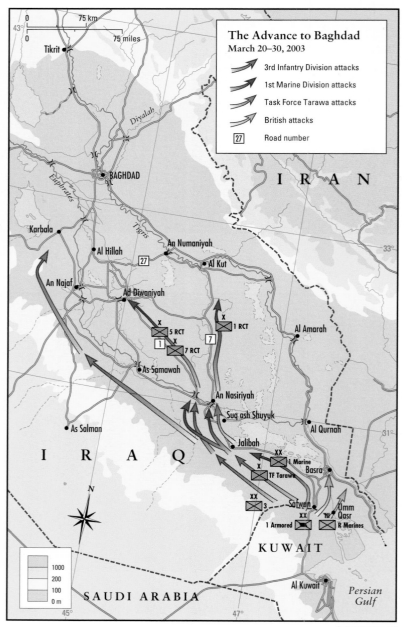

The Advance to Baghdad
March 20–30, 2003

3rd Infantry Division attacks

1st Marine Division attacks

Task Force Tarawa attacks

British attacks

27 Road number

Tikrit

Diyalah

BAGHDAD

IRAN

Karbala

Al Hillah

An Numaniyah

27

Al Kut

An Najaf

Ad Diwaniyah

X 5 RCT

X 1 RCT

Al Amarah

1

X 7 RCT

7

As Samawah

An Nasiriyah

Suq ash Shuyuk

Al Qurnah

As Salman

Jalibah

XX 1 Marine

I R A Q

X TF Tarawa

Basra

XX 3

Safwan

Umm
Qasr

XX 1 Armored

XX

XX R Marines

KUWAIT

1000
200
100
0 m

SAUDI ARABIA

Al Kuwait

Persian
Gulf

N

Cartographica Ltd

the attention of soldiers and cloud the judgment of leaders. Thus, the coming campaign would represent a test of not only how fast the 3rd Infantry Division could rush the gates of Baghdad but whether the division could accomplish that task without driving itself, emotionally as well as physically, into the ground.

Blount was the antithesis of the Pattonesque figure often associated with American armored commanders. In fact, he was more Lee than Patton. Cerebral and introspective, he expressed his southern upbringing in a gentlemanly, courteous manner. Nevertheless, he possessed the character of a soldier driven to succeed. Few men knew more about how to fight a division. Blount's soldiers trusted him because they knew from years of association that he was committed to preserving their lives. He recognized that his soldiers were confronting a march like that of Xenephon's ten thousand in the fourth century BC, who passed through this very region in the face of an enemy just as hostile and unfamiliar as the Iraqi soldiers now waiting beyond the berms of the Kuwaiti border. The 3rd Infantry Division's objective was Baghdad, more than 350 miles distant. The division would form the left hook of Third Army's assault on the Iraqi capital. The 1st Marine Division would provide the right hook, swinging north to come in from east of the Tigris. Success would depend on speed and the ability of the two phalanxes to synchronize their movements so that they could arrive simultaneously at Iraq's capital city.

The invasion of Iraq that began on March 20 had one simple, overarching mission: to end the tyrannical, dangerous regime of Saddam Hussein. Three imperatives governed the planning and conduct of that campaign. The first was self-protective: to find and neutralize Iraq's weapons of mass destruction, in order to prevent their use against Coalition forces. Intelligence at the time led commanders to believe strongly that the Iraqis possessed these weapons as well as the ruthlessness to use them. A corollary to the WMD objective was to preclude the Iraqis from firing Scuds at Israel and thus further inflaming tensions in the Middle East. A second imperative was political: to prevent Saddam from setting fire to Iraq's oil wells or dumping raw petroleum into the northern Gulf (as he had done in 1991) and to deliver humanitarian relief to the Iraqi people as soon as possible. These interventions would preserve Iraq's economic infrastructure and avoid an ecological disaster with international repercussions. The third imperative was strategic: to isolate and destroy the leaders and military forces of the Baathist regime, while minimizing civilian casualties and collateral damage.

How the Coalition achieved these objectives can be traced back to Operation Just Cause, which took down Manuel Noriega in December 1989.

THE PLANNING

A battle is a complicated operation that you prepare laboriously. If the enemy does this, you say to yourself, I will do that. If such and such happens, these are the steps I shall take to meet it. You think out every possible development and decide on the way to deal with the situation created. One of these developments occurs; you put your plan in operation, and everyone says "What genius . . . " whereas the credit is really due to the labor of preparation.

Ferdinand Foch, April 1919

In Panama in 1989, staff officers under General Max Thurmond, head of Southcom (Southern Command), with support from Lieutenant General Gary Luck, commander of XVIII Airborne Corps, created a plan for attacking twenty-seven critical targets simultaneously, or at least as close to simultaneously as human affairs will allow. After the successful execution of those strikes, Noriega's regime dissolved in less than twenty-four hours.

Barely a year later the American military confronted a new and very different challenge with the Iraqi invasion of Kuwait. General Norman Schwarzkopf's initial concept for the Gulf War would have put a marine division in charge of a holding-operation along the Saudi-Kuwait frontier, while XVIII Airborne Corps, spearheaded by the 24th Infantry Division, would have struck north in a single, narrow thrust to cut off and then destroy Iraqi forces in the Kuwaiti theater of operations. This first plan achieved notoriety among pundits as an unimaginative dash into the teeth of Iraq's military strength. But in retrospect—and we stress in retrospect—the plan would have worked as a preemptive, devastating strike against Saddam's military forces.

Still, the initial plan rested on a number of unknown factors. First, Coalition commanders had no clear idea how effective the Iraqi forces would prove to be; the picture that intelligence analysts were painting suggested considerable military competence. Also, the Coalition possessed far fewer reconnaissance capabilities than today—JSTARS and UAVs were still in development. Thus, H. R. McMaster and his cavalry troop were as surprised as the Iraqis when their Abrams tanks crested the ridge at 73 Easting and found themselves face to face with the enemy.

Concerned by these risks, Schwarzkopf and Colin Powell, then chairman of the Joint Chiefs of Staff, settled on a final plan that erred on the side of caution—a reflection no doubt of their grim experiences in Vietnam. Powell provided two divisions from Germany for the left hook, and with overwhelming force assembled in the desert, the Coalition crushed the Iraqis in a ground campaign that lasted only 100 hours. It was a decisive military victory, whatever the defects in the concept.

In the decade between the Gulf and Iraq wars, a number of factors changed to lower the need for overwhelming mass in removing Saddam from power. A new plan emerged from the fertile minds and experiences of three of the most imaginative military figures the United States produced in the twentieth century. The first was Luck himself, who in 1994 became head of the combined command in Korea. With the persona of a country boy (and a Ph.D. in systems analysis from George Washington University), Luck had formed a close working relationship with the new commander of I MEF, Lieutenant General Anthony Zinni. Witty and widely read, Zinni was the youngest son of Italian immigrants from Calabria and the first member of his family to go to college. He stood out as one of the most operationally brilliant generals the marines had ever produced. When he became Centcom commander in 1997, he turned to Luck, at that point retired from active service, as his mentor. Together, the two men addressed the problem of how the United States could overthrow Saddam Hussein in a swift and decisive campaign.

When Zinni himself retired, General Tommy Franks replaced him. The American military has never done a good job in educating its senior officers for the role of combatant commander, but Franks was a willing learner. The Luck-Zinni conversations now continued between Luck and Franks. Their discourse aimed to explore the advances in communications and reconnaissance that were occurring so rapidly within the military. Thus, the final plan for overthrowing the Iraqi regime owed its genesis to a complex interaction among military professionals at the highest levels.

As this plan would eventually make clear, the American military had come a long way from Desert Storm. Whereas the emphasis in 1991 had been on overwhelming force, the emphasis now, according to Luck, was on "overmatching power"—attacking the enemy across such a broad spectrum of capabilities that his military would suffer systemic collapse. Instead of focusing on overwhelming numbers, planners focused on electrons—sensors and information systems that displayed with greater fidelity than ever before what was happening on the battlefield. This allowed the Coalition to apply fewer numbers in precise ways aimed at the psychological dislocation of the enemy.

In preparing Centcom for possible operations against Iraq, Zinni had turned a set of service-oriented headquarters in the Middle East into joint task forces. Thus, Third Army became Joint Task Force Kuwait, and Centcom's Air Component Commander became Joint Task Force Southern Watch. Then, as the build-up for the invasion gathered momentum in 2002, Third Army found it relatively easy to integrate I MEF into its organization, which now became the Joint Force Land Component.

Superintending the planning and war gaming for an Iraq invasion was Tommy Franks, whose weathered exterior disguised a sharp and penetrating mind. In contrast with Schwarzkopf, Franks never let his ego get in the way of relations with his subordinate commanders. As one keen observer noted, "Tommy knows there's more to riding a horse than letting your feet hang down." Centcom proved most receptive to using graduates of the second-year staff college programs as major contributors to the planning of Operation Iraqi Freedom. In military planning, it used to be the iron majors and staff officers with stubby pencils in backrooms who transformed generals' conceptions into the movement of thousands of troops. Sometimes these individuals were brilliant; sometimes they were merely time-serving pedants. Today's planners, like Lieutenant Colonel Dave Johnson, are graduates of the second-year program at the service staff colleges, where they have been educated by a demanding history-based curriculum and the most modern computer-based simulations.

Experience in Afghanistan convinced Franks that the presence of special operations forces would increase the combat effectiveness of his command enormously. Thus, unlike the Gulf War, where

Schwarzkopf had refused to integrate special forces into the overall campaign plan, in the Iraq War Franks was delighted to involve special ops alongside his conventional forces.

Centcom's plan called for the main ground and air offensive to commence simultaneously. The plan presumed that an attack conducted in many dimensions—air, land, and sea—and timed to strike the Iraqis from many directions would achieve system-overload in Iraqi military and political organizations in which everything flowed from the center. As it turned out, the main aerial assault on Baghdad came after V Corps and I MEF were already deep inside Iraq. Unlike operations during World War II, the initial deployment of ground forces did not aim at seizing territory but simply at controlling it. The intention was to place U.S. ground forces as close as possible to Baghdad and establish final jump-off positions from which they could finish the campaign. For the army, this approach would not entail a huge risk because it was moving in from the deserts west of the Euphrates, where the Iraqis would have fewer opportunities to attack the lengthening logistical lines. Marine supply lines, however, would be more exposed to attack because I MEF's drive would push through Iraq's heavily populated sector between the Tigris and Euphrates rivers, terrain that Lieutenant General Jim Conway characterized as extremely difficult.

Franks and his subordinate commanders felt those risks were justified. Unlike their predecessors in the Gulf War, they understood how unprepared the Iraqis were to resist a major attack. With their huge advantage in reconnaissance and information systems, Coalition ground forces would have sufficient time to react to any threat the Iraqis mounted. The Iraqis, on the other hand, would be unable to react because the tempo of U.S. ground operations would be so fast. As with the French in 1940, every decision of the Iraqi high command would already have been overtaken by events when made. The simultaneity, speed, and unpredictability of U.S. ground operations would allow Coalition commanders to adapt to unforeseen situations, while the Iraqis would never be able to recover.

Centcom realized that the potential Achilles heel of the coming campaign would be the supply lines needed to keep the army and marine drives moving. Here, the army's logistical strength would play a major role in supporting the marines as well as its own soldiers. All the planners knew that the quantities of supplies, while adequate for projected needs, left little margin for error. In previous wars the American army had achieved success by smothering the enemy with superior numbers and mass—a concept that required mountains of supplies. In this war, things would be different. Mass would be sacrificed for speed, information, and precision killing power. Thus, the American command accepted the risk of going light. Success would rest on the accuracy of logistical calculations and the ability to keep supply lines open. Any unforeseen diminution in speed, however, would allow the enemy to turn a *blitzkrieg* into a campaign of attrition, which American commanders could not support at the end of a 350-mile tether.

Every echelon of command, from Frank's Centcom headquarters to corps, MEF, and divisional headquarters, spent most of the fall and early winter of 2002 planning and war-gaming the upcoming campaign. Meticulous planning, as well as serious thinking about how to adapt to the unexpected, were the new requirements of the day. The challenge in Iraq would be to improvise continuously while following the score. What the Coalition required was more along the lines of a jazz performance than an orchestral production.

On the other side of the hill, Saddam and his military advisers, such as they were, never had a clear idea of what was about to happen. Saddam's prewar actions, particularly with regard to U.N. inspections, suggest he never believed the Americans and their allies would attack. If they did, Iraq's military would aim to inflict the maximum number of casualties, so that the Americans would withdraw, as they had in Somalia and Vietnam. But even this minimalist strategy demanded a certain level of military effectiveness and competence—qualities in short supply in Saddam's regime.

Saddam's political needs largely determined Iraq's military plans. Above all, Saddam believed he needed to prevent a military coup in Baghdad and to use his forces throughout the country to suppress local rebellions. Consequently, when the Coalition's invasion began, Iraqi forces were in none of the places they should have been to be militarily effective. Moreover, the regime had undertaken no serious preparations to defend Baghdad, in part because its leaders feared that a concentration of forces in the city might set the stage for a coup and in part because they never really believed Coalition forces would penetrate that deeply into their country.

In addition, the United States' failed negotiations with Turkey over use of its territory in the event of an invasion suggested to Saddam that a ground war was far off; the 4th Infantry Division's equipment was still literally at sea when the conflict began. Moreover, the pattern of American wars since Panama suggested that a massive and sustained air campaign would precede a ground war against Iraq. Such a campaign would allow the Iraqis a considerable period to prepare. America's concern with casualties must also have suggested to the Iraqis and their Russian advisers that a ground campaign would be a cautious affair, following the pattern of the Gulf War. The slow forward movement of massive ground forces would afford Saddam the time he needed to appeal to the international community.

The regime's failure to prepare for the worst placed Iraq in an impossible position at the start of the war—one from which the Iraqis had no chance of recovering. In fact, the harder they attempted to grapple with the simultaneous and deadly thrusts that now befell them, the more hopeless their situation became.

V Corps' Advance

And Crispin Crispian shall ne'er go by,
From this day to the ending of the world,
But we in it shall be remembered;
We few, we happy few, we band of brothers;

William Shakespeare, *Henry V,* 1599

Centcom's plan called for the 3rd Infantry Division to move and fight in four ground maneuver formations. Major General Blount divided his maneuver battalions—nine armor and mechanized infantry— among the division's brigades to form three brigade combat teams (BCT), either infantry- or armor-heavy. Each was essentially a self-contained close combat unit which, thanks to the speed and killing power of Bradleys and Abrams tanks, had the ability to command as much ground as an entire division during the Cold War. Blount's 4th Brigade would fight as two distinct formations: one battalion each of Black Hawk and Apache helicopters would range well forward of the armored phalanx below, to shape the battlefield by attacking enemy formations. Behind the helicopters was the ground maneuver element of the 4th Brigade, the 7th Cavalry, a battalion-sized unit whose mission was to uncover the enemy for the heavier brigade combat team of the division to destroy.

Standing behind Blount's drive would be V Corps and its supporting forces. The corps commander was Lieutenant General William "Scott" Wallace, who had served as the commander and chief controller of the National Training Center, where he had built a reputation not only as a superb trainer but as an officer with clear insights into how an enemy army might best fight U.S. forces. Described often by his peers as taciturn and courtly, Wallace was responsible for coordinating logistical and combat operations from the Kuwait border all the way to downtown Baghdad. He knew that a ground force could not maintain the speed of its advance without some means to protect its rapidly lengthening supply lines. Here, the 101st Airborne Division fit the bill. With its great helicopter strength, it could provide cover for the supply lines and keep Iraqi forces at bay in cities and towns along the Euphrates. The commander of the Screaming Eagles was Major General David Petraeus. As a battalion commander in the 101st, he had been accidentally shot in the chest during a live-fire exercise at Fort Campbell, Kentucky, and he was lucky to be alive. He earned a doctorate in international relations from Princeton University in preparation for teaching at West Point. But academic life was just a detour that broadened Petraeus's horizons while doing nothing to diminish his reputation as a muddy boots soldier.

Wallace and the rest of the American command knew that time and distance were their real enemies. The 3rd Infantry Division would have to remain continuously on the move at a pace unprecedented in history. Fallen bridges, flooded lakes, and fortified urban areas could quickly turn this sweeping maneuver into a costly battle of attrition. Petraeus's helicopters would provide Wallace and Blount with the coverage and aerial mobility to extend the battlefield deep into the enemy's territory, particularly at night, while at the same time protecting the 3rd Infantry Division's lines of communication.

At nightfall on March 20, Apaches from the 4th Brigade were the first combat elements to go over the berm. Their immediate targets: eleven Iraqi outposts that were to provide early warning. Three hundred 155mm artillery rounds and Hellfire missiles eliminated the outposts before they could report. As soon as the enemy's observation posts were destroyed, Blount ordered the advance to begin. The 1st and 2nd BCTs poured through ten lanes previously cut in the frontier berm; in the process they destroyed a dozen Iraqi tanks just on the other side of the border. The 3rd BCT and the 7th Cavalry formed the second wave. They passed through the first two BCTs to take the lead in the advance on Tallil Airfield on the outskirts of An Nasiriyah, the division's first objective.

Blount's plan for the opening phase of the campaign combined audacity with trickery. Prewar intelligence had suggested that the Iraqis might expect the Americans to attempt to capture the bridges at An Nasiriyah, the first major crossing point of the Euphrates. Not to do so would force the Americans to swing westward into what was, from the Iraqi point of view, the inhospitable and treacherous desert and cross the Euphrates farther north at Karbala, a town virtually on the outskirts of Baghdad and within easy striking distance of Saddam's Republican Guard divisions. In fact, the Coalition war plan called for the 3rd Infantry Division to move as rapidly as possible to the Karbala Gap, before the Iraqis could grasp the threat. The 3rd Infantry Division was responsible for seizing the western bridge outside An Nasiriyah, for the 1st Marine Division's drive into the Mesopotamian Valley.

Blount employed his division in its first major engagement as a lure to draw the Iraqis into a firepower trap around Tallil. The American attack and the Iraqi response followed a pattern repeated time and again in the campaign. The firepower that preceded the arrival of the 7th Cavalry and the 3rd BCT on the outskirts of Tallil was far more effective in this war than such concentrations had been in 1991. Small teams of special operations forces, put in the area immediately before the war, provided targeting information for the 3rd Infantry Division's artillery. Armed with GPS and laser designators, these teams were able to call down precise artillery fires on the heads of those Iraqis who had dared to move forward. American artillery used an effective new precision munition—the SADARM projectile—for the first time in this war. This weapon ejected submunitions over the target area, which in turn carried onboard sensors to identify the signatures of armored vehicles and then attack them from above where even tanks are vulnerable. Thermal images of tanks erupting in flame on the horizon provided proof that American artillery had truly joined the precision age, albeit reluctantly.

Immediately after completing its antitank missions on Tallil, the division's artillery launched suppressive fire on deeper targets that might threaten the Apaches fanning out to the north. After the Apaches passed out of artillery range, the artillery shifted their guns to the Tallil airstrip, delivering a dense concentration of fire in front of the Abrams and Bradleys of the 3rd BCT as they passed over the airfield and pushed forward toward the western crossing site near An Nasiriyah. Shortly after midnight the Apaches spotted six troop-carrying vehicles and two tanks defending the crossing. Hellfire missiles destroyed them.

An hour later Task Force 2-69 Armor followed up the Apache strikes and attacked the Euphrates bridge. The 3rd Infantry Division's advance forces seized the bridgehead after two hours of sporadic fighting with Iraqi soldiers dug into sand-bagged bunkers. Two days later the marines would relieve the soldiers, and the 5th and 7th Regimental Combat Teams could begin to flow up Highway 1. By this time the remainder of the 3rd Infantry Division was advancing on the desert roads and tracks west of the Euphrates. The division had begun its 300-mile march to As Samawah and then on to An Najaf, occupied by the Republican Guard in the outer ring of defenses surrounding Baghdad. The Iraqis had at times fought hard around Tallil; but usually, regular units surrendered en masse after the ferocious American assault made them aware of the futility of resistance. Whatever remained of the 11th Iraqi Division evaporated so quickly that the defenders left behind copies of their war plan. It disclosed a scheme of defense from Kuwait to the Turkish border. The plan had already been overtaken by events. The one worrisome aspect of the fighting around the bridgehead above An Nasiriyah was the appearance of fanatical fedayeen at the side of regular army units. They would become a significant factor in the days ahead.

On March 21, the 1st BCT, along with many of the division's support troops, passed through the 3rd BCT and began a tortuous three-day march northward along Highway 28, called by Americans the pipeline road. The aim was to seize deployment and attack positions from which the division could strike and destroy the Republican Guard's Medina Division. The 3rd Infantry Division was now moving some 5,000 vehicles and 20,000 soldiers along two routes that converged on As Samawah. The two routes, code-named Hurricane and Tornado, began as dirt roads that eventually improved into a paved surface halfway to the objective. However, not long after the trek began, the division discovered that satellite imagery had hardly told the whole story. After enduring the abuse of a few seventy-ton Abrams tanks, road surfaces began to deteriorate rapidly. Even paved surfaces soon became sand traps. Adding to the difficulties, the movement of thousands of vehicles churned up the sand into a permanent reddish fog that smothered every piece of equipment and choked every throat.

After three days of fighting and movement, soldiers and their leaders found themselves at the limit of endurance and operational effectiveness. Accidents began to occur, as drivers fell asleep. Near As Samawah, the enemy intervened to make movement dangerous as well as exhausting. At the head of the division's advance, troopers of the 7th Cavalry encountered small, disorganized bands consisting of a fierce assortment of Baath officials, fedayeen, and other irregulars.

The Baathists in these bands were a sad lot. Mostly middle-aged men, they had been sent south to suppress the Shiites, and now they found themselves confronted with an enemy capable of blowing them to bits. With no prospects other than retribution at the hands of

Shiites who had endured decades of torture, rape, and murder, these pitiful men seemed to fight more out of helpless desperation than any lingering sense of patriotism or allegiance to Saddam Hussein.

The fedayeen and the soldiers of the Al Quts Brigades were cut from different cloth. The former originated in the fertile imagination of Saddam and his evil sons. Intrigued by the apparent success of Somali "technicals" in fighting against American rangers in the back streets of Mogadishu, Qusay and Uday established a force that mirrored the Somali technicals even down to arming pickups and SUVs with pedestal-mounted machine guns and rocket-propelled grenades. The 7th Cavalry reported that one fedayeen attack came from a motorcycle with a recoilless cannon strapped to its sidecar. Following the Somali example, Qusay ordered his legions of untrained "martyrs" to deploy in Iraqi cities along the Coalition's likely route to Baghdad. Division intelligence analysts knew about the irregulars, but they did not expect them to come out of the cities and attack Americans convoys in the desert.

No matter how badly trained the Iraqis were, their ambushes proved worrisome to fatigued cavalry soldiers, whose task was to push on toward Baghdad rather than engage in shoot-'em-ups with suicidal fanatics. The ambushes were short and sharp. A few fedayeen dismounts would place destroyed trucks or mines haphazardly across the road to create an obstacle. As soon as the armored column halted, the Iraqis would spring the ambush with a volley of RPG and automatic weapons fire. The most self-destructive of the lot would charge the tanks with guns blazing. Invariably, fire from the lead American vehicles would dispatch the attackers quickly and efficiently. In some cases, mobile technicals would rush the convoy, careening clumsily through the sand, firing wildly in the convoy's general direction. The results were the same: dead Iraqis and live Americans, largely unhurt but appalled and unnerved by the lunacy of their attackers.

As the Americans drew closer to As Samawah, fedayeen attacks increased and intensified. Meanwhile, regular troops and Baathists were shedding their uniforms to melt in with the general population, just as the fedayeen had done. All of these combatants were well versed in the rules of engagement that forbade Americans from firing on schools, mosques, hospitals, and cultural sites. As a result, the Iraqis sought out such places for headquarters, ammunition dumps, and firing positions. The troopers of the 7th Cavalry were among the first Coalition troops to discover that the most callous of the fedayeen pushed women and children to the front to act as human shields. In one case they watched a young woman break away from fedayeen who were taking shelter behind a group of civilians and run toward them. The fedayeen immediately killed her with a shot in the back.

On the road to As Samawah, the Iraqis began to employ artillery and mortars against the advancing Americans. Up to this point such barrages had been random and sporadic. The division's counter-battery radars, sited along the route of advance, picked up enemy rounds as soon as they left their tubes. Within seconds the source and location of the enemy was plotted; then guns linked digitally to the radar received the locations and blanketed the enemy position with artillery fire. By the time the division closed in on As Samawah, significant numbers of Iraqi regular soldiers had surrendered, providing intelligence officers with a steady stream of information about enemy positions and preparations, such as they were. The advance continued uninterrupted.

As the division's columns surrounded An Najaf, however, fuel and ammunition started to run low. The 230 fuel tankers established refuel points and began filling fuel tanks that were almost dry. By now the division had a clear idea of how Saddam's irregulars would attack. Blount's response was to isolate An Najaf—a major Shiite city of nearly half a million—from the north and east to prevent enemy paramilitaries from infiltrating and using it as a base to attack the 3rd Infantry Division's lines of supply.

On the afternoon of March 24 the 1st BCT established a blocking position north of An Najaf along Highway 9. The technicals appeared at nightfall mounted on SUVs and pickups. They continued their suicidal tactic of rushing at the Abrams and Bradleys, their guns firing. As intelligence later revealed, the enemy had concluded that the start of the *shamal* would allow them to infiltrate American positions. While the storm did limit the support soldiers could receive from the air, the Abrams and Bradleys used their thermal imaging sights to detect the fedayeen and destroy them, in fighting that was at times close and intense. Some fedayeen got within feet of American vehicles before being blown away by machine gun, chain gun, and cannon fire. On one occasion troopers from the 7th ran out of ammunition and, unable to receive resupplies in the intense fire fight, relied on captured AK-47s and ammunition to continue.

On the morning of March 25, the 7th Cavalry, supported by 2-69 Armor, attacked the main bridge across the Euphrates to close the cordon east of An Najaf. Again, resistance from the fedayeen was ferocious. Only two tanks got across the river before an Iraqi set off charges planted under the bridge. A few moments of panic ensued until engineers discovered that the bridge, though damaged, could still support tanks. By evening the fighting began to die down as the Iraqis ran out of enthusiasm and fedayeen.

DEEP ATTACK: THE 11TH ATTACK HELICOPTER REGIMENT

The Angel of Death has been abroad throughout the land; you may almost hear the beating of his wings.

John Bright, speech to the House of Commons, 1855

Wallace and Blount recognized the looming battle that was coming with the Medina Division and other Republican Guard formations. Both believed that Iraqi defenders needed to be attacked from the air before the 3rd Infantry Division reached Baghdad's defenses. In effect they were drawing on the army's Cold War concepts of Deep Battle and AirLand Battle. If that aerial attack did not occur, they feared that the 3rd Infantry Division, having fought its way across 300 miles of enemy territory, might no longer possess the combat power to break into the capital. They singled out the Medina Division as the likeliest candidate to be "shaped" by air force and helicopter strikes. It was the largest and most capable of the Republican Guard formations, and it sat deeply entrenched directly in the path of Blount's advance.

The deep attack plan called for the air force to wear the Medina down with precision weaponry. But Wallace and Blount worried that this division would be the most difficult to find and destroy with high-performance aircraft. Intelligence indicated that the Medina had skillfully dispersed its fighting elements within the suburbs and villages lying west of Baghdad. Much of its weaponry and support structure lay in or next to mosques, schools, and hospitals, as well as in public and private buildings. The only way to neutralize the Medina would be to attack it with low-flying helicopters. Wallace gave the mission to the 11th Attack Helicopter Regiment (AHR), which was directly assigned to V Corps.

What appeared at the time to be the only opportunity to attack the Medina came on the evening of March 22, as bad weather closed in from the west. Some operations are fated to go wrong from the start, and this was one. Laid on in haste, it never recovered its balance. The plans called for establishing a forward refueling point southwest of An Najaf on Objective Rams, captured earlier in the day by soldiers of the 3rd Infantry Division. The aviation commander chose Rams because it was closest to the target; thus, his helicopters could carry a heavier load of ammunition in place of fuel. But the fuel trucks and much of the regiment's command and control had to reach Rams by land convoy, and the convoy was already a full day behind schedule. It would be hard-pressed to arrive in time to provide fuel for all the helicopters. Moreover, the tactical assembly area chosen for the refueling operation was austere. Sand with the consistency of talcum powder formed opaque clouds as the helicopters started to land. A number of pilots experienced brownouts, where they lost their spatial orientation.

Because of delays and cancellations, the regimental staff was forced to communicate with V Corps over a single tactical satellite radio. Captain Karin Hobart, regimental intelligence officer, could obtain only the sparest data about the Medina. Over three hours late, just before dark, a portion of the fuel finally arrived. A complicated refueling operation had to take place in unfamiliar terrain and darkness. With the fuel situation deteriorating rapidly, the regimental commander reduced by a third the number of Apaches participating in the mission. The total strength of the attacking force would now be thirty-two Apaches. That decision in turn caused the regimental staff to reduce the number of targets at the last moment by a third. The Medina Division's 10th Brigade, which lay farthest to the east, would not be attacked at all.

At this point, events spiraled further out of control. News that the mission would have to begin three hours later than originally planned failed to reach those who were supposed to support the operation. The original fire plan had programmed air force fighters to take out the larger air defense systems that threatened the Apaches. The regiment had also designated "kill boxes"—territory cleared for engagement by supporting air force fighter aircraft. In addition, thirty-two army tactical missiles (ATACMS) were to be fired at the most critical air defense targets immediately before the Apaches reached the area. In fact, when the Apaches finally got off the ground, the suppressing fires had already occurred and an ominous quiet lay over the Iraqi landscape to the west of Baghdad. Adding to the sense of danger, intelligence picked up an increase in Iraqi cell phone and radio traffic immediately after the ATACMS strike. The enemy knew something was up, and he was clearly waiting.

From the pilots' point of view, the most disturbing aspect of the plan was the denial by V Corps of their request to attack the Medina Division from the west over Lake Razzazah and a virtually uninhabited Iraqi army maneuver training area. The only other alternative was from the south, a route that would take the helicopters dangerously close to Baghdad's suburbs. Because the power grid was still operating, reflected light from populated areas would silhouette the Apaches against the night sky, while hindering the use of night goggles. Nevertheless, despite these disturbing factors, the pilots were ready and eager to go.

Chief Warrant Officer John Tomblin and his frontseater, First Lieutenant Jason King, had a rough time getting off the ground. After pulling up, Tomblin felt his Apache shudder and wallow dangerously under its excessive weight of fuel, cannon shells, rockets, and Hellfire missiles. Six inches of fine dust thrown up by thirty-two helicopters blinded the entire formation, as they fought to gain a few feet of altitude and depart. One of the less experienced pilots from A Troop crashed on takeoff. For Tomblin and King, the 53-mile trip to the target was uneventful. Not so for some of their colleagues who were traveling on a parallel track to the east over more populated areas. Looking out their right window, the two pilots saw sheets of red, white, green, and yellow tracers reaching up to the formation almost from the moment of liftoff.

Just as they banked left into the objective, the bright lights below went out for two seconds, the apparent signal for the Iraqis on the ground to open up with everything they had. In effect, the Apaches had run into a low-tech ambush of small arms fire and RPGs. Tomblin's first indication that something was wrong came from the smell of burning electrical equipment. Looking down at a brightly lit cluster of buildings, he saw a lone man shooting an AK-47 at his helicopter. As he twisted reflexively, his helmet sight slewed the Apache's minigun directly at the enemy; a quick press on the trigger and the Iraqi soldier disappeared in a hail of exploding 30mm cannon fire.

At that moment, King took a slug in the throat. Tomblin heard the round's impact and saw the lieutenant's head lurch; other than the sound of labored breathing, he heard nothing more from his copilot. The patter and thump of hits increased as Tomblin fought to maintain stability, his flight controls becoming ever more sluggish and unresponsive. A glance to the right revealed that his wingman's engine was on fire. He pulled cautiously back on the stick to fall in behind his wingman, while spraying the ground in front of the helicopters with cannon fire. From his position in front, the wounded King could see the enemy tracers through his night vision goggles. At that moment, Tomblin was looking through his forward radar sensor and was unable to detect tracers. By pressing a bandage to his throat wound, King was at last able to speak and began directing Tomblin where to aim his cannon fire and where to fly to avoid enemy fire as much as possible.

With his instruments damaged and a wounded crewman on board, Tomblin swung his crippled bird to the south, dropped to 100 feet and accelerated to 130 knots. A few minutes later the assembly area appeared. Unable to find a safe spot to land amid the confusing swarm of helicopters seeking to let down, Tomblin gingerly lowered his aircraft on an open field 1,500 meters away and called for medical help. King was lucky to be alive—a half-inch in either direction and the bullet would have been fatal. King refused evacuation and, thoroughly bandaged but able to speak, he returned to flying duty a few days later,

The 11th Regiment's difficulties had not resulted from faulty doctrine, pilot incompetence, or design defects in the Apache. Hasty preparation, inadequate intelligence, a forewarned enemy, and an unfortunate selection of attack routes all had contributed to the failure. Nevertheless, in spite of the withering ground fire, all but one of the Apaches returned. The Iraqis held the crew of the downed helicopter captive until the end of the war, when the two pilots were rescued by marines. All but a few of the other damaged Apaches were flying within a couple of days.

Compared with the ill-fated 11th Attack Helicopter Regiment, the Apaches of the 101st Airborne Division had a number of advantages. The 101st never had serious problems with inadequate or missing ground support. The division's initial assault began with a ground convoy of over 2,700 vehicles that moved deep into Iraq, beginning March 22. By the end of the day that convoy had covered almost 200 miles before establishing a forward area refueling position (FARP) in the western desert. Only a day later the 3rd Battalion, 187th Airborne Infantry Battalion, air-assaulted aboard the division's Black Hawk helicopters to establish a FARP even farther into Iraq, this one located southwest of An Najaf and 385 miles away from the division's base camp in Kuwait.

Also unlike the 11th Attack Helicopter Regiment, the 101st had more than enough helicopters to conduct a robust maneuver campaign. When the 3rd Infantry Division ran short of ammunition, the 101st delivered over 3,000 artillery shells, each weighing more than 150 pounds, as well as 150 three-ton MLRS rocket pods. On March 28 after the *shamal* had abated, the division's Apaches mounted a series of successful aerial assaults, beginning with an attack on the Medina Division's 14th Armored Brigade. The 101st conducted the complex and seemingly thankless mission of protecting the 3rd Infantry Division's lengthening logistical tail. It also inherited the task, as the

3rd Infantry Division moved on to the Karbala Gap, of maintaining control of the various cities and towns on the west side of the Euphrates. Its helicopters were well-suited to reacting to and then destroying the various raids launched by Saddam's fedayeen from the cities and towns along the river.

Beginning on March 24 the vicious storm that had concerned planners of 11th Attack Helicopter Regiment's raid now assaulted ground operations with a vengeance. Troopers labeled it the "mother of all storms." The *shamal* blew for three days without relief. It had sustained winds of twenty-five knots, with gusts to fifty. Visibility with the naked eye shrank to less than 100 meters, grounding helicopters and some UAVs. For part of the storm, rain fell through the blowing clouds of fine sand. The result was blowing mud that coated everything.

While the storm was unwelcome, Wallace and his subordinates recognized that it offered time for forward units to resupply and refit. It also allowed them to stabilize worrisome areas left unattended or bypassed by the rapidity of the advance. As the storm closed in, 3rd Infantry Division's soldiers had reached the point where fatigue had begun to consume their attention. The exhaustion of much of V Corps was understandable, considering that in seventy-two hours it had moved 10,000 vehicles over 350 miles while fighting three different battles. Some units had nearly depleted their supplies of ammunition, while concerns mounted about units still engaged with the enemy as the storm increased in intensity. Wallace intended to stabilize his forces at Objective Rams before attacking through the Karbala Gap.

Contact with the fedayeen during the sandstorm reinforced the decision to halt for a period before resuming the advance. Senior commanders, marine as well as army, by now appreciated the intensity and fanaticism with which the fedayeen attacked. By coming out of the cities, the fedayeen provided Coalition ground forces with an opportunity to kill the enemy under conditions that maximized American firepower and minimized the destruction caused by the irregulars. The slaughtered would have no opportunity to make a last-ditch defense in the cities.

The fluidity of the Coalition's advance offered opportunities, but at times it also carried with it tragic consequences. On March 23, thirty-three soldiers in an eighteen-vehicle convoy from the 507th Maintenance Company strayed off the main route northwest and wandered into An Nasiriyah. The convoy continued through the city, observing large numbers of fedayeen, before it exited over the Saddam Canal. It then turned around and returned on exactly the same route. On the way back through An Nasiriyah, the Iraqis finally woke up and opened fire on the American vehicles. They killed eleven soldiers and captured six, while sixteen escaped. The resulting frenzy, exploited by media unclear about what was happening and often inclined to make a bad story worse, created an impression in the United States that the war was not going well. But Franks maintained a steady hand on the rudder, while soldiers and marines gathered their strength for the next push. Meanwhile, under the cover of the *shamal* the Iraqis would attempt to mass their forces, with disastrous results.

THE MARINE ADVANCE

The invaders drive north through the Iraqi desert in a Humvee, eating candy, dipping tobacco and singing songs . . . The four marines crammed into this vehicle—among the very first American troops who crossed into Iraq—are wired on a combination of caffeine, sleep deprivation, excitement and tedium . . . [Two of the marines] have already reached a profound conclusion about this campaign: the battlefield that is Iraq is filled with "fucking retards." There's the retard commander who took a wrong turn near the border . . . There are the hopeless retards in the battalion-support sections who screwed up the radios and didn't bring enough batteries to operate the Marine's thermal-imaging devices. But in their eyes, one retard reigns supreme: Saddam Hussein—"We already kicked his ass once," says Person, spitting a thick stream of tobacco juice out his window. "Then we let him go, and then he spends the next twelve years pissing us off even more. We don't want to be in this shit-hole country. We don't want to invade it. What a fucking retard."

Evan Wright, "The Killer Elite," *Rolling Stone,* June 2003

On March 20, at 8:30 p.m. local time, the 5th Marine Regimental Combat Team (RCT) crossed the berms delineating the border with Iraq. They were among the lead elements of the 1st Marine Division, the main combat division in I MEF. The 1st was the lineal descendant of the division that had seized the landing strip at Guadalcanal over sixty years earlier, thereby initiating the Battle of the Solomons. To the north, burning oil trenches lit by the Iraqis smoldered. The landscape, a dismal brown from horizon to horizon, was already littered with the wreckage left by air strikes. An embedded reporter described the scenery greeting the marines: "We are driving through a desert trash heap, periodically dotted with mud huts, small flocks of sheep and clusters of starved-looking, stick-figure cattle grazing on scrub brush. Once in a while you see wrecked vehicles: burnt-out car frames, perhaps left over from the first Gulf War, a wheel-less Toyota truck resting on its axles."[1]

Among the enlisted troops of all the services, the marines were on average the youngest. The great majority of the men in the 5th RCT were on their first enlistment, and most had joined the corps for the challenge it presented to macho seventeen- and eighteen-year-old males. As an embedded reporter observed: "[Young marines] are loud and rough. They have lots of tattoos. They'll ignore you or torment you if they think you're a fake. They'll do anything for you if they like you. One marine officer I knew liked to call his marines 'the most demented young people our society can produce.' He wasn't really kidding, but he still admired them. And I did, too."[2]

For a number of these young men, there seemed to be no understandable reason for embarking on military operations against what appeared to be a wretchedly poor Third World country, except perhaps that they were marines. However, the rationale for the conflict would become crystal clear to 1st Marine Division's commander, Major General James Mattis, after the war. In May 2003 an Iraqi came up to him and thanked him for the efforts the marines had made to free Iraq. It was too late for him, he said. During the time of the Baath, he had found the broken body of his twelve-year-old daughter on his doorstep, along with a videotape depicting her last two hours of life, as Saddam's thugs raped, tortured, and eventually killed her. But the Americans had saved others from a similar fate, he said, his eyes welling with tears.

The numbers alone give some idea of the commitment the marines made to this war. By the start of operations, the corps had deployed 100 percent of its tank and LAV (light armored vehicle) battalions, 55 percent of its artillery battalions, and 50 percent of its infantry battalions. Moreover, it accomplished this buildup of combat power in an astonishingly short period. Between January and March, 60,000 marines shipped out to the Gulf, where they linked up with their arriving combat equipment.

The mobile fighting power of the 1st Marine Division was concentrated in its three regimental combat teams. Each was more than a U.S. army brigade and certainly more than a traditional marine regiment. The 5th RCT consisted of the following: the 5th Marines, with its three infantry battalions; the 2nd battalion from the 11th Marine Artillery Regiment, for direct support; a light armored reconnaissance battalion, equipped with reconnaissance LAVs; an armored battalion, equipped with M1A1 Abrams tanks; a combat engineer company; a combat service support company; and other supporting organizations. Moreover, when the 5th RCT crossed the border into Iraq, it also possessed tactical control over the British Army's 7th Battalion Royal Horse Artillery, which detached to rejoin the British 1st Armoured Division after the marines reached the Rumaila oil fields. In total, 5th RCT contained 7,503 marines, sailors, U.S. and British soldiers. After the British moved on toward Basra, the regiment's strength dropped to between six and seven thousand men. For several days during the advance to Baghdad, the regiment added 900 marines and sailors of the 3rd Light Armored Reconnaissance Battalion to its strength.

In addition to his three maneuver RCTs, Mattis also commanded the 11th Marines, an artillery regiment, which brought additional firepower to the fight. Close and deadly air support for the 1st Marine Division came from the 3rd Marine Aircraft Wing, which was an integral component of the "marine air-ground task force" concept (MAGTF). The 3rd MAW was commanded by Major General James Amos, who had a tight working relationship with Mattis as well as with Lieutenant General Moseley, the joint air force component commander. The understanding among these three men allowed the MAW considerable latitude in using its air power to support the ground advance. The naval component commander, in turn, permitted the marines to use the big decks of their amphibious ships as light carriers. For a portion of the war, until the Harriers deployed forward, Amos sent his Cobra helicopters ashore and concentrated all his Harriers on the amphibious ships. This war would see little of the petty parochialism that too often marks interservice relations within the Beltway.

Amos used the Cobras as a hammer to smash the Iraqis immediately to the front of marine ground forces, while his Hornets and Harriers ranged deeper behind the lines to interdict Iraqi ground movements. What made the marine air ground system particularly effective was the willingness of the marine corps to detail its combat pilots down to maneuver-battalion company level to act as forward air controllers for close air support strikes. Amos even provided an extra flight officer for each battalion of the 1st Marine Division to ensure that his aircraft provided the most timely and effective air support possible. By the end of the war, 3rd MAW aircraft had flown 25,600 hours and 9,800 sorties; they had dropped 2,200 precision-guided munitions and 2,300 dumb bombs, for a total of 6.24 million pounds of ordnance.

The marine's task for the coming invasion was succinctly laid out by I MEF's commander, Lieutenant General James Conway, before the initiation of hostilities: "The purpose of this operation is to remove the Iraqi regime. We will support the CFLCC [combined forces land component commander] by rapidly defeating Iraqi forces in the MEF AO [area of operations] in order to protect the Main Effort's [V Corps'] eastern flank throughout the operation, and by isolating Baghdad from the east. Additionally, the early seizure of the key oil infrastructure will be central to preventing environmental disaster in the region while facilitating a smooth transition to a new Iraqi government." This statement suggests that I MEF was to have a supporting role in the overall execution of Operation Iraqi Freedom. Nevertheless, the marines displayed not only the tactical but the operational skill to form the other arm of the pincers which, with the 3rd Infantry Division, would envelop and then capture the Iraqi capital. As Conway suggested after the war, the marines' approach to their supporting role was to pick as many fights with the Iraqis as they could, keeping maximum pressure on the enemy from the beginning to the end of the campaign. When it was all over, the marines had demonstrated that they could conduct operations far from their natural habitat, the sea. The distance the marines covered in three weeks of military operations from Kuwait to Tikrit was equivalent to the distance from San Diego to San Francisco. I MEF's campaign reached even farther and deeper into Iraq than that of the army's V Corps.

Directly under Conway in I MEF's chain of command was Major General James Mattis of the 1st Marine Division. One year earlier, Mattis had commanded the two MEUs forming Task Force 58, which the marines deployed in southern Afghanistan in the war against the Taliban and Al Qaeda. One of his officers described the general as distant to those who did not know him, "but once he has decided you are worthy of trust, he will go to hell and back for you." Mattis's close relationship with his troops was partially based on his ability to speak their language. But he was also an avid student of military history and had much in common with the German field marshal Erwin Rommel, who, like Mattis, led his troops from the front. Mattis's "jump" command post consisted of an LAV with communications gear and three Humvees through which he kept in touch with his main headquarters and with Conway at I MEF.

From his lead position, Mattis stayed close to the regiments involved in the fiercest fighting and got a good sense for events on the battlefield. The general refused to believe that images on a computer screen in the quiet hum of a command post could tell him what he needed to know about how the battle was progressing and what his subordinates required. Mattis could be ruthless; he would relieve the commander of one of his regiments in the middle of a campaign. In the marines, only performance counts. Mattis picked several officers to act as what he called his "eyes only" representatives. They had no authority but, he said, like "Frederick the Great's focused telescope or Wellington's lieutenants in the Peninsula Campaign," they had the duty of wandering the battlefield to keep him informed of things they thought he needed to know: troops or officers who were exhausted by combat, supplies that were not reaching the front line, and the other human factors that can be crucial in combat. Equally important, Mattis attempted to understand the enemy he confronted. Here, he encountered considerable frustration. T. E. Lawrence had a better idea of the personality and capabilities of his Turkish adversaries in World War I, Mattis said, than he was ever able to get out of U.S. intelligence concerning the Iraqis.

The three regiments of the 1st Marine Division struck north into the Rumaila oil fields with the 1st RCT on the right, the 5th in the center, and the 7th on the left. Farther to the west lay Task Force Tarawa, following closely behind the 3rd Infantry Division on its way to An Nasiriyah. The Rumaila oil fields represent one of the world's great deposits of raw petroleum and gas—nearly 1,000 working wells (including the west Qurnah fields), as well as small fields lying farther to the east near Basra. The main field stretches from the Kuwait border for over fifty miles due north, parallel to the border with Iran.

The first and one of the most important tasks confronting 1st Marine Division was to secure these fields, with the help of special forces, and then pass control over to the British. It was then to turn west and move out as quickly as possible toward An Nasiriyah—the key to the road junctions leading north to Al Kut and northwest toward Baghdad. In two days the marines successfully achieved their first task. Late on the evening of March 22, the commander and assistant commander of the Iraqi Army's 51st Mechanized Division surrendered to the 3rd Amphibious Assault Battalion. Virtually nothing was left of the 51st—its soldiers were dead, POWs, or deserters. All three combat regiments of the 1st Marine Division now swung to the west to reach An Nasiriyah. Task Force Tarawa had already arrived in the area after occupying Jalibah air base. It had been forced to move through the desert to get to Jalibah because the 3rd Infantry Division's supply vehicles (which had movement priority) filled the roads. Ironically as it would turn out, among those army vehicles would be the ill-fated 507th Maintenance Company.

Task Force Tarawa was typical of the ad hoc units that the American military proved so capable of cobbling together in this war. Its heart consisted of the 2nd Marine Regiment from Camp Lejeune, reinforced to form the 2nd RCT. It would eventually receive the 24th MEU and the 15th MEU. Both MEUs would lend their aerial components to the 3rd Marine Aircraft Wing. In addition to the MEUs, Task Force Tarawa also received a combat engineer battalion and a company of Abrams to support its operations. Here, once again, U.S. forces were comfortable in creating an ad hoc unit that fit no known organizational framework. Common doctrine, training, and education gave commanders an inherent trust in the ability of disparate units to cooperate effectively on the battlefield.

The commander of Task Force Tarawa was Brigadier General Rick Natonski, a bigger and younger version of General Conway. Like Conway and Mattis, Natonski possessed the disarming eloquence of men who are far better read than they generally care to admit. Task Force Tarawa would have to address a number of I MEF's grittiest tasks, particularly in protecting the 1st Marine Division's logistical lines of communications. And like the troopers of the 82nd Airborne, the marines of the task force received little credit in the media for their critical role in the Coalition's victory.

THE BATTLE FOR AN NASIRIYAH

This is a gauntlet, men. This is what it's all about. If you ever thought you weren't going into combat in the marine corps, you were wrong. We're friggin gonna' run the gauntlet.

Captain Matt Reid, 3rd Battalion, 1st Marine Regiment,
quoted in *The Daily Telegraph, War on Saddam,* 2003

The first of these gritty tasks came in the Iraqi town of An Nasiriyah. After the fighting had ended, some young marine officers would complain that the army's 3rd Infantry Division had thrown rocks into a hornets' nest there and then moved on, leaving the marines to clean up the mess. In fact, whatever the 3rd Infantry Division left behind, marines were going to have to dig the fedayeen out of An Nasiriyah, just as soldiers from the 82nd and 101st were going to have to do in the cities and towns along the Euphrates to the north.

After leaving Jalibah air base in the early morning hours of March 23, Task Force Tarawa was to seize the bridges across the Euphrates and Saddam Canal in An Nasiriyah. Capturing these bridges would allow the 1st RCT to advance along Highway 7 north toward Al Kut. A second crossing lay to the west of An Nasiriyah and was already under the 3rd Infantry Division's control. It lay in the countryside outside the city limits and would provide the 5th and 7th RCTs with direct access to Highway 1, which led northwest toward Ad Diwaniyah. Conway and Mattis planned to use these two avenues of advance to confuse the Iraqi high command and to open up a back door to Baghdad. This concept of operations led to the fight for An Nasiriyah that would last for more than a week—a complication that had not been in the plan.

As with the British in the south, the marines had believed that the largely Shiite population of An Nasiriyah would welcome their liberation. The approaching marines failed to understand the deep fear the Baath inspired among the Shia. Nor did marine and Centcom intelligence pick up on the large numbers of fedayeen (including Syrians, Palestinians, Egyptians, and even some Chechens), regular soldiers from Iraq's 11th Infantry Division, and the usual assortment of Baath loyalists, all spoiling for a fight. These disparate groups, holed up in An Nasiriyah, intimidated the local population while they prepared to defend the city against the Americans.

The defenders of An Nasiriyah were under Ali Hassan al-Majid's command in southern Iraq. Majid—one of Saddam's relatives and most ruthless thugs—was more than willing to exploit the committed and to dragoon the unfortunate into making a determined last stand. Most of the foreign volunteers had come to Iraq because of a deep commitment to defending the Arab or Islamic world against Western interlopers. Yet, Saddam's regime had provided no reasonable training for the volunteers. After their arrival, they soon discovered that many among the Iraqi population viewed them with contempt and actually hoped the Americans would win. As one disillusioned fundamentalist, wounded in the war, told a British reporter in Beirut with considerable bitterness: "It was madness. We stayed at the front for five days with nothing to eat. I saw two dead bodies shot in the head by Iraqi soldiers. I went there to be a martyr, not to be murdered by a brother. We went there to help them liberate their country and all they did was shoot us in the back."[3] For the most part the fedayeen made ferocious fighters, but their hosts provided them with few of the skills by which they could make the Americans pay a price for their death. The marines would thus be the first, but not the last, to stand at the receiving end of attacks by Saddam's most fanatical defenders.

The first sign that something was not right came on the outskirts of An Nasiriyah. As the lead elements of the 1st Battalion, 2nd Marine Regiment (1/2), supported by tanks, approached the city, its marines got into a fire fight with Iraqis. They destroyed nine immobilized T-55 tanks—many without engines—that had been dug in to protect a railroad bridge just south of the Euphrates. At approximately the same time, the marines saw a U.S. army truck drive out of the city and head south toward them. They held their fire, but the truck turned around and then retreated back into An Nasiriyah.

Shortly thereafter, the truck reappeared and established contact with the marines. The soldiers on board indicated they were part of the 507th Maintenance Company and that there were wounded soldiers and damaged vehicles along the main road leading through the city. By taking a wrong turn, the 507th convoy had driven deep into the city and alerted the Iraqis that the Americans were coming. Not only that, but as a captured Iraqi officer suggested after the fight, the desperate efforts of some of the convoy to flee had given the Iraqi defenders a false sense of their own capabilities and the weakness of the Americans. The marines immediately proceeded north and rescued a dozen wounded soldiers.

The marines then refueled their tanks and headed to the Euphrates. The Iraqis had not blown the bridge over the river, but a fierce fire fight occurred, and the Iraqis were driven off with heavy casualties. Unfortunately, Bravo Company of 1/2 turned down the wrong side road in what was supposed to be an indirect approach to a second major bridge across the Saddam Canal. It immediately ran into a group of surprised Iraqis and, in a brief fire fight, killed them. But farther along, six of its vehicles became stuck in a sand bog, and the company's movement ceased entirely as the marines attempted to extract the vehicles from the powdery sand.

Charlie Company of 1/2 then resumed the advance to the Saddam Canal down An Nasiriyah's main road, soon to be called Ambush Alley by the marines. The company reached its target, but things soon "went to hell in a hand basket," as one marine reported. Supported by Abrams tanks, the marines made a successful crossing, but one of their amphibious assault vehicles (AAVs) was hit by an RPG on the bridge. With the gear on the outside of the vehicle already burning, the AAV barely made it across. On the other side of the canal, the marines inside the AAV discovered that the ramp was jammed, so they had to crawl through the escape hatches to get out. Four marines inside were wounded. As one marine described the scene: "It was mayhem, everyone was screaming."[4] But worse was to come. Almost immediately thereafter, an A-10 Warthog, supposedly providing close air support, strafed the north side of the bridge, destroying another AAV and killing six marines with "friendly fire."

Now in serious trouble with a huge fire fight on their hands—to some of the survivors, reminiscent of what had occurred on the streets of Mogadishu in 1993—the marines of Charlie Company confronted the task of getting their wounded back by vehicle. A medical evacuation helicopter was out of the question because of intense incoming RPG and small arms fire. The officers on the spot decided to send a convoy of six vehicles back south along Ambush Alley. The convoy moved out and within 500 yards ran into another ambush. A barrage of RPGs and small arms fire destroyed two vehicles, killing most of the marines inside. Two other vehicles were badly damaged. The survivors crawled into a nearby building to continue the fight. As evening fell, they believed they were there for the night. However, two hours later a "gunny" (gunnery sergeant) with an Abrams and two Humvees showed up at the building's door. The marines jumped aboard, "sticking out everywhere," and the vehicles ran a mad dash south through the rest of Ambush Alley to safety.[5] The marines had arrived at An Nasiriyah. As their commander commented after the war, they had never expected to see the level of sustained resistance that they had encountered.

The fight for the bridgehead continued all night. A Cobra pilot providing close air support over the Saddam Canal reported after the war:

> That night, we returned to where the Grunts were located where we had left them to go get gas. It's dark now. The Marine vehicles are parked in a coiled formation . . . so that each individual vehicle can fire in a specific direction to protect the rest of the vehicles in the coil. Each tank and LAV is assigned a particular sector of fire. As we

approached, we could see that they were in a pretty decent dog fight. As we moved to get over their position, fire is going out in every direction from their coil. TOW missiles, 25mm chain gun, M-1 tank main gun, and heavy machine gun fire. We were so low over them the firing from the machine guns made your teeth rattle. Every couple of minutes, a FAC [forward air controller] would give me a rollout heading, and I'd either ripple a pod of rockets, or blast away with cannon. Everything was danger close.[6]

It was going to take considerable fighting to clear An Nasiriyah of fedayeen and Baathist resistance. By the morning of March 24, Task Force Tarawa had a secure hold over both bridges and had suppressed some of the danger along Ambush Alley. Nevertheless, the avenue was sufficiently long for the Iraqis to infiltrate fedayeen teams and establish small ambush points. Mattis, Natonski, and Conway determined to take the risk of moving the 1st RCT straight through An Nasiriyah along Ambush Alley, then across the bridges and on up to Highway 7. From the operational perspective, it was crucial that 1st RCT threaten Al Kut along the Tigris as soon as possible and present the Iraqis with what appeared to be two threats to central Iraq and eventually Baghdad.

Meanwhile, the move by 5th and 7th RCTs was developing satisfactorily, since the bridge they were crossing to reach Highway 1 lay outside the urban area. Their only difficulty lay in the traffic jams that soon developed as large numbers of vehicles tried to cross this choke point. The first winds of the *shamal* did not help matters.

For the marines of the 1st RCT, it was a different story. The movement through An Nasiriyah was conducted under RPG, small arms, and sometimes mortar fire. The 3rd Battalion, 1st Marine Regiment

(3/1), led the way. The next morning the 1st Marine Division's reconnaissance battalion crossed. Its embedded reporter later recorded:

> Just after sunrise, [the] seventy-vehicle convoy rolls over
> the bridge on the Euphrates and enters An Nasiriyah.
> It's one of those sprawling Third World mud-brick-and-
> cinder-block cities that probably looks pretty badly
> rubbled even on a good day. This morning, smoke curls
> from collapsed structures. Most buildings facing the
> road are pockmarked and cratered. Cobras fly overhead
> spitting machine-gun fire. Dogs roam the ruins . . . A
> few vehicles come under machine-gun and RPG fire.
> The Recon Marines return the fire and redecorate an
> apartment building with about a dozen grenades fired
> from a Mark-19. In an hour we clear the outer limits of
> the city and start to head north. Dead bodies are scat-
> tered along the edge of the road. Most are men, enemy
> fighters, some with weapons still in their hands . . .
> There are shot-up cars and trucks with bodies hang-
> ing over the edges. We pass a bus, smashed and burned,
> with charred remains sitting upright in some windows.
> There's a man with no head in the road and a dead little
> girl, too, about three or four, lying on her back. She's
> wearing a dress and has no legs.[7]

From the Coalition's point of view, the gamble worked. With relatively few casualties, the 1st RCT was through the city and headed
seemingly in the direction of Al Kut, a town lying on the banks of the
Tigris. It was here that the Turks had defeated the British in 1916 during the British Army's disastrous Mesopotamian campaign. The marines had successfully accomplished one of the most difficult tasks

ground forces confront in war: in military terms, it is called a forward passage of lines under fire.

However, Task Force Tarawa's problems with An Nasiriyah had not been solved. It had to ensure the safety of the supply lines through the city that ran north to Highway 7 and 1st RCT, and the only way to achieve that goal was to clean out An Nasiriyah. The only way to do *that* was by killing the Baathists and the fedayeen who still remained alive after the first several days of fighting. Natonski's problems were further exacerbated by the *shamal,* which not only reduced the air support he received but worsened the conditions under which his marines had to fight. And all the while, raids and ambushes by Iraqis destroyed vehicles, kept his marines on edge, and threatened the convoys running down Ambush Alley. But slowly Natonski's task force mastered the situation. Marine sniper teams and special forces infiltrated the city to kill fedayeen and Baath officials as they attempted to move about. The establishment of a cordon around the city choked off reinforcements. On several occasions, the marines stopped busloads of young Arab men, many from outside Iraq, cleanly shaven and military in appearance, and sent them straight to the POW camps they had set up.

As the marines battered away at the Saddam loyalists, intelligence steadily improved. Increasingly, the Shia came forward to direct the marines to fedayeen and Baathist administrative centers. Marine precision air strikes quickly destroyed these command centers, as well as front line positions and ambush points. Slowly but steadily the fedayeen's ability to sustain the fight waned. This combination of improving intelligence and special forces enabled the rescue of Private Jessica Lynch. An Iraqi walk-in informed the marines where her Iraqi captors were holding her, and then he returned to the hospital to determine the security around her room. That intelligence allowed a combination of marines, SEALS, and rangers to put together the complex mission that rescued her. The marine diversion that set the stage for this special forces operation was led by a Royal Marine Commando, Major Mike Tanner, who was on an exchange tour with the U.S. Marines. The first SEAL into her room called out: "Jessica Lynch, we're United States soldiers and we're here to protect you and take you home."[8]

Surrounded by a marine cordon outside the city, the Baath and fedayeen inside An Nasiriyah were slowly strangled by the pressure that Task Force Tarawa applied. But it was not until the beginning of April that the city was truly cleared out and convoys could run through without fear of ambush. By then Task Force Tarawa was beginning to head north to support the ever-lengthening lines of communications of the 1st Marine Division, as its spearheads moved toward the Tigris and their appointment in Baghdad. During the fiercest fighting in An Nasiriyah, 1st Marine Division's drive up Highways 7 and 1 had proceeded, although the *shamal* slowed the advance considerably. The terrain was anything but desertlike. After the war, Mattis recalled that he never saw desert terrain after crossing the Euphrates. Central Iraq, he indicated, was extraordinarily difficult to traverse and could have presented a tremendous challenge to his advance, had his opponents been half-way competent. But "Iraqi generals," he added, "couldn't carry a bucket of rocks."

As the marines advanced along Highways 1 and 7, they ran into a series of ambushes, almost all conducted incompetently—a nuisance, but nothing that presented a real challenge. By March 27, 1st RCT had reached Qalat Sukkar, two thirds of the way to Al Kut, while the 5th RCT, leading the drive down Highway 1, had nearly reached Ad Diwaniyah. At this point, the I MEF and 1st Marine Division were on the way to setting the trap for the Iraqis. Meanwhile, to the north, around-the-clock bombing was wrecking Iraq's military forces.

A Meeting of the Minds

Indeed, it is because of our orderly temper that we are brave in war and wise in counsel—brave in war, because self-control is the chief element in self-respect, and respect of self, in turn, is the chief element in courage . . . We are educated . . . not to be so ultra-clever in useless accomplishments as to disparage our enemy's military preparations in brave words and then fail to go through with the business in corresponding deeds.

Thucydides, *History of the Peloponnesian War*,
spoken by King Archidamus to the Spartan Assembly, fifth century BC

In less than a week the Americans had achieved a stunning advance deep into enemy territory, setting the scene for the final chapter of the Baath regime. Nevertheless, a number of disturbing issues confronted them as the *shamal* blew itself out on March 26. On that day a crucial meeting took place at General Conway's I MEF headquarters. McKiernan and Wallace both flew in to determine what the next move would be. While the *shamal* had provided a brief respite to some of their soldiers and marines, the logistical situation was serious for everyone. Blount's 3rd Infantry Division had consumed virtually all of its supplies over the course of the campaign thus far. Moreover, the lead army and marine units were engaged in a series of nasty fire fights in An Nasiriyah, As Samawah, and An Najaf that were distracting the focus of V Corps and I MEF. The need to protect lengthy logistical lines was dissipating combat power in a number of meaningless engagements.

Fierce attack by fedayeen along the Euphrates was having a significant impact on the conduct of operations. Blount's 3rd Infantry

Division, spread out over the entire length of the lines of communications, was highly vulnerable. Its 3rd Brigade Combat Team extended from As Samawah to An Najaf. The 2nd BCT was isolating An Najaf with a portion of the 7th Cavalry, while the 1st BCT was fighting for control of the river crossing site outside the city. Wallace argued that unless these brigades were freed from their current missions, V Corps and 3rd Infantry Division would barely be able to scrape together two brigades for the attack on the Karbala Gap.

McKiernan agreed. Consequently, with Franks' consent, Third Army released its reserve brigade from the 82nd Airborne to take over the fight at As Samawah and the protection of the 3rd Infantry Division's lines of communications, aided by the 101st Airborne Division. Once this was sorted out, 3rd Infantry Division would regain full control of its combat power for the job of driving through the Karbala Gap and on to Baghdad. But that was only one of the steps that needed to be taken. The second was the establishment of a fully functioning forward supply base at Objective Rams near An Najaf. Wallace estimated that the corps needed to stockpile at least three to four days of supplies—and probably five to six days—in order for the 3rd Infantry Division to have the legs to push through to Baghdad.

Before the meeting broke up, the senior commanders agreed that they had to create three basic conditions before launching the final offensive against the capital. First, they needed to clear up the lines of communications, so that supplies could flow smoothly forward. Second, they needed to establish three to four days of supplies in the forward supply dumps, so they could sustain significant fighting as they surrounded Baghdad. And third, they needed a clearer idea of the strength and position of the Republican Guard on the other side of the hill. In the coming four days their troops would establish these conditions and set the stage for the battle of Baghdad.

4

The British War in the South

We go to liberate not to conquer. We will not fly our flags in
their country. We are entering Iraq to free a people, and the only
flag which will be flown is their own. Show respect for them.
There are some who will not be alive shortly. Those who do not
want to go on that journey, we will not send. As for the others, I
expect you to rock their world. Wipe them out if that is what
they choose. But if you are ferocious in battle, remember to be
magnanimous in victory.

LIEUTENANT COLONEL TIM COLLINS,
from a speech to the 1st Battalion Royal Irish Regiment, March 2003

By mid-day on April 6, 2003—"a terribly long day,"
one battle group commander recalled—the Desert
Rats of Britain's 7th Armoured Regiment had fought their way through
to the main road junction in Basra. Around them, the square was dec-

orated with ghastly symbols of the Baath regime. The statue of Saddam towering above their heads was no surprise—representations of the tyrant were ubiquitous in Iraq. But troops were unprepared for the huge, garish dolphin rising out of the ground with an Iraqi soldier riding on its back. This statue was supposedly a metaphor for the successful Iraqi defense of Basra and the Shatt al Arab waterway—the strategic gateway to the Tigris and Euphrates Rivers—in the war against Iran fifteen years earlier. But it was in effect a monument to the Iraqi Shiite conscripts slaughtered in Saddam's war against the Iranians.

The junction where the troops now stood was known as the gateway to the city, and according to Iraqis, "He who holds the gateway holds Basra." One British officer, perhaps metaphorically inspired himself, described what occurred next: "We kicked the door, and it fell in." From this point, resistance in Basra collapsed as the British pushed ever deeper into the city, demonstrating to the local Shiite population that the time of the Baath was over.

During the course of the twentieth century, Great Britain has been the United States' staunchest ally, in both war and peace. Operation Iraqi Freedom—the first major conflict of the twenty-first century—continued that tradition. The hero of this latest episode was Prime Minister Tony Blair, who risked his career, his reputation among his countrymen, his international influence, and his position in history to stand with the United States in Iraq. Confronted by fierce opposition from within his own Labour Party, Blair provided the leadership, drive, foresight, and moral conviction that put British troops on the ground for the opening day of the war. Moreover, he did all this in the face of vast demonstrations in downtown London in February 2003 during which more than a million marched to protest the Blair government's support of the war—demonstrations that rivaled those of the anti-Vietnam crusade in the 1960s.

Why Blair took this thorny route in the face of such resolute opposition is not easy to determine. Perhaps part of his stand was due to political expediency, a desire to make sure that Britain maintained its connection across the Atlantic in opposition to Jacques Chirac's vision of a Europe united under the French banner against America's hegemonic muscle. Perhaps the prime minister also recognized that without Saddam's removal a stable Middle East in the near future was simply a mirage. Perhaps most likely Blair felt a deep antipathy to the odious tyranny that Saddam represented and believed that even a liberal government had a responsibility to employ military force against such a regime. Or perhaps it was a genuine fear, based on intelligence reports, that Saddam was developing weapons of mass destruction that he could deploy or distribute at will—a factor that Saddam's previous track record suggested as a possibility. Most likely, it was some combination of the above.

Whatever the reasons, during 2002 Blair followed a consistent line in saying that he would support the United States, come what may, should the Bush administration desire to terminate the Baath regime. And in early January 2003, the British government began dispatching substantial military forces to the Persian Gulf. On the evening of March 20, 2003, the British 1st Armoured Division crossed into Iraq, led by the U.S. 15th Marine Expeditionary Unit (MEU). The immediate target was the Rumaila oil fields and the oil terminals on the Al-Faw Peninsula. The 7th Armoured Brigade and the 16th Air Assault Brigade would provide back-up to special forces in taking the oil fields. Royal Marine Commandos were already moving with U.S. navy SEALs to seize the petroleum facilities on the peninsula. The Iraq War had begun, and the British were in it as major participants.

The presence of a full British division with approximately 20,000 soldiers represented a more significant contribution to this war than to the Gulf War of 1991. In that earlier conflict, the British division was just one of more than ten divisions put in the field to liberate Kuwait. A number of other nations, including France, had also provided division-sized formations. But in 2003 the British supplied nearly one third of the land power, one of the three-plus divisions with which the American-led Coalition would begin the invasion of Iraq, and a significant portion of the air power. Great Britain was the only nation other than the United States to commit more than a token military force to the fight.

The British role in the campaign would also be significantly greater than in 1991. The ground invasion of Iraq could not have begun on March 20 if the British division had not been in place and prepared to act. The British took on two immediate assignments: preventing the Iraqis from torching the oil wells in the Rumaila fields and from dumping millions of gallons of raw petroleum into the northern Persian Gulf, as they had done in 1991. In that effort, the British would work with U.S. marines and special operations forces. Next, the British were to liberate the port of Umm Qasr, the terminal through which humanitarian aid would flow to the Shia in the south. The 1st Armoured Division was then to push on to Basra and besiege Iraq's "second city." British forces executed these four missions with their usual professionalism and panache.

For a variety of reasons, the British were not to attempt to liberate Basra immediately. Coalition commanders feared that an attack on the city which ran into difficulties might encourage Iraqi resistance in Baghdad. At the very least, an early attack on Basra would signal to Saddam's officers how the Coalition might assault their capital. But most important, the 7th Armoured Brigade might be needed further north, if the U.S. marines got into trouble. They would also provide a screen if units of the Iraqis moved out of their positions along the Iranian border to threaten I MEF's southern flank.

The 1st Armoured Division consisted of the 3rd Marine Commando Brigade, the 16th Air Assault Brigade, and the 7th Armoured

Brigade. This was not the mix the British would have wished to send to the Gulf. The division's make-up reflected the constraints of time and logistics created by the late decision—not made until the end of December—to deploy British forces to Kuwait. As it turned out, the division offered an ideal set of capabilities for the missions it would execute. The 3rd Commando's amphibious capabilities proved crucial in seizing the Al-Faw Peninsula, its oil terminals, and refineries. The commandos and light infantry in the 16th Air Assault Brigade delivered the manpower necessary to seal Basra off from the outside and, later in the war, go in after Baath resisters. The 16th's Parachute Regiment would also provide security for the supply convoys moving north to support the U.S. marines and east to support British troops around Basra. Finally, the heavy armor and firepower in the 7th Armoured Brigade, with its Challenger II tanks and Warrior light armored fighting vehicles reinforced with additional infantry from the 20th Brigade, allowed the British to punch through the Iraqi divisions and cordon off Basra.

THE BACKGROUND: PLANNING AND DEPLOYMENT

Seldom have democracies gone into a war in an atmosphere of such moral and logical confusion. The soldiers have stopped thinking about it and have absorbed themselves in the comforting drills and routines of their calling. The civilians in their path have no such solace.

PATRICK BISHOP, dispatch from the Kuwait border, March 19, 2003

In the period after the Gulf War, the British governments of John Major and Tony Blair proved the most steadfast of all America's allies in supporting U.S. efforts to contain Saddam Hussein. RAF fighter aircraft consistently enforced the no-fly zones in northern and southern Iraq. And in the dreadful aftermath of September 11, Britain was the first among America's allies to offer its full and complete support in the war on terror. Prime Minister Blair himself flew to Washington and was in attendance when President Bush declared war on Al Qaeda and international terrorism. In the fighting that followed, British Special Air Service troops were active participants in the effort to overthrow the Taliban and clean out the nest of terrorists in Afghanistan.

The British were also first to join in deliberations on overthrowing Iraq's Baath regime. In September 2002 Blair gave clear warning that his administration agreed with Bush that the overthrow of Saddam was a necessary precondition for stability in the Middle East. Not only Labour's back benchers but many front benchers as well were less than enthusiastic about the direction British foreign policy was taking, however, and they forced Blair to extract concessions from the United States.

The most important was a commitment to present the case for military action against Iraq to the U.N. and to seek an international coalition. This route was fraught with danger from the Bush administration's point of view, since if Saddam proved even partially cooperative with weapons inspections, the basis for an invasion would evaporate, along with British support. But as usual the Iraqis acted in a way that only reinforced the arguments of U.S. hardliners. And then to help Blair with the parliamentary opposition within his own party, French President Jacques Chirac obdurately rejected *any* military action against Iraq, no matter what evidence U.N. inspectors turned up. This provoked a major reversal in British public opinion, which had exhibited considerable doubt about operations in the Gulf.

British military strategists had actively participated in U.S. war games and planning exercises dealing with the Middle East since 1995. Prior to spring 2002 they had focused largely on supporting an American drive north from Kuwait to Baghdad. But in June of that year, as the possibility of war grew, Centcom tasked British forces to participate in the drive from Turkey through northern Iraq, to seize Tikrit and eventually push on to Baghdad. In this plan, only a portion of the 3rd Commando Brigade would remain in the south to help U.S. marines clean up the Al-Faw Peninsula and the Rumaila oil fields. Who instituted this shift from south to north, and why, is not entirely clear. Lieutenant General David McKiernan, Third Army commander and a close friend of the British from his days with the Allied Rapid Reaction Corps (ARRC), appears to have offered the British and the ARRC control of operations in northern Iraq. But because ARRC is a NATO organization, the Blair government turned the proposal down.

As negotiations with the Turks dragged on into December, British and Centcom planners increasingly recognized that, even if the Turks were to allow the American 4th Infantry Division onto their territory, they would not allow the British to be part of the northern operation. Why the Turks held such an attitude was never clear. The best that British officers could offer was that several senior Turkish generals still resented Britain's role in the 1932 Treaty of Lausanne which awarded Mosul, with its rich oil fields, to Iraq. Strange as it may seem to many Americans who have never lived in the southern part of the United States, history has an odd way of lingering around for decades to affect the contemporary landscape.

On December 28, convinced that the Turks would not yield, the British exercised their option of operating from Kuwait. In a hurry, they now confronted the need to reoganize their deployment, logistical support, and operational focus. And with the Americans talking about beginning operations in March before the summer heated up, there was precious little time. Once again, as they had done during the Falklands and in the Gulf War, the British displayed an extraordinary ability to improvise. Senior military commanders and their political leaders made the decision to send out the 7th Armoured Brigade (the

Desert Rats) from Germany. The presence of one Royal Marine Commando already in the Gulf region made it easy to decide to ship out another commando with sufficient army support to build the marine force up to brigade strength. Finally, the 16th Air Assault was dispatched because of the relative lightness of its equipment and its required support.

The ten weeks that the British had available to deploy a division to the Gulf had to include a massive program to desertize the Challenger II tanks coming from garrisons in Germany. The experiences of a 2002 deployment to Oman undoubtedly helped, as did considerable work over the intervening years to make the British army more "expeditionary." Nevertheless, the Scots Guards would only complete their combat preparations on March 17, barely three days before ground operations would begin. Moreover, the weakness of the 3rd Commando Brigade in armor may have represented a major contributing factor to I MEF's decision to provide the British with the 15th MEU, which could deliver an additional heavy punch to aid the commandoes in securing the oil fields.

Placement of the 1st Armoured Division under I MEF turned out to be an inspired decision. The British would work well with the MEF staff, especially Lieutenant General James Conway, who proved supportive, tactful, and understanding of British needs and perceptions. The maneuver war doctrines that the British army and the U.S. marines shared made it easy for officers from the two nations to communicate and to operate together effectively.

Nevertheless, British preparations exhibited some considerable deficiencies, particularly in logistics. Supply troops received inadequate small arms ammunition to defend themselves—a real concern for the convoys that had to run through the troubled rear areas during the invasion's first days, when large numbers of fedayeen were still about. Like many of their American counterparts, some British logistics had moved to a just-in-time mentality, which one British officer described as *"definitely not"* a success. In the end, the British got their troops, equipment, and logistical support out to the Gulf from garrisons in the United Kingdom and Germany, but it was a terribly close-run thing.

Immediately before the war began, the commander of I MEF came out to the 1st Armoured Division to give a rousing speech to the headquarters and troops. Introduced by the division's commander, Major General Robin Brims, Conway's message was simple and direct: once again the Americans were delighted to have British troops at their side as allies. With that, the British troops prepared to move forward to their jump off points. Only time would tell whether they had positioned themselves to "fight at the right place and at the right time."

UMM QASR AND BASRA: THE START

On board the Chinook I remember thinking, "What the hell am I doing here? Have I gone crazy? We're flying low in order to sneak beneath Iraqi radar, making us sitting ducks for anyone with a decent rifle. And we're going to land right on top of our intended target, the main southern Iraqi oil installation on the Al-Faw Peninsula. We're not landing a few kilometers away so we can then advance towards it, we're actually going to land right on top of it! I must be crazy; we're all crazy."

CLIVE MYRIE, BBC reporter,
"Al-Faw Peninsula: Securing the Oil Fields," late March 2003

Two surprises awaited the British from the outset of military operations. The first was how completely unprepared the Iraqis actually were to fight. The second was the depth of control that the Baath

Party was able to exercise over the population, even the Shia in the south, where the British expected to be greeted as liberators. In addition, the British soon discovered that the Baathists were able to put out large numbers of fanatical party loyalists along with a number of fedayeen from other Arab countries who were willing to resist to the death. While they might have lacked military skills—and most were largely untrained—from the point of view of the British, these irregulars still had to be killed. As long as they lived, they added to the party's ability to control the local Shiite population and caused considerable dislocation to British forces with their sporadic attacks on frontline troops, rear areas, and the numerous supply convoys running to and from Kuwait.

To the front and left of the British was the 1st Marine Division. Brims deployed his own brigades in the following manner: On the far left of the British line was the 16th Air Assault Brigade; it would sweep north of Umm Qasr and set up blocking positions along Highway 6, the main highway from Baghdad to Basra. In the center, the 7th Armoured Brigade would also sweep north of Umm Qasr to strike as fast as possible at Basra. And to the south the 3rd Commando Brigade would seize much of the Rumaila oil fields and the oil terminals on the Al-Faw Peninsula, with help from British and American special forces and U.S. marines.

The 15th MEU would lead the British 3rd Commando Brigade out from forward deployment areas in Kuwait. After moving through the Rumaila oil fields, 15th MEU would then swing to the west and eventually join up with Task Force Tarawa. In addition to U.S. marine support, the 3rd Commando's Brigade Commander, Brigadier Jim Dutton, would receive support from special operations forces: U.S. SEALs and British SAS (Special Air Service) and SBS (Special Boat Service, the amphibious version of the SAS) to conduct the initial attack and ensure that the oil fields and terminals would fall into

Coalition hands. A substantial air component, including heavy helicopters, would assist in seizing the oil facilities at the earliest possible moment and providing air support. These disparate forces would work together effectively throughout initial operations.

The Al-Faw Peninsula and the marshes that surround it were a patchwork of canals and waterways that took the Royal Marines, SBS, and various naval units over a week to clean out. But the strategic and political task of seizing the oil terminals was immediately successful. A four-hour bombardment by British and U.S. artillery located on Bubiyan Island—in Kuwaiti territory—softened up the Iraqi forces before the Royal Marine Commandos and special forces moved out. Naval gunfire from the frigate *HMS Marlborough* and the *Chatham*, each firing 4.5″ guns, supplemented the land-based artillery. In the original plan, B-52s were supposed to rain down additional munitions on the Iraqis, but they were needed elsewhere. In their stead, AC-130 gunships and the low-flying A-10 Warthogs, with their Gatling cannons, helped suppress Iraqi resistance.

Landed by MH53 Pavelow and Chinook helicopters, the initial teams of SEALs, Royal Navy landing strip specialists, and Royal Marines from 40 Commando destroyed enemy forces before they could damage the oil facilities. The attack caught the Iraqis by surprise. Some fire fights ensued, but local defense was inadequate, and the Iraqis were unprepared to blow up the main pumping facilities and send petroleum gushing into the Gulf. The success of the initial strike bode well for future joint operations involving the Americans and British.

Meanwhile, to the north the 15th MEU led the rest of the 3rd Commando Brigade in its move to make contact with special forces that would help them secure the eastern portion of the Rumaila oil fields. Commanded by Colonel Thomas D. Waldhauser, the 15th MEU provided 2,000 marines, four Abrams tanks, sixteen amtracks, and a number of Cobra attack helicopters, to add some welcome strength to the mission. The link-up with the special ops units already holding the oil fields occurred quickly. As on the Al-Faw Peninsula, the timing and speed of the Coalition's ground offensive caught the enemy off guard. Consequently, the Iraqis were able to set fire to only seven of more than 1,000 well heads in the region. Equally important, they were unable to destroy the gas-oil separation facilities that would be critical to the resumption of Iraq's oil exports.

By early on the morning of March 21, U.S. marines had seized the port area of Umm Qasr and gained control of the bridges to the north of the city. They immediately turned the ground over to the British and continued on their way to link up with Task Force Tarawa. Unfortunately, 3rd Commando, with its mission to clear the Al-Faw Peninsula and open up the waterway to the port of Umm Qasr, did not possess sufficient marines to clear out the city itself. As a result, the British soon ran into hit-and-run raids launched by fedayeen. These raids never posed a tactical threat to the Coalition's lines of communications, but they were a persistent nuisance, and over the next several days they did kill people.

During its first twenty-four hours of battle the success of the 1st Armoured Division had been considerable. Casualties had been relatively light, but a helicopter accident on the first night suggested that the war would not be fought without cost. An American CH-46 crashed, killing its crew of four U.S. marines along with eight British servicemen—five Royal Marines, two army gunners, and a Royal Navy specialist. Given the conditions under which helicopter pilots flew during the war, particularly at night, through dust, and close to the ground, it is surprising that the Coalition did not lose more helicopters to accidents. Following his first experiences in flying a helicopter in combat, one U.S. Marine Corps pilot noted the difficulties he encountered even with technological aids:

For those of you who haven't looked through a pair of
NVGs [night vision goggles], they are built for use in
darkness. If there is too much light, then they don't work
correctly. The worst time to fly on the goggles is right after sunset . . . The sand in the air is something that we
hadn't dealt with too much in training. In accordance
with our peacetime training rules, if visibility is poor,
you don't fly. Common sense—safety. But in war . . .
[when] lives are at stake, sometimes you have to push
the edge of the envelope and deal with conditions that
you're not normally accustomed. With the reduced visibility and lack of moon that night, I can say that was
the darkest night I have ever flown in my life . . . This
was dark. Seat-cushion-clenched-in-your-butt dark. Not
only did sand hang in the air to minimize horizontal visibility, but also the desert we were flying over was completely smooth and lacked any detail. You couldn't tell,
from two-hundred feet above ground level, how high
you were. No depth perception. You couldn't see obstacles until you were right on top of them. That's a bit
nerve-wracking.[1]

On March 21 and 22, while 3rd Commando Brigade was seizing
the southern-most riverine waterways of Iraq, the 7th Armoured, with
the 16th Air Assault on its left, swung by Umm Qasr toward the Shatt
al Arab tidal river, where the Tigris and Euphrates run together. These
brigades were also supposed to prevent the Iraqis from blowing up important oil facilities: the main pumping station at Az Zubayr (captured by the 7th Armoured) and the oil wells farther to the west (secured by the 16th Air Assault). After accomplishing those tasks, the
two brigades followed closely on the heels of the 1st Marine Division

in its drive north. Just short of the waterway, the 7th Tank Brigade relieved the 7th Marine Regiment, while farther to the north the 16th Air Assault Brigade relieved the 5th Marines. The movement of the U.S. marines up to the Shatt al Arab probably reflected planning worries within I MEF about whether the British 7th Armoured Brigade would be able to roll at the start of the war. But the 7th Armoured was ready, and within little over a day it would move from the Iraq-Kuwait border all the way to the outskirts of Basra, a distance of seventy miles.

At this early point in the war, direct cooperation between major units of the British army and the American marines ended. Nevertheless, so closely were the two allied forces tied together that G Battery of the Parachute Regiment would remain attached to the 11th Marine Artillery Regiment up to the fighting in An Nasiriyah far to the west of Basra. During heavy fighting around that city, the British artillerymen would render signal support to the hard-pressed marines. In a short description of his experiences written after the war, a British paratroop sergeant in the battery witnessed the strength of the marine division as it moved to the northwest: "After traveling west on route Tampa towards the stronghold of An Nasiriyah the awesome size of the U.S. marine corps became obvious. From Rumaila to the outskirts of An Nasiriyah there seemed to be a continuous moving convoy of amphibious vehicles, M1 Abrams, and Humvees, a spectacle not seen in recent history."[2]

The British advance over the next several days went relatively smoothly. No regular Iraqi army units appeared to oppose them. Thus, 16th Air Assault Brigade established its blocking positions on Highway 6 from Baghdad to pick up any Iraqi movements that might threaten the British positions around Basra. At the same time, 7th Armoured Brigade swung into position on the outskirts of Basra's suburbs. The advance had crossed the area supposedly defended by the 51st Division of Iraq's regular army; but by the time operations began, most of that division's Shiite conscripts had already been convinced to desert by propaganda leaflets and Coalition air attacks. Only a few thousand remained in the ranks to surrender to British and American troops.

The 7th Armoured Brigade had been substantially reorganized in Kuwait while it prepared for military operations. Here the British were following a pattern that would influence American forces: reorganizing and task organizing ad hoc units that did not fit the normal charts of military organization and equipment. Instead of the usual three battalions, the 7th Armoured Brigade was now organized into four battle groups, each of which contained armor as well as infantry mounted in armored personnel carriers.

Attached to each of these battle groups were two companies of mechanized infantry drawn from the 20th Armoured Brigade. For example, Lieutenant Colonel Hugh Blackman, commander of one of these battle groups, had two companies of Irish Guards under his command. Tank and infantry cooperation had not been common in the British army over the course of the past decade, according to Blackman. Luckily, the Challenger II (unlike the Abrams) still had a connection for a telephone line that allowed the tankers inside to talk to the infantry on the outside while remaining buttoned up. The willingness of the British to cross-attach and exploit ad hoc units was underlined when they dispatched a squadron of tanks from the 7th Armoured to the 3rd Commando Brigade to provide that unit with some heavy support as fighting intensified around Basra. Such cross-attachments would also occur in U.S. forces between the 3rd Infantry Division and the 101st whenever light units required added firepower and armored protection.

At this point, with the inhabited areas of Umm Qasr largely bypassed and the siege of Basra beginning, things appeared to go badly wrong, at least in the eyes of the world's media. When Umm Qasr's port fell, British Defence Secretary Geoff Hoon had described that city as similar to Southhampton. A Royal Marine squadie caught the actual state of affairs more accurately: "It's not at all like Southhampton: there's no beer, no prostitutes, and they're shooting at us. It's more like Portsmouth." Indeed, the fedayeen were shooting at anyone who came close to Basra's urban areas. Because of the rapid movement of American and British troops out of southern Iraq in the drive to the north, parties of fedayeen made the rear areas dangerous places indeed for Coalition forces. Yet, the danger was only occasional, and the media's emphasis on the actions of the fedayeen was out of all proportion to their actual military effectiveness.

THE FALL OF BASRA

We were hurtling off into battle, the Warrior rocking from side to side as it raced across rough terrain and towards a compound where some of the most hardened of Saddam's Fedayeen militia were making a last stand. Inside the Warrior, the heat was stifling and my shirt was drenched in sweat within the first few seconds. As the noise of machine-gun and tank fire resonated around us, and Cobra attack helicopters hovered overhead, I tightened the strap of my helmet and fastened up my flak jacket . . . At first, things seemed to have quietened down a little. There were just sporadic bursts of fire. Then, suddenly, something much louder and right next to us: bullets raking a low wall, no more than a few feet away.

BEN BROWN, BBC reporter,
"Basra—The Second City Falls," early April 2003

Despite the British (and American) expectation that the Shia in both Umm Qasr and Basra would immediately overthrow the Baath regime and welcome Coalition forces as liberators, this did not happen, at least not at the beginning of the prolonged siege of Basra. The Shia's memory of their rebellion in 1991, encouraged by the United States and then murderously suppressed by Saddam's thugs as the Americans stood aside, was painful and deep. As long as the Baath Party activists and the fedayeen remained in place throughout Basra, the Shia would not dare to revolt again.

British commanders realized almost immediately that the Baathists were firmly in control. Here they were helped considerably by the human intelligence network that MI6, the British secret service, had established throughout Basra in the decade after the Gulf War. They had even recruited a high-ranking military figure in Basra. In the run-up to the war, that network had expanded, so that British intelligence possessed an accurate and up-to-date picture of what was happening in the city.

The Baathist police and military in Basra were led by Ali Hassan al-Majid, better known in the Western press as Chemical Ali, one of the leading figures in Iraq and a close associate of Saddam. Majid had begun his ignoble career as a motorcycle driver in the army, but his penchant for violence and his ruthlessness soon launched him on a successful career in Saddam's regime. On his way to the top he married the daughter of Saddam's predecessor, al-Bakr, but smoothly switched his loyalty to Saddam when he became dictator. A member of the Revolutionary Command Council, Chemical Ali had served as defense minister and had headed the security and intelligence agencies.

In 1988 Saddam ordered Majid to bring the Kurds to heel. His measures bordered on genocide. They included the use of poison gas against Kurdish villages—perhaps the only time that a regime has used chemical weapons against its own population. He displayed neither remorse nor contrition afterward for his actions. A taped conversation with subordinates, discovered by Western intelligence agencies in the aftermath of the Gulf War, suggested the measure of the man as well as the regime that made him one of its chief leaders: "I will kill them all with chemical weapons . . . Who is going to say anything? The international community? Fuck them."[3]

In 1990 Saddam awarded Majid for his bloody successes in northern Iraq with the governorship of Iraq's "nineteenth" province, Kuwait. In that job he instituted a reign of terror to destroy the Kuwaitis' sense of independence—a campaign terminated only by Operation Desert Storm. Majid then turned his talents to suppressing the Shia uprising in the aftermath of the Gulf War. Iraqi exiles have estimated that Chemical Ali's forces executed upwards of 50,000 Shiite rebels in that effort. In 1996 he was in charge of the operation that murdered Saddam's traitorous sons-in-law—his own nephews—after their return from Jordan, where they had cooperated extensively with American intelligence agents.

Whatever his failures as a military commander or as a politician, Majid knew how to keep a tight rein on the population of the south. Now charged by Saddam with safeguarding the region, Chemical Ali put up a reasonable defense. He did not hold a strong hand, however. The units of the regular army that collected in Basra, consisting of Shiite conscripts, were virtually useless. The fedayeen that Qusay Hussein supplied for Basra's defense were deeply fanatical and prepared to die for the regime but had virtually no military training beyond a few hours spent on learning how to fire AK-47s or RPGs. They had little hope of anything short of death when they came up against professional soldiers. As for Baath Party loyalists in the city, they fully understood what kind of fate awaited them at the hands of Shiite mobs, should the regime collapse. Their role was largely to keep the urban population under firm control. They were thugs, desperate to be sure, but not fighters by any means.

With this weak hand, Majid devised a political and military approach that aimed to achieve two goals: to keep tight control over Basra's Shiite population to the very end; and to draw the British into fighting within the city. The confusing urban landscape would maximize civilian casualties, he believed, and take a heavy toll on British forces—all of which was aimed at influencing civilian public opinion in the Arab and Western worlds.

But the British refused to be drawn into fighting in Basra until they were ready. They intentionally kept the cordon around Basra loose, allowing considerable movement in and out of the city. The down side of this strategy was that the Baath militia and fedayeen could use the fleeing crowds as human shields. The Baathists also enthusiastically mortared fleeing civilians, as a warning to those remaining under their control and for the propaganda value that dying civilians would have in the West, where the media would view the killing of any civilians as being the result of Coalition military actions. The Baath even sent tanks out to the edge of their lines of control and then backed them into urban areas, teasing British troops to follow. The British refused to respond to such ruses beyond destroying Iraqi tanks or other vehicles that came within range of the Challengers' 120mm guns.

On the up side, looser control of access allowed the British to infiltrate their own agents, sniper teams, and SAS patrols in and out of the city. What was clear to British military commanders almost immediately was that the Baathists held the Shia in a vise, and only gradual, carefully calculated military and political action could loosen it.

After initial attacks by fedayeen, some of whom raised white flags before opening fire, others of whom had launched rockets-propelled grenades, British troops settled down. Over the night of March 26–27 a force of regular Iraqi army tanks headed out from Basra. Spies in the city had already reported to British intelligence that the Baathists had dragooned the unwilling soldiers into making the raid by threatening to kill their families. As the Baathists put it to the soldiers, if they went out to attack the British, only they would die. In fact, a number were able to surrender, but many perished as the Challengers blasted rounds into their vehicles. The Iraqi T-55 tanks did not even make a dent in British armor. One officer suggested that the contest was like "a bicycle against a motor car."[4] No British tanks were damaged in the skirmish.

By the night of March 27–28 the British felt comfortable enough with the situation to send more snipers into Basra. In addition, small raiding teams of Warrior armored personnel vehicles attacked areas of the city now supposedly free (according to intelligence sources) of significant Iraqi military forces or irregulars. The aim of all these probing attacks was at first largely psychological—to warn Baath loyalists and fedayeen that they had no sanctuary, no place to hide where the British could not target them, even in the heart of Basra. At the same time, the attacks underlined to the Shia that the British were moving slowly but deliberately toward the city's liberation. The larger aim was to ensure that the city could be taken without heavy losses to the Coalition or extensive collateral damage to the Shia.

One of the British officers who participated in the siege from the beginning did not find the penchant of Iraqis to play dead, use white flags to cover their attacks, or even hide behind civilian shields particularly disconcerting. But the countermeasures that British troops were forced to take in response did raise doubts in his mind, since they were all operating under the glare of BBC cameras. He worried that television images of his soldiers wandering around the battlefield shooting what appeared to be dead Iraqis would go down badly among civilians back home, who had little understanding, much less experience, with the brutal, harsh realities of war.

Initially, sniper teams were sent to pick off the fedayeen raiding parties that were attacking British checkpoints. These raiding parties consisted of up to twenty ill-trained "martyrs," largely armed with AK-47 rifles and RPGs. Sometimes they would receive support from mortars that could deliver sporadic and haphazard fire. Enemy losses began well before the Iraqis reached British positions, as snipers dropped them seemingly out of the blue. As they closed in on British forces, they were in a hopeless situation, up against well-trained, disciplined troops. As one Basra resident recalled after the war, the fedayeen would move out in parties of twenty, and barely two or three of their number would return. Nevertheless, whatever the military difficulties the Baath confronted, they still possessed the political and policing power to crush any Shiite uprising within the city.

At the end of March, the British began to launch swift raids into the city from various points on the periphery, this time to test Baath defenses as well as to infiltrate sniper teams deeper into the urban landscape. British commanders coordinated these raids carefully with human intelligence from agents on the inside. Snipers began the task of picking off not only the fedayeen but Baath Party operatives at ranges up to 400 yards. The latter were usually easily identifiable by their penchant for ordering others about and using cell phones. Major Ben Farell, commanding officer of 2nd Company, 1st Battalion Royal Irish Guards, characterized their efforts this way: "Our snipers are working in pairs, infiltrating the enemy's territory, to give us very good observation of what is going on inside Basra and to shoot the enemy as well when the opportunity arises . . . They don't kill large numbers, but the psychological effect and the denial of freedom of movement of the enemy is vast."[5]

The sniper teams also served as intelligence gatherers. As one of Major Farell's snipers told a reporter in early April: "It's a bit scary going into buildings because they haven't been cleared and we don't know if they have left any booby traps for us. But once we are here they don't know where we are and it feels OK. We can report back what is going on—to call in air strikes or direct artillery—and if they are within range of our rifles we will shoot them."[6]

Lance Corporal Vincent Polus, who had three kills in eight days, commented to a *London Daily Telegraph* reporter that "your eyes are on the target all the time, you keep your eyes on that area. If a target comes into view you report it to command and ask permission to fire, then you check your elevation and adjust the wind. You have to get the breathing right, a couple of deep breaths, then you start breathing again normally and as you start to release your breath you squeeze the trigger. That's the moment you are at your most steady."[7]

In early April the British stepped up their pressure on the Baathists in Basra. Raids by Warrior armored vehicles were targeting specific places in the city that British intelligence had identified as Baath hideouts. Again, the emphasis was on the psychological impact these raids would have not only on the Baathists—by increasing their sense of vulnerability—but also on the Shia.

It was now clear that the British were aiming to kill or capture all Baathist Party members in and around Basra. In propaganda leaflets scattered throughout the city, the message to the Shia was, "We will not desert you this time. Trust us and be patient."[8] British deliberation and caution was beginning to pay off. As Warrior raids struck into Basra day after day, Shiite locals proved increasingly willing to point out where the fedayeen and Baath activists were hiding or where they had stashed weapons and supplies. While the locals were not yet ready to jump off the fence, during the first couple of days in April they were clearly beginning to lean toward the Coalition.

As the 7th Armoured Brigade stepped up its activities on the outskirts of Basra, others were putting direct pressure on the Baath leadership inside the city. There are virtually no open-source discussions of what the SBS and SAS were up to in Basra throughout the siege, except to suggest they targeted Baathist and fedayeen centers for Coalition aircraft to attack with JDAMs and other precision weapons. After someone in Basra gave away Chemical Ali's hiding place on April 5, a JDAM attack destroyed the building, and for a time Coalition intelligence believed Majid was dead. That "success" appears less likely from what is now known. But at the time, news of Majid's supposed death spread rapidly throughout Basra and clearly weakened the Baathists' control over the city. Another JDAM attack, again most probably directed by special forces teams within the city, hit a major meeting of Baath leaders, killing most of them.

On Sunday, April 6, the British launched a three-pronged attack into the city with battle groups of the 7th Armoured Regiment consisting of Challenger IIs and Warriors. The initial plan of attack was to punch deep into the city and then pull back out at night. The operation went so well, however, that British commanders could only conclude that the Baath system was now collapsing. They decided to stick around. The initial fighting took place in a factory complex where there were no civilians, so the British could call in air support, particularly from Cobra attack helicopters. ANGLICO (Air-Naval-Gunfire Liaison Company) teams of U.S. marines interspersed among the British attacking columns provided communication links to the Cobras—as well as translation between the two forces "separated by a common language."

The operation on this "terribly long day" was going so successfully that Major General Brims decided to finish off the Iraqis with a final stroke. One battle group, which had done much of the fighting in the factory complex, now moved against an area that was known as the College of Literature but which was in fact a university. This would be the last fedayeen stronghold, defended by over 300 fanatics, mostly from other Arab countries. The university had become a focal point for international terrorists. Passports and other documents from Tunisia, Morocco, Algeria, Syria, and other Middle Eastern countries were found in the wreckage. Here occurred one of the few intelligence failures of the siege of Basra—the existence of a fedayeen stronghold in the university was unexpected.

Clearance of the university grounds took approximately four hours. The British could not use Cobra or artillery support, nor could they identify clear military targets on the ground. Warrior infantry squads, with supporting fire from Challengers and the Warriors themselves, had to winkle out the Iraqis room by room, building by building. In the words of a British officer, "It all came down to good old-fashioned bayonet and rifle work."

By now the local Shia were out in the streets. Delightedly, they indicated to British soldiers where the fedayeen were hiding and where ambush points might be set up. In many areas they participated actively in hunting down and killing Baathists and fedayeen. Once the British troops of the 7th Armoured Brigade had secured the university grounds, they set it up as a forward operating base and remained in the city for the duration. Baath rule over Basra was over.

The next morning, the paras (Parachute Regiment) of the 16th Brigade moved into the old city to finish off the Baathists in the narrow streets where the Challengers and Warriors would have had difficulty maneuvering. As it turned out, the paras were not needed, because the Baath and the fedayeen were everywhere on the run. In their movement through areas untouched by the 7th Armoured the day before, the paras ran into very little resistance and suffered virtually no casualties. By day's end they began moving out of the city.

At this point an incident occurred that underlined how much the events of spring 1991 had burned their way into the collective memory of the Shia. As the paras withdrew, Shia crowds began throwing rocks at British tanks and armored personnel carriers. One of the battle group commanders immediately sensed what was happening. He ordered his tank and armored personnel carrier crews, as well as the infantry, to get out of the vehicles, take off their helmets, stow most of their weapons on their vehicles, and walk out into the agitated crowd. Immediately the rock throwing ended and members of the crowd again smiled and clapped hands for the British troops. The Shiites understood that the British were in Basra to stay.

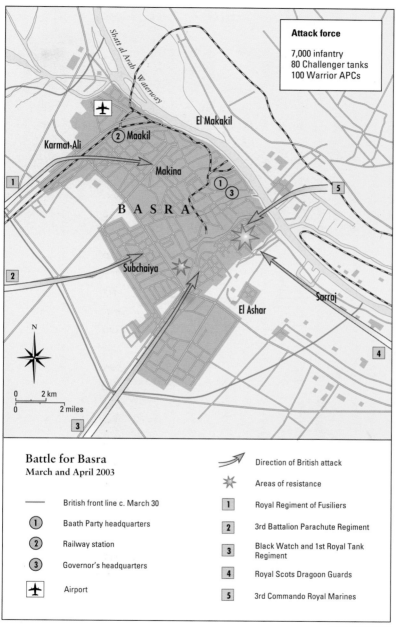

Attack force

7,000 infantry
80 Challenger tanks
100 Warrior APCs

El Makakil

Karmat-Ali

② Maakil

Makina

B A S R A

① ③

Subchaiya

El Ashar

Sarraj

N

0   2 km
0   2 miles

Battle for Basra
March and April 2003

—— British front line c. March 30

① Baath Party headquarters

② Railway station

③ Governor's headquarters

✈ Airport

⇗ Direction of British attack

✳ Areas of resistance

1 Royal Regiment of Fusiliers

2 3rd Battalion Parachute Regiment

3 Black Watch and 1st Royal Tank Regiment

4 Royal Scots Dragoon Guards

5 3rd Commando Royal Marines

Cartographica Ltd

Top: Royal Engineers prepare their reconnaissance vehicle for desert action in the days immediately before the invasion. Bottom: Royal Marines from 42 Commando fire a Milan wire-guided missile at Iraqis defending the Al-Faw Peninsula.

Top: An Iraqi soldier lies dead at the entrance to his bunker. He was killed by British troops as they cleared the Al-Faw Peninsula on March 22. Bottom: Kuwaiti firefighters work on March 27 to extinguish one of the nine oil well blazes set by Iraqis in the Rumaila oil fields.

AP Photo/Tony Nicoletti

AP Photo/Terry Richards

Top: A Warrior armored personnel carrier of the Scots Dragoon Guards, part of the fabled Desert Rats (7th Armoured Division), moves up to cover one of the exits from Basra on March 24. Bottom: Iraqi irregulars surrender to Royal Marine Commandos near Basra on March 30. A Chinese-manufactured Iraqi T-55 tank smolders in the background.

Royal Marine Commandos secure Umm Qasr on April 1. Through this port city, humanitarian aid would soon begin flowing to southern Iraq.

Above: During the fighting around Basra, Shiites flee the city for the safety of British positions. A dead T-55 sits directly behind them. Top right: A truckload of tomatoes bound for Basra undergoes inspection at a British road block on March 29. By keeping the cordon loose, the British were able to smuggle their own intelligence teams into the city. Bottom right: British infantry attached to the 7th Armoured Brigade participate in urban combat to break the back of Baathist resistance.

AP Photo/Anja Niedringhaus

Mirrorpix/Getty Images

AP Photo/Julie Jacobson

AP Photo/Markus Schreiber

Top: A CH-46E Sea Knight of the 3rd Marine Aircraft Wing passes over a herd of camels in southern Iraq. This helicopter provided much of the heavy airlift for troops on the ground. Bottom: Two F/A-18 Hornets light their burners and are hurled skyward from the aircraft carrier *USS Harry S. Truman* on March 26 to participate in the air campaign.

Top: A UH-60 Black Hawk helicopter flies low over the Euphrates, carrying troops from the 101st Airborne into battle. The range and survivability of the Black Hawk allowed American infantrymen to advance hundreds of miles into Iraqi territory. Bottom: Ordnance, with Hornets in the background, awaits in the hanger deck of the *USS Kitty Hawk* in the northern Persian Gulf on April 9.

An F-15E Strike Eagle drops GBU-27 laser-guided bombs on its target.

Over Kuwait, a KC-10 refuels a marine F/A-18 flying off the *USS Nimitz*.

The workhorse of the air campaign, the B-1 dropped more bombs than any other aircraft in the Iraq War.

The results of a 5,000-pound precision strike—a small hole in the ceiling and vast wreckage inside the building—illuminate the difficulty of battle damage assessment during the course of an air campaign.

Top: The AC-130 carries a 105mm cannon on the left side of the aircraft. This gunship provided air support for special operations forces in northern Iraq and elsewhere during the war. Bottom: Two marine AV-8B Harriers prepare for launch off the deck of the *USS Bon Homme Richard* on April 5.

Captain Kim Campbell examines the damage inflicted on her A-10 Warthog over Baghdad on April 7. Among fixed-wing aircraft, the Warthog, flying at low altitude and providing close air support, bore the brunt of Iraqi anti-aircraft fire.

Top: Paratroopers of the army's 173rd Airborne Brigade move toward a waiting C-17 for the flight to northern Iraq. They would secure the Bashur airfield and ready it for heavy aircraft. Bottom: With C-17s carrying vehicles, ammunition, supplies, and reinforcements now landing at Bashur, soldiers of the 173rd were in a position to open a second front in the north and provide protection for the Kurds.

Patrick Barth/Getty Images

Special forces from 10th Group create a surrogate army with Kurdish Peshmerga guerillas and capture the northern cities of Mosul and Kirkuk.

Top: A special ops soldier engages the enemy from the bed of his combat vehicle, a modified Toyota pickup truck. These soldiers infiltrated Baghdad early in the war and became the eyes and ears for regular units arriving during the first week of April. Bottom: In the western desert, special forces, using an assortment of civilian and military equipment, secure the main highway from Jordan to Baghdad.

Widespread looting accompanied celebrations over the collapse of Baath rule. The looting was less pervasive than in Baghdad, but the British ran into some difficulties not only in dampening down the theft but in preventing large crowds of Iraqis from taking matters into their own hands and lynching looters they caught. They did manage to foil an attempt to loot a liquor store in downtown Basra that contained what one officer described as "the largest collection of single malt whiskeys he had seen outside of the liquor stores at Gatwick and Heathrow."

In conclusion, the British participation in the ground war to liberate Iraq and overthrow Saddam's regime underlined a new reality: allies of the United States can and will bring significant forces to the conduct of American military operations in the future. The performance of the British 1st Armoured Division should put paid to the nonsense that allies can no longer fight effectively alongside the technologically advanced military forces of the United States. The British proved adaptable, flexible, and formidable on the battlefields of southern Iraq. They also displayed their ability to work within the doctrinal framework and culture of the American marines.

Perhaps most important from a military point of view, the British performance in the Iraq War underlined how the skillful use of human intelligence, particularly in an urban environment, provides the crucial edge in combat. The British had invested considerable effort in establishing an intelligence network in Basra before the war began. Once in combat, they were able to extend and deepen that network by infiltrating agents and SAS teams into the city. The combination of clear human intelligence, special operations, and raids into the city provided British commanders with what the Germans call *Finger-spitzengefühl,* feeling at the end of one's fingers—a sense for when the Baath regime within the city was ready to collapse.

5

The Air War

War applied as much to the strategic air offensive waged over Europe's skies through five-and-a-half bitter years as [it] did to the sailors and soldiers on the distant seas or in the mud and sand below. Occasionally the airman may have felt himself living and fighting in a new dimension, just as the air force commander may have sometimes felt he enjoyed a freedom of manoeuvre denied to admirals and generals below. But the airmen died, and the air force commander was defeated and stalemated unless the laws were kept. When they were kept, success came; until they could be kept, hope was kept alive by courage alone.

ANTHONY VERRIER, *The Bomber Offensive*, 1968

Sometime after 1 a.m. on the morning of March 20 (Riyadh time), Lieutenant General Michael "Buzz" Moseley received an urgent telephone call from the chairman of the Joint Chiefs of Staff, General Richard Meyers. The chairman asked Centcom's air component commander whether his F-117s could attack a discrete target in downtown Baghdad before dawn. Moseley replied in the affirmative. An indistinct exchange ensued on the other end, and then Meyers returned to the line to give Moseley the coordinates and the order to execute. Moseley asked the chairman to please ensure that General Tommy Franks was informed, and with that the phone call ended. This tense conversation set the war against Iraq in motion a day and a half earlier than had been planned.

To execute a stealth attack on such short notice was unprecedented, but the target was even more unprecedented—it was Saddam Hussein himself. U.S. intelligence indicated that he and his murderous sons, Qusay and Uday, along with other Baathist leaders, were meeting at that very moment in a three-building compound in the capital. Lieutenant Colonel David Toomey and Major Mark Hoehn were to execute the mission. So little time remained before dawn, when stealth would only protect against radar, not daylight, they could not perform the usual detailed calculations and preparations—examination of the enemy's defenses, the best ingress and egress routes to the target, coordination of tanker linkup and frequencies. Normally, this alone was a six-hour job. Instead, Toomey and Hoehn planned out only the most basic elements of their mission, almost on the back of an envelope, while crew chiefs performed last-minute checks. The rest was left to chance. Fortunately, the armorers had already loaded two EGBU-27 bunker-busting bombs, which had just arrived in the theater, onto Toomey's aircraft, thereby saving 30 minutes.

To reach Baghdad from Kuwait in the last minutes of darkness, the two F-117s of the Eighth "Black Sheep" Fighter Squadron had to be airborne by approximately 3:30 a.m. They launched within two hours of receiving their orders—at 3:38 local time. As the aircraft neared the capital, the GPS unit on one of Toomey's bombs went dead. He worked desperately to reset the faulty guidance system and got it working just in time to drop both of his 2,000-pound bombs at 5:36 Baghdad time. All four bombs from the F-117s hit their target squarely.

Saddam and his sons were not in the shelter where intelligence suggested they might be, however; or if they were, somehow they escaped. Still, as a result of this preemptive strike, Saddam knew for sure that he and his thugs were hunted men and that Coalition aircraft would seek them out, should any one of their entourage betray their location—a factor that could only have exacerbated suspicion and paranoia within the Iraqi leadership while making the task of commanding Iraq's military forces from Baghdad virtually impossible.

The history of air campaigns is perhaps the most difficult for the military historian to depict, and the Iraq War is no exception. Whatever the difficulties in writing a history of ground war, at least the ebb and flow of troops provide patterns on which to construct a narrative. The key events announce themselves, victors and vanquished are generally obvious, and outcomes can be traced back to specific decisions, events, and trends. In effect, the historian can trace the course of maneuver to establish what soldiers term "ground truth." Air war, by contrast, offers no such clarity. It involves hundreds, if not thousands of aircraft. The incidents and battles occur at blinding speed. There are no clear markers to indicate exactly what happened except perhaps the number of aircraft lost. Effects are equally hard to evaluate, especially during a conflict in progress. Damage to ground targets by bombs or strafing may appear to be massive, when in fact it has little impact on the enemy's ability to fight. At other times the destruction from air attacks may be devastating, but no reliable way exists to measure damage until the conflict is over.

In the Iraq War, despite extraordinary reconnaissance technologies, assessment of damage from aerial bombardment—battle damage assessment, in military parlance—remained an intractable problem, as the March 20 effort to decapitate the Iraqi regime illustrates. For weeks, the Coalition could not determine whether that strike had killed or injured Saddam, his sons, or other key leaders. And even today American intelligence has no clear idea of exactly what the result of that attack was. The effects of many air strikes in this war were impossible to assess until Coalition forces actually put their boots on the ground, and even then the outcome could remain uncertain.

Only after a conflict is over—and sometimes long after—can the historian, with access to the documents on both sides, untangle the real effects that bombing and missile attacks have had on an enemy. In the case of World War II, decades passed before a clear picture of the crucial role of the air campaign began to emerge—one that the hoary myths perpetrated by popular historians continue to cloud even today. A final difficulty for the historian lies in the fact that more often than not the greatest damage caused by air attacks lies in the psychological realm, in the minds of enemy combatants or civilians—a domain that is frequently opaque to examination.

That said, Coalition commanders and their subordinates in the Iraq War enjoyed unmatched transparency as to what the Iraqis were doing, for two reasons. First, unmanned aerial vehicles (UAVs) and satellite reconnaissance provided a clearer picture of what was happening on the ground than at any time in the history of war. Second, the speed of ground operations allowed commanders to sense the impact that the air campaign was having on the enemy. In this war it is almost impossible to divide the air and ground campaigns into neat segments. While one can state with great assurance that air power was a crucial factor in the Coalition's victory, the degree of that contribution is simply not open to exact measurement. There were, in fact, no boundaries between the air and ground campaigns—perhaps the surest indicator of how conjoined this campaign was, in the final analysis.

BACKGROUND

The implication that *cannot* be drawn from . . . experience, however, is that friction has been permanently eliminated . . . Exactly how frictional imbalances might ultimately manifest [themselves] in this "technologically altered" set of conditions is hard to anticipate. What can be said with confidence, though, is that . . . friction will probably manifest itself in other ways or in areas that we may not even be able to predict.

BARRY D. WATTS, Clausewitzian Friction and Future War, 1996

To understand how far the U.S. military has advanced in both technology and joint warfare in the Iraq conflict, one only needs to go back twelve years, to Operation Desert Storm. In the immediate aftermath of Iraq's invasion of Kuwait, America's political and military leadership struggled to come to grips with the problems involved in planning a campaign to defeat Iraqi forces and liberate Kuwait. Nowhere was this struggle more urgent than among airmen. Their initial concepts for an air campaign were not imaginative, to say the least. Tactical Air Command's plan for the Gulf War looked astonishingly like the inept and ill-fated Rolling Thunder campaign the United States had waged against North Vietnam from 1965 through 1968. The navy's concept did not win any awards for creativity, either; it suggested that the air force and navy carve up the theater into two separate route packages, that is, geographical areas, just as the two services had done in North Vietnam.

U.S. airmen had not conducted a major air campaign for over twenty years, and they were largely unprepared intellectually for what was to come. From 1970 to 1990 virtually all of their planning had focused either on nuclear war with the Soviet Union or on a massive conventional and nuclear war in Central Europe. Neither of those scenarios provided any realistic analog for thinking about how to conduct an air campaign—much less an air *and* ground campaign—against a Third World country like Iraq. Adding to their difficulties was the appearance on the scene of substantial improvements in technologies, including brand new capabilities, the implications of which few senior officers had seriously considered—and in some cases did not even know existed.

For all these reasons, in 1991 initial thinking about an air campaign was unsatisfactory from the point of view of not only the theater commander, General Norman Schwarzkopf, but also the chairman of the Joint Chiefs of Staff, General Colin Powell. Both wanted to see more imagination—a plan that might substantially disrupt and erode Iraqi military power before a ground campaign began. They got much of what they wished for when a relatively obscure colonel on the air staff in Washington, John Warden, brought forward a plan, Instant Thunder, aimed at striking a debilitating aerial blow at the heart of Saddam's regime at the immediate onset of hostilities. Warden argued his plan widely in Washington before flying to Riyadh at the end of August 1990 to brief the air component commander, Lieutenant General Chuck Horner. Horner was not impressed. As he pointed out to Warden, there were only enough bombs in the theater for a six-to-eight-day campaign, and virtually no U.S. troops had arrived on the ground. So what was going to happen if the Iraqis did not surrender after a week?

Warden was shipped unceremoniously back to Washington, but Horner kept one of his accompanying officers, Lieutenant Colonel Dave Deptula (now a major general), whom he knew and regarded highly. He teamed Deptula with Brigadier General "Buster" Glosson, who had been dumped in a dead-end job in the Middle East after being fired from the air staff. The creation of a "special planning staff" under these two officers allowed Horner to prepare a strategic campaign against Iraq in great secrecy and assemble a number of first-class officers to assist him in addressing the problems raised by Iraq's sophisticated air defenses. One wit characterized the planning cell as the Black Hole, since bright officers were sucked in, never to reemerge—at least until the war was over. The name stuck.

Glosson and Deptula proved to be a highly creative team, which focused the planning on gaining results or effects rather than simply attacking targets. For example, in striking the sector operating centers that controlled the Iraqi air defense system, instead of using six LGBs (as intelligence planners suggested) to destroy the structure totally, Glosson and Deptula figured that one direct hit by a 2,000-pound bomb would discourage survivors from returning to work in the building. They were right. Thus, by focusing on the psychological as well as the physical impact of aerial bombardment, they saved five bombs to use on other targets. Moreover, they recognized the crucial advantages of stealth in penetrating to the heart of Iraq at the onset of the air campaign. Their planning was so insightful, in fact, that the initial night's attack on Iraq's air defense system caused its complete collapse within the first three to four hours. It never functioned as an integrated system again.

From the perspective of the early twenty-first century, we can easily forget how strange and new stealth and cruise missiles really were in the American arsenal of 1990. Even though precision weapons had been around since America's last year in Vietnam, most U.S. war doctrine was predicated on the use of what today are called "dumb" bombs. Moreover, stealth was a highly guarded secret for most of the 1980s—so much so that few of the air force's senior commanders fully understood its capabilities or potential. The planners in Black Hole understood perfectly. They did an extraordinary job in reconceiving the context of war in light of the combat potential of these new and improved technologies.

Nevertheless, the air campaign of January and February 1991 ran into a few problems. First, the air and land campaigns were sequential, not integrated. For the first thirty-eight days, while Coalition air power blasted infrastructure targets throughout Iraq, ground forces remained stationary. A second problem was the fact that the strategic air campaign in Iraq remained separate from the air effort in Kuwait, the sole aim of which was to demolish military equipment rather than destroy the ability of Iraq's ground forces to cooperate on the battlefield. And finally, after the incident at the Al Firdos bunker, where nearly

300 Iraqi civilians died from two 2,000-pound LGBs after taking shelter in a below-ground command and control center, the air campaign backed off from attacking Saddam's political infrastructure, including his secret police.

Finally, when ground operations began, there was relatively little synergy between the ground and air campaigns, largely because bad weather prevented aircraft from providing close air support. And no precision munitions existed that Coalition aircraft could drop from high altitude and guide to their target through the sandstorm that battered Coalition forces advancing through the desert. A larger problem, of course, was the fact that the ground campaign was launched so late in the game; Horner's pilots could do very little to stop Iraqi forces who were fleeing faster than Coalition forces were advancing.

The air war against Iraq in 2003 was substantially different. To begin with, while planners in the Gulf War had had to husband precision assets carefully, because they had so few, in this war virtually every sortie possessed precision capabilities. The B-2, for example, could carry up to sixteen JDAMs, sixteen JSOWs, or eight GBU-37/BLU-113s. The B-1 could carry an even heavier load: twenty-four JDAMs, twelve EGBU-27s, or thirty WCMDs. Moreover, virtually every fighter aircraft in the Coalition inventories—RAF as well as USAF—was capable of dropping precision munitions, either LGBs or JDAMs.

The proliferation of precision capaabilities and weapons allowed a more flexible targeting regime. Moreover, the various aerial control agencies were now able to redirect aircraft already in the air over Iraq, so they could either strike targets of opportunity or support troops on the ground that had run into trouble. Precision weapons also allowed Coalition fighters to fly at altitudes above enemy flak or shoulder-fired heat-seeking missiles and still hit their targets within several meters' accuracy, even when they could not see the target.

The only Iraqi weapons that could reach Coalition aircraft were surface-to-air (SAM) missiles, guided by radars on the ground. A moment of electronic emission by an Iraqi radar immediately invited a deadly response by a HARM missile fired by Coalition countermeasure aircraft. On occasion the Iraqis fired without radar guidance, but these blind firings inevitably missed. It appears that one errant SAM fell to earth in a downtown market in Baghdad early in the war. Of all the Coalition fighters, only the A-10 Warthog tended to work at low altitude consistently, and then largely because its most effective weapon, a 30mm Gatling cannon firing depleted uranium rounds, could only work at low altitude.

If these advantages were not enough, Coalition air forces also enjoyed air supremacy throughout the war. This resulted from a number of factors stretching back to the Gulf War, during which Coalition air power had destroyed Iraq's integrated air defense system almost completely. The Iraqis might have been able to rebuild at least some of their capabilities in the 1990s had the northern and southern no-fly zones not been created in response to Saddam's ferocious attacks on the Kurdish rebels in the north and the Shia in the south. These no-fly zones denied Saddam's pilots the use of a substantial portion of Iraq's air space. As British and American aircraft patrolled the skies between the two wars, Saddam could not resist ordering his air defenders to fire at the intruders with SAMs and anti-aircraft guns. The pilots of the Coalition aircraft were authorized to fire back, usually with HARM missiles, which homed in on the radar transmissions guiding the SAMs. By the late 1990s British Tornado pilots were referring to these aerial missions over the no-fly zones as "recreational bombing." HARM-bearing aircraft were so ubiquitous over Iraq in the 1990s that "Iraqi radar [became] a no-show" in the 2003 campaign, according to one air force observer.[1]

In effect, then, the Coalition waged a twelve-year air campaign against Iraq's air defense system before the first shot was fired in the actual war. The months running up to the war saw a significant increase in aerial operations over the no-fly zones. In the last month, a ferocious bombing campaign finished off Iraq's air defense system, while UAVs, U-2s, other intelligence aircraft, and satellites formed a "ruthless, staring constellation looking at Baghdad." As one air force senior official explained, intelligence, surveillance, and reconnaissance (ISR) aircraft allowed planners to do detailed change analysis: "What blips were there now that weren't there before? . . . They were moving every 4–5 hours. We focused all our ISR in there, and we pieced together where those guys were."[2] Thus, by the start of the war, there was little that the Coalition did not know about how the Iraqis would attempt to defend themselves. Perhaps the only surprise was Iraq's failure to get a single sortie into the air during the conflict.

The sensor systems available to Coalition commanders were far better at detecting, tracking, and discriminating among Iraqi ground movements than had been the case even in Afghanistan. UAVs accounted for much of the improved sensor capabilities. But the war also suggested that the full potential of UAVs has not been reached. American airmen—particularly in the air force—have yet to invest sufficiently in UAVs to turn this interesting and important technological advance into a reconnaissance and weapons system that could change the way U.S. military forces fight wars. Nevertheless, the Coalition brought ten different UAVs to the battle arena. At one end of the spectrum, the air force's high altitude RQ-4A Global Hawk could survey enormous expanses of territory. At the other end of the spectrum, the marine corps' back-packable Dragon Eye surveillance drone could be deployed quickly, for short-distance reconnaissance. The layered coverage of this family of UAVs enabled Coalition commanders to track the enemy's movements, often with enough fidelity and consistency to understand the enemy's intentions better than the Iraqis themselves.

Long-range UAVs, like the Predator, provided useful intelligence while flying over dangerous places such as Baghdad, but what its feeds could relay back to those on the ground was considerably limited. The problem lay in the fact that UAVs detect thermal-energy sources rather than ambient light. As a commentator on the use of Predator feeds during the fighting in Afghanistan noted: "Although the forward-looking infrared was at its highest magnification level for most of the battle, the images left much to be desired. Consequently one can describe the video taken of the battle of Takur Ghar as nearing only 20/200 visual acuity. Regardless, even with improved acuity, it would have been difficult to ascertain what was transpiring below."[3]

The potential of UAVs in combat was illustrated by the performance of Britain's relatively unsophisticated Phoenix. On one occasion a sergeant, flying the Phoenix at its maximum range of 60 kilometers, spotted a concentration of Iraqi soldiers and vehicles. On his own initiative, even though he had no experience as a forward air controller, he called in an F-18 aircraft to strike the Iraqis. Other Phoenix operators called down mortar and artillery fire on concentrations of enemy troops. In one case they used the Phoenix and artillery fire to destroy Iraqi naval craft operating in the Shatt al Arab waterway. And finally, during the period when the advance of the 1st Marine Division toward Baghdad began to pull the marines away from the British 1st Armoured Division, the British sent several Phoenixes on one-way missions of 120 miles to ensure that the Iraqis were not moving to take advantage of the growing gap.

The most important reconnaissance tool on the battlefield for both ground and air alike was the Joint Surveillance and Target Radar System (JSTARS). This aircraft possesses a twenty-four-foot radar antenna that scans the landscape and allows its on-board controllers to pick up objects moving along the ground at great distances. Though still under development in 1991, JSTARS was sent out to the Kuwaiti theater during Desert Storm, where it performed useful service. By the time of the Iraq War, the air force possessed fourteen JSTARS aircraft capable of maintaining twenty-four-hour coverage of the battlefield. JSTARS' operators could now pick up virtually any vehicular ground movements and pass that information along to army and air force stations on the ground. Commanders could then warn ground forces of possible attack, while at the same time committing aircraft to wiping out the Iraqi units. Moreover, the lack of any significant air defenses allowed JSTARS aircraft to operate deep inside Iraq, thus significantly increasing their ability to pick up ground activity. Even during the *shamal,* Coalition forces—ground as well as air—had an accurate and up-to-date picture of what the main mechanized forces of the enemy were up to.

THE AIR CAMPAIGN

Day after day, as weather and equipment permitted, B-17s and B-24s went out, dropped their deadly loads, and turned homeward. The immediate result of their strikes could be photographed and assessed by intelligence officers in categories reminiscent of high school "grades"—bombing was excellent, good, fair, or poor. But rarely was a single mission or series of missions decisive . . . the effects of the bombing were gradual, cumulative, and during the course of the campaign rarely measurable with any degree of assurance . . . Drama hovered close to each plane which sortied . . . [but] the big show itself was in 1942–1943 flat, repetitive, without climax.

WESLEY FRANK CRAVEN AND JAMES LEA CATE,
The Army Air Forces in World War II, 1983

For air commanders, the sudden F-117 attack on Saddam's hideaway in the early hours of March 20, prior to the announced date of the war, caused some dislocation of plans. A substantial amount of the

Coalition air effort over the daylight hours of March 20 and 21 focused on aiding ground forces that were already beginning to move into Iraq from their initial deployment bases in the deserts of Kuwait. However, the Air Tasking Order was simply not flexible enough for a full-scale, all-out attack on Baghdad to take place that night. Thus, the night of March 20–21 saw rather sporadic strikes on leadership and command and control targets throughout Iraq. Three U.S. warships (the destroyer *USS McCain* and the attack submarines *USS Columbia* and *USS Providence*) and two Royal Navy submarines (*HMS Turbulent* and *HMS Splendid*) fired off 36 Tomahawk cruise missiles at the capital, while Coalition aircraft struck a number of targets throughout the country. The Iraqis, for their part, managed to fire off six Ababil-100 tactical ballistic missiles against various targets in Kuwait. Patriots shot down four of the missiles; the other two missed their target (which was Tactical Assembly Area Fox) entirely.

It was not until the night of March 21–22 that the full panoply of Coalition air power would rain down on Baghdad. F-117s, B-2s, B-1s, a variety of fighter aircraft, and cruise missiles all contributed to the spectacle of violent explosions that echoed throughout the capital. Brilliant footage by the various news agencies and correspondents, all of whom were paying huge sums to the Iraqi government for the privilege of reporting live from Baghdad, provided the rest of the world with a brief glimpse of the aerial firepower the Coalition was bringing to bear on the Iraqis.

One British observer of the scene, Wing Commander Derek Wilson, who commanded a Tornado squadron and flew a mission on the night of "shock and awe," reported about his experience:

> Baghdad was ablaze. There were explosions going off every few seconds. We had anti-aircraft fire to one side and multiple rocket launches were used against us, putting

up about eight to ten missiles. We could see them, but
they were never a threat . . . When we got up we had to
fly through a wall of coalition aircraft waiting to go in
behind us. We found our way through. It was in some
ways the most dangerous part. There was so much up
there. I have never seen anything like it . . . When we approached Baghdad it was a red glow on the horizon. The
missiles were already doing their work . . . I would not
have wanted to be on the receiving end.[4]

The phrase "shock and awe" suggested the hope of some at higher
policy levels of the administration that the initial aerial assault would
cause the collapse of the Baath regime—yet another indication of the
United States' underestimation of the sustaining power of tyranny.
The initial air attacks on Baghdad had no hope of bringing about a regime change, no matter how impressive the pyrotechnic display may
have appeared in images conveyed around the world. Over 500 high-
value targets within the confines of Baghdad were off limits to air
strike. Some of these targets were removed from the initial list because
of overconfidence that the massive attack would lead to the immediate
collapse of the regime. As one officer at the Combined Air Operations
Center at Prince Sultan air base in Saudi Arabia put it: "There was a
hope that there would be a complete and utter collapse of the regime
early on. In order to let that come to fruition, [air commanders] initially held back those targets."[5]

A number of the targets spared represented essential elements of
Saddam's command and control system. Here appeared one of the
ambiguities in air war: perhaps there was no harm in leaving so many
lines of communications to Baghdad open, since most Iraqi commanders fully understood the danger of passing along bad news to the
boss. Nevertheless, some significant targets were off limits to attack

because of a pervasive fear of civilian casualties. In the end, the Iraqi population, for the most part—except for those whom the attacks directly impacted—were not overly affected by the Coalition's air offensive. As one Iraqi commented to an American reporter after an attack on a Baghdad telephone exchange: "Speaking logically, they are precise, even if the goal is inhuman . . . With all of America's power, we expected the strike to be more devastating, we expected it to be leveled to the ground."[6]

Two target systems in particular could have had a considerable impact on the conduct of the war had they been struck earlier in the conflict. The first involved the regime's propaganda outlets—Iraqi television and radio. For much of the war, Saddam's propaganda was blaring into the gullible ears of his supporters and those who remembered the terrible events of spring 1991. Ironically, at the war's end when U.S. soldiers and marines were battering the final miles toward Baghdad, Iraqi propaganda that proclaimed American defeats may have facilitated the collapse, as Sunni Iraqis finally were forced to confront the discrepancy between the propaganda they were hearing and the reality they could see with their own eyes. But in the war's early days, most Iraqis must have taken the continued, uninterrupted broadcasts of the Baath regime as clear evidence that Saddam was still in control.

Equally puzzling was the failure to attack the electrical grid, particularly since specially designed Tomahawk missiles could throw out carbon filament wires that can short out transforming stations without doing serious long-term damage to the system. Such weapons had been enormously effective on the first night of attack in 1991, but they were not used until late in this conflict. Thus, the world was treated to the rather bizarre image of bombs exploding all over downtown Baghdad while the capital remained fully lit.

Still, the massive night attack was an impressive display of military muscle. Navy special mission C-130s dropped three air force Firebee target drones—two others were ground-launched—which immediately attracted the attention of Iraqi air defenses. As Iraqi anti-aircraft guns blasted away into the night skies with no hope of hitting anything, the drones dropped chaff all over the city, confusing the Iraqis even further. Meanwhile, below the drones, cruise missiles were flying in and hitting sites throughout the city, while F-117s, soaring unseen above it all, dropped their bombs with precision on a variety of high-payoff targets.

The use of drones (which are just early-model UAVs) continued into the daylight hours. Two older Predator UAVs, stripped of all their highly classified gear, flew over Baghdad to tease out any remaining Iraqi radars that dared to light up. Neither Predator was hit, which says a great deal about the state of Iraqi air defenses. When they eventually ran out of fuel and crashed into the Tigris and a lake near the river, the world was treated to the spectacle of Iraqi militiamen shooting into the reeds and marshes, trying to hit downed pilots.

The numbers tell the story of the massive assault on Baghdad throughout the night. The Coalition launched 600 cruise missiles: 500 off of thirty U.S. and British ships and 100 from air force bombers. Out of approximately 1,500 missions flown over the course of the night, over 700 were strike aircraft which hit approximately 1,000 targets. The British were able that night to showcase their own technologies, when the RAF fired off its new Storm Shadow missile from Tornadoes, with full success. The reach of Coalition air power is suggested by the bases from which its aircraft were coming: Whiteman Air Force Base in Missouri, Diego Garcia in the Indian Ocean, Upper Hayford in the United Kingdom, five aircraft carriers in the Persian Gulf and the Mediterranean, and over thirty bases scattered throughout the Middle East from Turkey to the Persian Gulf. Despite all the fireworks, Coalition air commanders took great pains to prevent civilian casualties and collateral damage. Coalition aircraft struck none of the bridges over the Euphrates and Tigris Rivers, as they had done in 1991, because these would be used in the immediate future by U.S. and British ground forces.

For the third straight night there was no significant response from the Iraqis. The few radars that were turned on were immediately terminated. The Iraqis flew no sorties. They did fire a few SAMs, but none with tracking radar. While considerable anti-aircraft fire added to the spectacle in the skies over Baghdad and other Iraqi cities, it usually occurred after the bombs had already fallen and inflicted no damage on Coalition aircraft. General Horner had described the air campaign against the Iraqis in the last stages of Desert Storm as being like hitting a "tethered goat"; that was an apt description of what Iraq's position looked like at the *beginning* of this second Iraq war.

The night of March 22–23 saw a considerable difference in targeting from the night before. Perhaps the change reflected the previous night's success with precision weapons, or perhaps it was an indication of the increasing resistance Coalition soldiers and marines were encountering on the ground—resistance at a level that caught commanders and planners by surprise. More strike sorties (800) were launched than on the previous day, but the number of preplanned targets dropped by nearly 50 percent, while the number of cruise missiles fired dropped by nearly a third.

A substantial number of the sorties were being provided with their targets while in the air. These "on-call" sorties largely were to support ground forces in contact with the enemy or to attack Iraqi forces moving forward to participate in fights along the Euphrates. These latter targets were supplied by JSTARS. Over the course of the next two days (March 23–24 and 24–25) the Coalition launched between 1,500 and 2,000 sorties. During each twenty-four-hour period, approximately 500 of the targets were preplanned; the others were targets of opportunity (where aircraft received their strike mission in flight) or close air support missions (where teams on the ground called in strikes against enemy forces in close proximity to Coalition ground forces). The Iraqis managed to fire only one tactical ballistic missile, which was intercepted and destroyed by a Patriot battery. A Patriot battery also locked on to one of the Coalition's own F-16s, which promptly replied by firing off an HARM that destroyed the offending radar. Fortunately, no soldiers were killed.

On March 25, as the *shamal* blew in from the west, ground forces were already running into fierce and unexpected resistance as well as logistic difficulties resulting from the distances they had already covered. Many observers from safe perches in the United States emphasized the "exhaustion" of the ground offensive. In reality, the *shamal,* with its heavy winds, blowing sands, and rain squalls, provided Coalition air forces with a brilliant tactical opportunity.

Saddam and his chief lieutenants calculated that since Coalition close support aircraft were grounded, they could move their forces forward to engage Coalition troops. Certainly from the Iraqi perspective, that decision made eminent good sense; in 1991 bad weather had indeed incapacitated the air campaign. But this time around Saddam was making a disastrous mistake. Throughout the three days of the *shamal,* JSTARS and the fleet of long-range UAVs watched the Iraqis concentrate their forces and begin their deployments toward V Corps and I MEF. By this point in the war, Moseley was so confident that the entire Iraqi air defense had been crushed that he was willing to deploy the JSTARS aircraft deep into Iraq's air space. Coordinates on Iraqi movements were immediately passed along to high-flying B-1s or fighter bombers in the area, most of which possessed infrared capabilities that allowed them to penetrate the blowing sands and illuminate moving targets far below.

Lieutenant Colonel Robert Givens, operations officer of the 524th

Fighter Squadron, equipped with F-16s, was able to use his on-board infrared sensors to pick up a group of Iraqi vehicles whose movement army drones had detected. Givens then dropped his 500-pound GBU-12s, destroying eight tanks and infantry fighting vehicles belonging to the Republican Guard Medina Division. During heavy fighting near An Najaf, UAVs and JSTARS picked up a compact formation of Iraqi T-72 tanks and other armored vehicles moving forward to attack. Four GPS-guided bombs were sufficient to take out no less than thirty of the vehicles and halt the formation before it could deploy an attack. Throughout the three days and nights of the *shamal,* Coalition aircraft struck Iraqi forces as they were deploying or attacking marines and soldiers on the ground.

The physical destruction that Coalition air power was able to achieve would become apparent as V Corps and I MEF soldiers and marines counted the burning hulks of Republican Guard vehicles that littered their advance through the Karbala Gap and along the Tigris toward Baghdad. But the psychological damage done to Iraqi soldiers who survived these air attacks must have been equally horrific. Told by their commanders that the *shamal* would protect them from air attack, the destruction that seemingly came from nowhere must have broken the will of many to fight. Such unrecorded incidents represent precisely the inherent difficulty in assessing fully the extent of the contribution that air power made to the Coalition's victory. Evidence in the *Gulf War Air Power Survey,* which examined the debriefing reports of Iraqi POWs in the 1991 war, makes clear that air attacks had a devastating impact on the morale of officers and soldiers and increased their willingness to surrender.[7] Air attacks must have had a similar effect in this conflict, but we will not know for sure until the results of interrogations are available.

As the sandstorm abated on March 28, Iraqi efforts to redeploy in Baghdad's defense died down just as Coalition ground forces—

refreshed, resupplied, and cognizant of their superiority over the Iraqis, owing in part to the cover provided from the air—prepared to resume the march on Baghdad. The number of missions flown throughout this period remained close to 2,000 daily. So heavy was the effort that at one point during the night of March 27–28 marine computers picked up nearly 1,000 aircraft flying over southern Iraq either entering or exiting their respective kill boxes. It was the first time since the *shamal* had begun three nights before that the Coalition was able to get its full complement of aircraft into the fight.

The large number of missions being flown deep into Iraq, either to attack command and control targets around Baghdad or in support of ground forces as they approached the capital, placed considerable strain on the aerial tanker fleet. The KC-135s, the mainstay of aerial refueling since the late 1950s, were clearly nearing the end of their useful life, while the newer KC-10s were too few. Here British tankers made a substantial contribution, because RAF aircraft used the same probe and drogue system employed by U.S. marine and navy aircraft. Thus, the British were able to take some of the load off the American tanker fleet.

Planners between the two wars seriously underestimated the importance of tankers. Only Kuwait's three air bases were close enough to allow Coalition fighter bombers to reach deep into Iraq without being refueled in the air. The other 55 bases within reasonable range of Baghdad all required that attacking aircraft be refueled both entering and exiting the arena. The Coalition tanker fleet supplied almost as much fuel in the Iraq War as their predecessors had during the Gulf War, but with a fleet only two thirds as large.

After the *shamal*, as Coalition forces closed in on Baghdad, the air campaign shifted its focus to supporting ground troops. Two thirds of Coalition strike sorties now targeted the Republican Guard or the fedayeen. For example, on the evening of April 4 a marine Hunter UAV picked up the movement of a substantial number of Iraqi tanks and artillery pieces as they attempted to deploy out of the capital under the cover of darkness. The senior watch officer in 3rd Marine Aircraft Wing's combat operations center forwarded the coordinates to Harriers and F/A-18 Hornets overhead. The resulting attacks destroyed approximately eighty vehicles and killed a considerable number of Iraqis. The effect of these strikes on the morale of the survivors can only be imagined.

With the capture and rehabilitation of the Iraqi air force base at Tallil, the 3rd Marine Aircraft Wing and the RAF were able to create a forward rearming and refueling point for their Harriers 100 miles inside Iraq. Within a short time the air force would move some of its A-10s onto Tallil's tarmac, allowing the close air support to remain immediately responsive to the needs of ground forces. Having this base for refueling also took pressure off the hard-pressed tanker fleet.

By the first week of April, Iraqi high command had realized how dangerously near to Baghdad marines and soldiers were. But the wild shuffling of Iraqi ground units to meet those threats only increased the number of targets for air attack. By April 4, 85 percent of the Coalition's air effort was focused on destroying Iraqi ground forces, particularly the Medina, Baghdad, and Hammurabi divisions, which were defending the Karbala Gap and the approaches to Baghdad. On that date army intelligence reported the Hammurabi Division down to 44 percent of its peacetime combat effectiveness, with some officers estimating the division's fighting ability even lower; the figure for the Medina Division was barely 18 percent. This rapid rate of attrition left the Iraqis with virtually no means to defend their capital. Whether Saddam and his chief lieutenants were ever informed about the state of affairs of their ground forces is unknown. But with Coalition air forces clearly on the hunt for them, they undoubtedly had other things on their mind.

The battle for Baghdad represented the end of the conventional war in Iraq. To a considerable extent it expired with a whimper rather than a bang. Coalition commanders, the media, and legions of military commentators had all expected the Iraqis to put up a sustained and effective defense of their capital, the heart of the Baath regime. But as it turned out, Saddam and his military commanders had done no better job in preparing the capital's defense than they had in preparing the rest of the country for war. Saddam's paranoiac fears of internal rebellion, as well as the incapacity of his military and civilian bureaucracy to tell him the truth, prevented the regime from putting up a credible defense. "Baghdad Bob," the information minister, fully understood that American tanks on the opposite bank of the Tigris were on their way into the city. Nevertheless, they might shoot at him and miss, but if he said the wrong thing to the international media, Saddam would ensure that he would die.

As Coalition ground forces approached Baghdad, the air and ground battles merged into a single, conjoined fight. The course of the ground campaign will become clearer as historians digest what happened and where. The air contribution will remain murky and uncertain. How, for example, can historians ever evaluate the second-order effects of a bombing attack that destroyed, say, ten vehicles but persuaded 200 Republican Guard soldiers to shed their uniforms and melt back into the civilian population? What is certain is that the experience of army and air force units in working together considerably improved their level of cooperation and lethality in the final stages of the approach to Baghdad. The marines already possessed that symbiosis between air and ground. In fact, a major portion of the marines' success in advancing through the central valley between the great rivers was due to their ability to work their air and ground forces as a single team.

Even though the emphasis of the air campaign was now on supporting the ground forces, air attacks continued to knock out command and control centers in Baghdad and go after the regime's leadership. In a twenty-four-hour period, I MEF's air-ground team finished off the Republican Guard division near Al Kut and destroyed much of the remainder of the Al Nida Republican Guard Division on the road to Baghdad. Meanwhile, the 3rd Infantry Division had reached and captured Saddam International Airport, soon to be renamed. The seizure of the airport immediately opened up the possibility of flying C-130s into Baghdad and thus providing emergency resupply of critical items to the army. It also sounded the death knell of the Baath regime. The door to Baghdad lay open.

In the early afternoon of April 7 U.S. intelligence intercepted cell phone traffic suggesting that Saddam and his sons were meeting at a site in Baghdad's Al Mansur district. The CAOC (Coalition Air Operations Center) immediately passed the coordinates to one of the B-1 bombers that orbited over Iraq twenty-four hours a day. The B-1 had just refueled and was coming off the tanker. As its weapons systems officer later recalled: "When we got that it was a priority leadership target, immediately you get kind of an adrenaline rush. The words that were used when we got passed the coordinates [were] that this was 'the big one.' We knew we had to react quickly to it."[8] Minutes later the bomber was over downtown Baghdad and the bunker-busting bombs were dropped from 20,000 feet. Apparently Saddam was not at the location and had dodged another bullet. But the message U.S. air power sent was clear enough: we can go after you anytime, day or night.

Early in the second week of April, it was clear that the conventional war in Iraq was virtually over. On April 8 Coalition intelligence reported that the three Republican Guard divisions immediately outside the capital had broken up into a number of disparate units that were fighting without any coherent plan or order. Of the approximately 850 tanks these units had possessed at the start of the war, only 19 remained. Of 550 artillery pieces, only 40 were usable. By April 11 the Coalition had destroyed Iraqi forces in the environs of Baghdad, and only a few bashed and bloodied units remained to put up token resistance in Saddam's home town of Tikrit to the north.

"Who destroyed what" would in the end represent only meaningless statistics. The ground offensive had forced the Republican Guard and other units to concentrate their troops in areas where Coalition air power could devastate them. Day and night it had pounded the Iraqis, destroying morale as well as equipment and lives. But dispersion was hardly a viable alternative for the Iraqis, because Coalition ground forces would then have been able to kill them with ease. In every respect the air campaign had been an integral part of a truly joint military operation.

Still, the numbers that sum up the air campaign—if not its meaning or indirect contribution—are indeed impressive, even when compared with the Gulf War. That earlier conflict lasted forty-two days, while the Iraq War lasted only twenty-three days. During the former the first Coalition flew approximately 126,645 total sorties; during the Iraq War the second Coalition flew approximately 36,275 sorties, for an average of 1,576 per day. Of the 36,275 sorties, 14,050 were strike sorties—the great majority conducted by precision aircraft, most of which carried more than one precision weapon. Whereas barely 7 percent of the strike sorties had used precision munitions in the earlier conflict, nearly 65 percent of the weapons dropped in the Iraq War were precision munitions, possessing an order of magnitude greater killing power than conventional dumb bombs.

To keep the massive effort going day after day, the RAF and the USAF had to fly 7,525 tanker sorties that unloaded over 310 million pounds of fuel (46 million gallons) to the thirsty fighter and bomber aircraft flying north. The great workhorse in this campaign was the B-1 bomber. It flew less than 2 percent of the sorties in the Iraq

War but delivered approximately 50 percent of all the JDAMs dropped during the conflict. The Coalition lost only two fixed-wing aircraft to enemy action, an A-10 over Baghdad and an F-15E near Tikrit. The A-10 pilot was rescued; the two F-15 crew members were killed. In addition, for reasons that remain unclear, a Patriot missile shot down a Tornado, killing both crew members with "friendly fire."

LESSONS LEARNED

Air power is the most difficult of all forms of military force to measure or even to express in precise terms.

WINSTON S. CHURCHILL, *The Second World War,* 1948

In 1991, in the midst of the Coalition aerial assault on Baghdad, an Iraqi woman noted the following in her diary over the course of the forty-day campaign:

DAY FOUR: In the evening we cook potatoes in the fireplace . . . I make a dynamite punch with Aquavit, vodka, and fresh orange juice . . .

DAY SEVEN: The worst has happened: we have to drink warm beer . . . we opened a bottle of champagne and ate *mesoukhia* and a million other things. I wish that our stock of food would finish so that we could eat a little less . . .

DAY TWENTY: It has now been three weeks. Forty-four thousand air raids. I have another leak in the water system . . .

DAY THIRTY-FOUR: Tim brought faxes from Sol, Dood, and Charlie, our first contacts with family and friends— a break in our isolation. We had a super barbeque lunch today, a lovely day but quite noisy.[9]

Whatever damage Desert Storm's air campaign managed to do to Iraq's infrastructure—and it was considerable—aerial attacks had relatively little impact on the minds and hearts of Iraq's civilian population in 1991. There is considerable irony here, because most military theorists of the 1920s and 1930s posited that air power was a weapon that should attack exclusively the morale of the enemy. Yet, everything that has occurred over the course of the past decade has pushed doctrine in the opposite direction. The prevailing view appears to be that the precision capabilities of modern air power developed over the past three decades have now ruled out civilian casualties.

The aerial campaign that accompanied the Iraq War had even less impact on the general population than Desert Storm twelve years earlier. Women, children, and parents who lost husbands, fathers, or sons in the army were of course emotionally devastated and would likely suffer financially in the coming years. But there were no incidents comparable to the Al Firdos bunker bombing, and Coalition air attacks rarely struck Iraqi civilians. The widely reported hit on an open-air market, supposedly by a cruise missile, was most probably accomplished by an unguided Iraqi SAM that fell to earth after running out of fuel. In Afghanistan, according to current estimates, one civilian died for every twelve munitions dropped during the air war. In the Iraq War, one civilian died for every thirty-five munitions dropped. Yet, in the end what so often matters in war is the perception of observers and the media. The deaths of so few Iraqi civilians over the course of this month-long campaign was quite simply not news; thirty or forty casualties all at once in a Baghdad market, on the other hand, was news indeed, regardless of who fired the missile. In order to reduce the number of casualties among civilians and avoid other collateral damage, this war, as well as the war in Afghanistan, saw the bizarre situation in which military lawyers assigned to the various commands participated in making targeting decisions. Their presence was simply a reflection of the American desire to provide legal cover.

The air campaign's psychological effect on Iraqi *combatants* is another story. We can relatively easily tote up the number of tanks, artillery pieces, vehicles, and key targets attacked and destroyed by air strikes, but how does one assess the impact of air attacks on the minds of enemy officers and soldiers? If the Gulf War is any guide, the effects were considerable, and joint commanders and airmen should not lose sight of the psychological dimension of aerial attack as they plan and prepare for future wars.

Despite the strictures under which the air campaign against Iraq was conducted, its effectiveness was impressive, and at times devastating, throughout the conflict. Perhaps the most important contribution made by the air campaign was establishing air supremacy. Coalition ground forces never saw a single enemy aircraft overhead during the entire course of the war. The massive (and vulnerable) deployment and projection of soldiers and marines took place under an umbrella of aerial protection. The hallmark of the American way of war since Sicily in 1943 has been air superiority. U.S. ground forces have rarely had to deal with enemy aircraft overhead, and that air superiority has allowed U.S. ground forces the freedom to maneuver audaciously with the confidence that their supply lines as well as the firing line would be safe from enemy air attack. In Desert Storm air superiority, gained in the first hours of the war, soon gave way to air supremacy. In Iraqi Freedom the Coalition started off from day one with complete control of the air space. As one senior air force general suggested, "You can do everything with air superiority, but nothing without it."

Ironically, that achievement allowed bomber and fighter bomber fleets to become aerial truckers, conveying great amounts of ordnance north and dropping it on targets flushed out by the speed and ferocity of the Coalition ground forces' advance. This leads to the second enormous contribution that air power made. It lay not in the ability to attack strategic targets such as power grids and communication centers but in the consistent, devastating strikes against Iraqi ground forces. Such support came in two distinct forms.

The first was interdiction of the enemy's troops as they concentrated and then advanced in an effort to close with the marine and army spearheads. This occurred even faster than intelligence could keep track of the results. The combined-arms team thus placed the Iraqis on the horns of a dilemma. They could either remain dispersed and hidden from the air, thereby laying themselves open to destruction by ground forces, or they could concentrate to withstand ground attack, leading to even swifter destruction from above. The second form of air support was close air support of the Coalition's own troops. Here the army and the air force could still learn a good deal from the marines. The fact that marine aviators were routinely embedded in marine battalions allowed for more skillful use of direct precision weapons to support ground troops.

Nevertheless, whatever advantages the marines enjoyed with their more responsive air power from the 3rd Marine Aircraft Wing, air force aircraft provided crucial support to the 3rd Infantry Division. Iraqis in contact with Coalition ground forces died in huge numbers from precision strikes and in some cases from conventional dumb bombs. The A-10 with its 30mm cannon and ability to survive in a dangerous low-altitude environment once again proved the wisdom of those congressional legislators who forced an unwilling air force hierarchy to buy the plane in the 1970s.

What were the shortcomings of the overall air campaign, from the American perspective? Although intelligence by technical means—reconnaissance platforms and sensors, including those in space—provided critical support, human intelligence was sparse and often misleading. As has become apparent over the past two decades, intelligence gathered by thinking human beings, with their ability to interpret local languages, customs, and cultures, is a depressingly weak link in America's attempt to grasp the nature of its opponents and their capabilities. For all the talk of effects-based operations and operational net assessment, the failure to understand the enemy where he lives—his culture, his values, his political system—quickly leads up a dark path where any assumption will do. Nothing in the ahistoricism of the current generation suggests that such weaknesses will be addressed, much less amended, at any time in the near future.

What was particularly impressive about air power in the Iraq War was the ability of the command and control system to retarget aircraft in the air and assign them new targets that had only recently popped up from UAV or other sensors. That capability approached real-time targeting and allowed the Coalition to attack the enemy as he began to move. Yet, the very communication capabilities that enabled such flexibility can be used for top-down control rather than true, real-time execution.

Dangerous tendencies in this direction remain alive and well in the American military, especially within the soul of the air force. For decades the air force has trumpeted its desire to have centralized control of air assets but to execute its missions in a decentralized fashion. With its ability to reassign missions to aircraft literally on the fly during this campaign, the air force lived up to its doctrinal statement of decentralized execution—one which it had rarely honored in the past.

On the other side of the ledger is the belief among some airmen (and others) that the increasing powers of computer and sensor technologies will eventually allow centralized control *and* centralized execution. To go down that road would be to follow in the disastrous footsteps of Robert McNamara and his minions in the 1960s. Whether commanders eager to control the battlefield themselves or lawyers desirous of limiting collateral damage (which they know little about) assume control at the center, such a result would be the end of flexibility and truly decentralized execution.

We close this chapter with a note of warning. The conflict with Iraq engaged an enemy who had virtually no military capabilities left after an air war of attrition lasting over twelve years. Consequently, the conventional phase of the conflict was extremely lopsided and brief. The aftermath, however, is proving more troublesome and unmanageable, and in this phase of the conflict cruise missiles are of little value. The ability of bombers and strike aircraft to hit a number of targets with precision does indeed represent a significant step forward in technological capabilities; and once air supremacy is achieved, these capabilities allow the projection of almost unlimited firepower against specific targets of value to the enemy. Nevertheless, unless advances in air power are coupled with intelligent thinking—by planners on the ground—about the nature of one's opponent and of wars and their aftermath, past, present, and future, these improved technologies will ensure only that political and military defeats will come later, and at greater cost.

6

The End of the Campaign

All the business of war, and all the business of life, is to endeavor
to find out what you don't know by what you do; that's what I
call "guessing what was on the other side of the hill."

DUKE OF WELLINGTON (1769–1852)

The end of the sandstorm in the south brought relief to marines and soldiers alike. Resupplied and
somewhat rested, they were ready to continue their drive on Baghdad.
However, the *shamal* had been anything but a pause for the Iraqis,
who had attempted to move their forces under cover of the clouds of
dust. But the dust did not protect them from the prying eyes of UAVs
and JSTARS, which saw their movements and relayed the intelligence
to the aircraft waiting overhead. The Iraqis died by the thousands, and
the detritus of smashed equipment American ground forces passed on
the highways leading to Baghdad stood as mute testimony to the
death that had rained down on Saddam's legions.

The story of the military collapse of the Iraqi regime in the last days of March and the first week in April involves a set of coherent and effective operations that ran concurrently—the campaign in the north, the drive through the Karbala Gap by the 3rd Infantry Division, and the advance of the 1st Marine Division across the Tigris at An Numaniyah. We begin in the north, where special forces, supported by airborne troopers and marines, presented a direct and palpable threat to Saddam's regime from the Kurdish provinces near Mosul and Kirkuk.

THE NORTHERN AND SPECIAL OPERATIONS CAMPAIGN

Who dares, wins.

                    Motto of the British Special Air Service

After spectacular successes in Afghanistan, Franks had enough confidence in the capabilities of special operations forces to give them the responsibility of controlling and dominating almost two thirds of Iraq. He was fortunate that many of those who had participated in the destruction of the Taliban were available for the Iraqi campaign, including Brigadier General Gary Harrell. After decades of operations, in virtually every American combat theater, Harrell still maintained the appearance of a college linebacker. As with most special operations soldiers, his personality and leadership style contrasted with his Rambo-like exterior. Jovial, collegial, and often self-deprecating, Harrell knew how to build and lead a team of warriors, much as he had led an outstanding football team in his younger days.

Franks assigned him two missions: first, protect Centcom's left flank by controlling the immense western deserts of Iraq. Harrell gave this task to the 5th Special Forces Group under the command of Colonel John Mulholland. A few thousand soldiers would seize and then dominate the entire western desert from the Euphrates to Iraq's borders with Syria and Jordan. This vast wasteland became a maneuver area for American, British, and Australian special forces, backed up by tanks and artillery. Their task included isolating Iraq's borders to prevent the Baath from escaping or from evacuating weapons of mass destruction to their neighbors Syria and Jordan. The special forces also effectively closed down the "Scud boxes"—areas the Iraqis had used to launch missiles against Saudi Arabia and Israel during the Gulf War. In addition, these units single-handedly secured critical airfields in the western desert, both to deny them to the Iraqis and open them up for Coalition aircraft. Many of 5th Group's missions are still active and remain highly classified today.

Second, Harrell was to use the 10th Special Forces Group to open a second front in northern Iraq. Franks needed this both to destroy terrorist camps of Ansar al-Islam, widely believed to be partners with Al Qaeda, and to detain Iraqi regular forces so they would not move to the defense of Baghdad. The refusal of the Turks to allow the U.S. 4th Infantry Division to deploy through their territory had created a vacuum. To maintain a viable threat from the north until Harrell could get his force in place, Franks kept negotiations with the Turks going, even though there was little chance of resolution. The ships with the 4th Infantry Division's equipment on board lingered in the eastern Mediterranean to the last moment.

Harrell's mission was delicate. He had to create enough combat power using surrogate Kurdish forces to threaten the Iraqis while not allowing the Kurds themselves to become so powerful that the Turks would intervene. His center of gravity would be the key cities of Mosul and Kirkuk and the oil fields in the north.

The northern mission belonged to the 10th Special Forces Group commanded by Colonel Charlie Cleveland, a West Point grad and son of a career enlisted man. Cleveland had an affinity for motorcycles and a talent for gaining the unquestioned allegiance of his soldiers. Years of training and exercises provided Cleveland with an understanding of the cultures in the region. The experience of special forces in building a surrogate army out of the Afghan Northern Alliance's militia, along with the skill these soldiers had acquired employing twenty-first-century precision-bombing techniques against medieval enemies, allowed his unit to achieve similar successes among the Kurds.

Cleveland's Task Force Viking mission began in earnest in mid-February 2003 when small special forces units deployed from Europe to establish a forward operating base in Constanta, Romania. They would thus be within range of the northern Iraqi combat zone. Refusal of the Turks to grant overflight rights made the infiltration by MC-130 aircraft both circuitous and dangerous. When the group began infiltrating in earnest on March 20, the MC-130s flew from Romania, detoured over Greece, and dog-legged across the eastern Mediterranean to land and refuel in Jordan before continuing into Iraq. The transports made the final run into Bashur Airbase at night; they flew at fifty feet to avoid enemy radar. But the Iraqis still managed to shoot up three aircraft severely.

Task Force Viking consisted of the 2nd and 3rd Battalions from 10th Group, augmented by the 3rd Battalion of 3rd Group. The latter was equipped with specially modified Humvees, called ground mobility vehicles. Each GMV was a self-contained command and control headquarters, a fighting platform, and an armored recreational vehicle, all in one. The vehicles variously carried several calibers of machine guns, from heavy .50 caliber to light 5.56mm, Mark 19 grenade launchers, sniper rifles, shot guns, Stinger shoulder-fired anti-aircraft missiles, and the new Javelin fire-and-forget antitank missiles. The onboard command center consisted of sophisticated communications gear, GPS, and lasers to designate targets for air strikes. The soldiers in 10th Group traveled aboard militarized versions of Land Rover SUVs equipped with automatic weapons and communications mounts. Unfortunately, little strategic airlift was available early in the campaign, and the Land Rovers remained in Romania until the end of March. Cleveland's soldiers had to make do with any form of transport they could pick up inside Kurdish areas. As a result, they traveled about in buses, pickups, and the occasional taxi. Cleveland's personal command post was an ancient Toyota Land Cruiser equipped with blue velvet seats and a jury-rigged stereo, along with a liberal assortment of Arab music CDs.

Cleveland's partner in the operation was air force Colonel O. G. Mannion, who commanded the 352nd Special Operations Group. Unlike most air force pilots, Mannion had spent virtually his entire career flying special ops missions. He agreed to serve as Cleveland's deputy, as well as air commander. Mannion's skill as a special ops airman would be tested. The Coalition could not have executed the northern campaign without the firepower of air force and navy fighters and AC-130 gunships. And until late in the campaign, aircraft could only reach the theater across a tenuous aerial bridge between Romania and Bashur.

Cleveland's mission was to create and advise a surrogate army consisting of his troops in alliance with two militias: the Kurdish Democratic Party (KDP), consisting of 45,000 soldiers, and the Party for a Unified Kurdistan (PUK), with 20,000 soldiers. The American command referred to these two organizations as the "Peshmerga." They were essentially two political parties, each of which maintained a military force loyal to its individual leader. The Kurdish leaders used their militia to control their turf and to protect themselves against any competing military organizations.

And there was no shortage of odd military organizations inside the 200-mile Green Line—a de facto border within Iraq that separated Iraqis from the Kurds. The BADR corps, a strange assortment of Iraqi expatriates sponsored by Iran, occupied a piece of Iraqi territory east of Mosul astride the border between Iran and Iraq. Iran also sponsored

Ansar al-Islam, a terrorist group of approximately 1,000 men, roughly a tenth of whom were confirmed Al Qaeda terrorists recently escaped from Afghanistan. The Americans were particularly keen to take on Ansar al-Islam as payback for the World Trade Center and Pentagon attacks. Saddam had his own expatriate band, the MeK, consisting of about 3,000 well-trained and equipped Iranians engaged in a campaign against the mullahs in the western Iranian provinces. In spite of their prewar affiliation, American special ops soldiers respected the skill and fighting abilities of the MeK.

Saddam positioned one Republican Guard and three regular army corps along the Green Line. Uday Hussein was particularly distrustful of the regulars and dispatched his fedayeen to stiffen their resolve. He purchased additional insurance by scattering special security teams just behind the lines with the mission to execute any regulars who refused to fight. From this Rubik's Cube of byzantine politics, Cleveland formed a partnership with the Kurds, while keeping his indigenous allies firmly in hand. Likewise, he knew that taking on the Iraqi regulars would require a subtle combination of overwhelming force occasionally moderated with persuasion, guile, and diplomacy—and cash.

The Coalition and conventional side of Cleveland's operational environment was equally complex. During the campaign, he would have operating in his area the army's 173rd Airborne Brigade from Vicenza, Italy, an armored task force from the 1st Armored Division in Germany, and the 26th Marine Expeditionary Unit. He would also receive one battalion of reinforcements—1-14 Infantry—from the 10th Mountain Division, and operational control of Task Force 7, a highly classified British special forces unit. Two civil affairs units, one regular and one from the National Guard, would eventually provide him with the capability necessary for gaining control of Kirkuk and Mosul. In circumstances increasingly characteristic of American special operations, Cleveland orchestrated or influenced the actions of approximately 80,000 soldiers from three countries and virtually every service and component.

The 10th Group had three missions. The first was to attack the Ansar al-Islam terrorist base camps along the Iranian border. Cleveland's soldiers saw this mission as a chance to kill as many Al Qaeda as they could. As a condition for joining the Coalition, the Kurds insisted these terrorists be eliminated before turning south toward Mosul and Kirkuk. The second mission was to lead the surrogate Kurdish army in its attack on Iraqi forces defending the Green Line. Harrell recognized that Cleveland's organization would be outnumbered and isolated deep in Iraq. His guidance to Cleveland was to be cautious: "Push them as much as you can and take as much ground as they will give you." Harrell shouldered the responsibility of negotiating with the Turks on Cleveland's behalf to ensure that the Kurds' approach to the oil fields near Kirkuk would not alarm the Turks. Cleveland's third mission was to capture the oil fields and secure and stabilize the northern cities of Kirkuk and Mosul.

The greatest challenge lay in gaining the trust of the Kurds, who were disenchanted from past experiences with the United States. Cleveland intended to use Operation Viking Hammer—the mission to destroy Ansar al-Islam—as a means to demonstrate not only the power of American technology but the strength of American resolve. The operation had been in the works for at least a month. Teams from the 3rd Battalion, 10th Special Forces Group, infiltrated in February to establish contact with Peshmerga fighters. Each side took the other's measure.

The Ansar al-Islam occupied approximately 300 square kilometers of Iraqi territory. The terrorist camps were tucked into low creases between some of the most mountainous and inhospitable terrain in the Middle East. Lieutenant Colonel Ken Tovo, commander of the 3rd Battalion, 10th Special Forces, chose to approach the terrorist camp at night and begin the attack in daylight along six different prongs or axes leading toward the largest terrorist camp in the Sargat Valley. The 1,000-plus terrorists in the valley had prepared a string of bunkered fighting positions spread several hundred meters apart along each avenue of approach. They were armed with AK-47s, machine guns, RPGs, and a few heavy mortars and artillery pieces in questionable states of repair.

Tovo organized his Peshmerga fighters into six groups, each supported by one of his A Teams. The Kurds traveled lightly, dressed in short-sleeved shirts, track suits, and tennis shoes. Their weapons were much like those of the terrorists. The Americans, by contrast, were loaded like pack mules, carrying weapons, radios, laptops, laser designators, and a full load of batteries, food, and ammunition.

The advance began in the early morning on March 27 and immediately ran into concentrated enemy AK-47, sniper, machine gun, and occasional heavy mortar fire. For a day and a half the Peshmerga forces and their American allies clambered across the high ridgelines leading to the camps, with slopes so steep attackers literally had to climb hand-over-hand to advance in some places. The A teams took out bunkers one at a time by calling in close air support from navy fighters flying off the aircraft carriers *Roosevelt* and *Truman* and AC-130 Spectre gunships orbiting overhead. As usual, the enemy's ignorance of American technology and fighting techniques contributed to their destruction. After watching their sturdily built bunkers disappear in a cloud of debris after hits by 2,000-pound JDAMs, the enemy rushed to occupy two-man fighting positions. Sensors aboard Spectre easily picked out the radiated heat from enemy soldiers and slammed 105mm cannon shells into their positions. When the Peshmerga and Americans arrived at the camp deep inside the Sargat Valley, they found nothing standing. Dead terrorists littered the ground around the flattened buildings.

With the terrorist threat to the rear eliminated, the Peshmerga turned south to assault the Green Line. The ineptitude of the three regular corps in the defense was staggering even by Iraqi standards. Instead of falling back, dispersing, and seeking cover from air strikes, the Iraqis moved forward and silhouetted their fighting positions on the crests of the hills, ridges, and mountaintops that defined the course of the Green Line, making themselves clear targets.

The success of American firepower in the Ansar al-Islam fight convinced the Kurds they had chosen the winning side, and they eagerly sought to exploit their newly acquired friends. Aware of Turkish nervousness, the Americans were careful to temper Kurdish enthusiasm. The offensive against the Green Line sought to push the Iraqis off their positions by use of aerial precision firepower, followed by cautious advances toward Kirkuk and Mosul. Occasionally after the Iraqi regulars retreated, the Americans would hear the sounds of small arms fire coming from behind enemy lines. Soon the regulars would reappear and commence a more spirited defense. Later, the Americans learned that Saddam's special security teams had executed the regular army soldiers for deserting.

The commander of B Detachment 370 received the mission of defeating the XV Corps, the single most important Iraqi force. The first objective was Bushman—an expansive ridge complex encompassing the high ground south of Bardarash and north of Bashiqah. The Iraqi 108th Infantry Brigade with supporting elements from the 16th Division held the area.

An AC-130 fired the first shots at two battalions of the 108th Brigade. Exposed in open terrain to the gunship's infrared sensors, the Iraqis found no place to hide. Throughout the night and into the following morning, enemy casualty collection points filled with victims, as the Iraqis desperately attempted to hold. In the afternoon, the Peshmerga exploited a weak point in the Iraqi front lines to gain a foothold on the ridgeline. The Iraqis attempted to drive the Kurds back, but AC-130s devastated the attackers. In desperation, the enemy sought to escape American firepower by hugging the Peshmerga positions. The green berets then used a combination of infrared strobe lights and chemlights to trace the Kurdish front lines, so that gunships could target aerial strikes within 100 meters. Over the next four days continued ground attacks by the Kurds, aided by deadly precision strikes from the air, crushed the remaining elements of the 108th Brigade.

Meanwhile, conventional forces began to arrive to bolster the Kurds and heighten the northern threat in Iraqi minds. The 173rd Airborne Brigade, stationed in Vicenza, provided the initial force. The target was Bashur airfield. Its lengthy runway would allow air-landed reinforcements brought in by C-130s and later with C-17s, the latter capable of delivering Abrams tanks and other heavy equipment.

The first airborne assault struck early in the morning on March 26, when over 1,000 paratroopers with their heavy equipment jumped from seventeen C-17s 500 feet above the drop zone. After landing, the paratroopers shed their harnesses and secured the airfield and terrain from which they could defend their bridgehead. Artillerymen hastily derigged howitzers and prepared their guns for firing. Other soldiers scrambled through the bundles to identify the pallets and move their loads to the airfield. On the ground, elements of the 10th Special Forces Group met the paratroopers on the airfield and introduced them to the unmilitary but fierce Peshmerga guerrillas.

Twenty air force specialists in runway repair jumped with the paratroopers and immediately went into action to ready the runway for heavy aircraft. Within a matter of hours, C-17s were landing with heavy combat loads and reinforcements. Over the next four days the air force landed an additional 2,000 soldiers and almost 400 vehicles.

Quickly securing the area around the airfield, the 173rd, under its commander, Colonel William Mayville, was in position to provide protection to the Kurds, should the Iraqis make a major move north.

As the Peshmerga applied pressure on the collapsing Iraqi military, the Americans flew in heavier forces. By the end of the first week of April, McKiernan and his staff called forward an armored task force, delivered by air from Germany to reinforce the 173rd. The armored force was small—only a tank and mechanized company of five Abrams and five Bradleys plus a command element from the 1st Battalion, 63rd Armor, part of the 1st Infantry Division stationed in Germany. Additional combat forces followed, including an infantry company mounted in lighter M-113 armored personnel carriers transported by C-130. The challenge of conducting such operations in the future was illustrated by the fact that this single force required thirty C-17 sorties to deliver, thirteen more than needed to move the entire airborne assault echelon of the 173rd from Vicenza to Bashur.

While the Americans were beefing up their conventional forces, the Kurds, with the deadly assistance of U.S. special force advisers and Coalition air power, continued the war on Iraqi positions north of Mosul. While A Teams from the 3rd Special Forces Group were finishing off Bushman, another team was planning an assault on Maqloub Mountain, the only piece of significant terrain between Coalition forces and Mosul. The mountain had considerable political significance for the Kurds because it overwatched the gateway to Mosul, which stood only fifteen kilometers south. It was important enough for the commander of 3rd Group to dispatch two of his invaluable GMVs as reinforcements.

The planning for the mission brought to bear the full spectrum of special operations capabilities. Three days of AC-130 gunship activity had already broken the defenders' morale. The plan called for the special forces teams to use lasers to control joint aerial firepower from a distance. Other green berets would accompany Peshmerga infantry on foot as they cleared villages and advanced over the top of the mountain. As one team finished clearing the towns near Maqloub, another mounted in Land Rovers immediately began an armed reconnaissance, which quickly turned into a victorious advance when the Kurds discovered the Iraqis had bolted.

Once the brittle Green Line defenses collapsed, the road opened to Kirkuk and Mosul. Two days after the fall of Baghdad, Cleveland, his staff, and a hundred Peshmerga militia drove their convoy of Toyotas and pickups cautiously into the outskirts of Mosul. It was night and the power grid had collapsed. The Baathists had fled, leaving behind only the bodies of Saddam's special execution squads, who themselves had been executed by departing regular soldiers in retribution for the slaughter on the Green Line only a week before. The darkness was broken by points of light from burning tires and oil-filled barrels that served to mark city blocks which competing sheiks claimed as their territory. To Cleveland, the scene was shockingly reminiscent of the movie *Escape from New York,* complete with the sounds of gunfire and the taunts of warring gangs. The Coalition owned Mosul. But Cleveland felt the chaos wrought by war would not dissipate anytime soon. He was right.

V CORPS RESUMES ITS NORTHWARD DRIVE

Chariots strong, horses fast, troops valiant, weapons sharp—so that when they hear the drums beat the attack they are happy.

CHANG YU, 1100

By the last days of March, the decisions taken in the meeting on the 26th among senior American generals—McKiernan, Conway, and

Wallace—had begun to have a salutary effect on the overall situation of V Corps and I MEF. McKiernan and his corps commanders, with Franks participating by video-teleconferencing, had come to grips with the operational, logistical, and strategic problems they confronted. Having advanced almost to the Karbala Gap, 3rd Infantry Division was seriously short of supplies. The marines were in a less difficult position with respect to supplies, but they too were engaged in fire fights with the fedayeen. The strength of Iraqi forces, particularly the Republican Guard, that lay in front of V Corps and I MEF was not yet clear to commanders.

Distressing to all was the reaction of the American media. Words like "stalemate" and "quagmire," along with dire references to Vietnam, were being bandied about by commentators and reporters on the major networks. The talk in the media was that the current pause would have to be extended indefinitely to allow invading forces to clear out the cities and towns along the Euphrates and muster additional reinforcements from outside the theater. Only then could the advance resume. The four generals did not share this pessimism. They believed that the fighting skills of their marines and soldiers would allow U.S. forces simultaneously to clear the cities, protect the lengthening supply lines, and drive into Baghdad successfully without a hiatus. Franks approved the order turning his reserve force—a brigade from the 82nd Airborne—over to V Corps. Paratroopers from the 82nd, along with the air assault troops of the 101st, would assume the task of emptying the pockets of Iraqi resistance at As Samawah and An Najaf, thus freeing up the brigades of the 3rd Infantry Division to battle through the Karbala Gap. The next several days would see an emphasis on redeploying the 3rd Infantry Division to the north and building up its supplies. What Wallace could not yet know was the extent of the damage that air power had already inflicted on the Republican Guard during the *shamal*. The devastation of these attacks would gradually emerge over the coming days and reinforce Wallace's willingness to launch the final confrontations of the war.

Like the 1st Marine Division's commander, General James Mattis, Wallace maintained a forward headquarters close behind his lead units. This headquarters was remarkable for its economy: barely eighty soldiers, three command and control vehicles, and ten other support vehicles. The communications gear and the available bandwidth were sufficient to keep the general in touch with his rear area headquarters as well as with Franks. By positioning himself close to the front, Wallace could monitor the divisional command nets, stay in touch with his front line commanders, and develop a real feel for what was happening on the ground.

To resolve the problem of fedayeen in the cities, Wallace and his subordinates would use their armor to destroy the enemy's heavy equipment, "technicals," and bunker complexes. Light infantry would immediately follow on the heels of the armor to police the dazed and broken remnants of Iraqi resistance. The brigade from the 82nd, despite the relative lightness of its weapons, was particularly well prepared for the fighting to come near As Samawah. Its commander, Major General Chuck Swannack, had been a plebe in Wallace's company at West Point. He had also served as commander of the Joint Readiness Training Center at Fort Polk, Louisiana, where in "Jetertown," a replica of Third World cities, the army trained its soldiers to fight in an urban environment. There was not much the Iraqis could serve up that Swannack had not already inflicted on those who had come through his center. After being given the mission to secure As Samawah, Swannack, half in jest, commented to Wallace, "This is just another Jetertown." Wallace replied, "Yeah, a Jetertown with half a million people!" Working alongside the soldiers of the 82nd and the 101st in clearing out the fedayeen nests along the Euphrates were some small armored task forces of the 3rd Infantry Division.

A *Washington Post* reporter embedded with the forces going into As Samawah described the fighting that finally broke Iraqi resistance on April 4: "The city of Samawah reveals itself in the luminescent glow of tracers fired from an AC-130 gunship flying somewhere overhead. Jagged outlines of palms define the banks of the Euphrates River. Brick perimeters of low buildings appear and then vanish with the fade of the illuminations. The breeze of the city carries diluted hints of burning. Close, the smells are of chewing tobacco and the sour infantrymen who haven't showered in weeks . . . Dressed in full 'battle-rattle'—30-pounds of flak jackets, Kevlar helmets, M-4 carbine rifles, canteens, protective masks—many of these guys know what this place looks like without using the night-vision scopes."[1] In the vicious fights that flared along the Euphrates at the end of March into early April, soldiers like these set the conditions that allowed the 3rd Infantry Division to press on to Baghdad.

On March 30, V Corps began a five-dimensional maneuver to clear its communications and to confuse the Iraqis about the direction from which the actual drive on Baghdad would come. The plan called for the 3rd Infantry Division to make the main attack with 3/7 Cavalry leading two BCTs in a rush directly into the Karbala Gap. Four feints would accompany the main attack. The remaining 3rd Infantry Division would attack toward the Euphrates, capturing the bridges between Al Hillah an Karbala. The 101st would conduct two "demonstrations" from An Najaf to Al Hillah. Elements of the 101st Attack Helicopter Brigade would conduct a daylight armed reconnaissance to the west of Karbala, with the added intention of confusing the Iraqis as to the actual direction of the corps' attack.

With this five-pronged assault, Wallace aimed to suggest to the Iraqis that the Americans were about to drive up Highway 8 to attack Baghdad. If Saddam and his sons swallowed the bait, they would swing the Republican Guard out of its positions facing west and reorient them to the southwest. That move would provide the Coalition with opportunities to wreak havoc from the air. At the same time it would leave Baghdad uncovered and vulnerable to the main thrust by the entire 3rd Infantry Division, which would push through the narrow gap between Karbala and Lake Razzazah.

To the south of V Corps, the marine advance was reinforcing the army's deception efforts. The 1st Marine Division continued to push its 5th and 7th RCTs past Ad Diwaniyah along Highway 1, contributing to the Iraqi misperception that the drive on Baghdad was coming from the south. In fact, the marines were about to swing almost due east along Highway 27, cross the Tigris, and approach Baghdad from the southeast. The Iraqi leadeship took the bait. Thus, one saw a situation where operational maneuver set almost perfect conditions for U.S. forces to fire on their enemy, while at the same time drawing the Iraqi defenders away from the very areas where the actual arms of the pincers would close on the capital city. And as the Iraqis moved their troops, they died.

The fight to protect the supply lines began on March 30 when 200 sorties by Black Hawk and Chinook helicopters from the 101st, flying over 300 miles from their bases inside Kuwait, airlifted two brigade combat teams to surround An Najaf. The city presented General David Petraeus and his commanders with a number of problems. A rock escarpment to the south provided a natural protective shield, which the fedayeen had reinforced with numerous bunkers and concealed fighting positions dug haphazardly under palm trees and beneath protective walls and buildings. Like most of the urban landscape of central Iraq, An Najaf consisted of low flat-roofed buildings made of concrete block. The streets were wide in the newer parts of town and narrow in the older center. The city's key feature was the tomb and surrounding areas of the Golden Dome Mosque of Ali, son-in-law of the Prophet Muhammad, a location particularly sacred to the Shia.

The air assault deposited Petraeus's infantry in a series of landing zones around An Najaf. Three battalions of the 1st BCT, reinforced by an attached battalion of Task Force 1-70 Armor, moved toward the city from the southwest along Highway 8 and and from the southeast toward the Golden Dome Mosque. Elements of the 2nd BCT completed the city's isolation from the north, northeast, and west. Having relatively little armor, Petraeus had to be deliberate in the 101st's clearing actions. One of his primary targets was the Baath headquarters, which took a hit from two 2,000-pound JDAMs. The major clearing operation would be assigned to 1st Brigade, supported by Task Force 1-70's heavy armor, air force and navy precision weaponry, and the division's helicopters—the eyes and ears of the force.

In essence, the helicopters were high-altitude observation posts and precision firepower platforms immediately available to support the infantry on the ground. The helicopters prevented the enemy from escaping, denied the fedayeen any chance of reinforcement, and provided immediate, responsive "standoff" fires. Soldiers maneuvering beneath the Apaches killed Iraqis who exposed themselves in attempts to shoot down helicopters with RPGs and small arms fire, as had occurred in Somalia. The lighter OH-58D Kiowa Warrior scout helicopters, with their smaller size, tighter turning radius, and lethal weaponry, proved particularly effective in cities. With their doors removed for better visibility, the Kiowa Warriors literally hovered over the infantry to draw fire, spot for the grunts, and deliver over-the-shoulder fires directly into buildings. While a portion of the Apache force was also involved in these support operations, others flew on the eastern side of the Euphrates and destroyed over 200 enemy vehicles. By April 1, the fierce intimidation imposed by infantry, tank, artillery, and air power, combined with tactful coercion orchestrated by interpreters and civil affairs soldiers, gave the 101st the upper hand in An Najaf.

A key element in Wallace's five-pronged deception was the "demonstration" conducted south of Al Hillah by the 2nd BCT of the 101st on April 2. As the fighting in An Najaf died down, V Corps ordered Petraeus to clear the fedayeen out of Al Hillah. The 101st aimed to destroy the Republican Guard units that had been pulled south to defend Highway 8 and the southwestern approaches to Baghdad. By pinning the Iraqis down, the 101st would prevent them from transferring forces to meet the main blow that Blount's division was now preparing north of Karbala. This effort would also prevent the Iraqis from reacting to the marines' crossing of the Tigris. The Republican Guard presence in Al Hillah was substantial, since the Iraqis believed the main American thrust would come through this area. In the ensuing fight, the 101st confronted one of the few coherent and cohesive defense efforts by a unit of the Republican Guard—in this case a reinforced battalion from the Hammurabi Division,

On April 3, Petraeus's 2nd BCT used Black Hawks to launch an assault on an area south of the city. As at An Najaf, JDAMs preceded the advance. The air strikes targeted barracks, Baath Party headquarters, and defensive positions. The Iraqis responded with a respectable barrage directed at tank and infantry formations approaching the city. Immediately, U.S. radars picked up the location of the Hammurabi's artillery, and the Iraqis died in blasts of counter-battery fire. As the 101st troopers worked their way into the city, helicopters again provided devastating support from overhead. The demonstration turned vicious, as soldiers fought from tank turrets and from atop Bradleys and alongside infantrymen clearing bunkers and trenches. During a week's fighting, air strikes by attack helicopters and fighter bombers pulverized Iraqi positions in a city consisting largely of Shiites. By the end of the battle, the 101st had fired off 114 ATACMS, 3,000 artillery rounds, and 1,000 Hellfire missiles. Air force and navy fighters provided an additional 135 close air support sorties, each one of which was capable of dropping several precision-guided bombs on targets marked by forces on the ground.

While a portion of the 101st was drawn into heavy fighting in Karbala, Petraeus's 2nd BCT continued its long, drawn-out struggle with the fedayeen in Al Hillah. On April 8, the fighting was particularly severe. Petraeus the scholar had only a few moments to reflect on the fact that the battle being waged by his twenty-first-century force against a twentieth-century opponent was being fought within sight of the Temple of Nebuchadnezzar, built in the sixth century BC. The ferocity of the Iraqi defenders forced Petraeus to commit his 3rd BCT to finish the job in the center of the city. The 101st was engaged in struggling through a series of berms, RPG ambushes, and bunkers established by regular troops. This was one of the few cases in the war where the Iraqis gave any indication of having thought through some of the implications of what U.S. air power could do to their defensive schemes. They rarely presented a massed target; they were careful to move only when necessary; and they hid from aerial observation, including sensors and aerial platforms. But in the end, all of this did them no good. By April 10, the 101st had cleared out the entire city.

In their close support missions as well as their interdiction attacks in the areas around Al Hillah, the helicopters of the 101st had proven their worth. Just in the number of enemy vehicles destroyed, the Apache and Kiowa helicopters had achieved impressive scores: 256 air defense sites and vehicles, 110 artillery rockets and guns, 287 tanks and other armored fighting vehicles, 800 other vehicles, and innumerable enemy bunkers and defensive positions.

CROSSING THE KARBALA GAP AND CAPTURING THE AIRPORT

I don't want to say that we're surrounded—but we're being fired at from all sides!

Unidentified sergeant in A troop
fighting at Saddam International Airport, April 3, 2003

Over the course of March 29 and 30, the 3rd BCT—relieved from the fight around As Samawah by the brigade from the 82nd—rejoined the 3rd Infantry Division north of An Najaf. It would now become the spearhead for the advance on Baghdad. With information from prisoner of war reports, captured documents, and the detailed surveillance by JSTARS and UAVs, commanders knew that U.S. aircraft had already ravaged Republican Guard units defending the capital. As a consequence of those attacks, neither intelligence officers nor ground commanders could discern the intention of the Iraqi high command from the broken fragments of troops they were encountering. But the Iraqi high command, such as it was, probably had no clearer picture of where its units were or what they were trying to do than the Americans did. It appears that Uday and Qusay were attempting to run the war from Baghdad; but with military experience that did not extend beyond torturing the defenseless, they proved as inept as their father at orchestrating a campaign.

Luckily for the 3rd Infantry Division, the Iraqis focused so much attention on the 101st's efforts along the Euphrates and the marine advance beyond Ad Diwaniyah that they never appreciated the 3rd Infantry Division's concentration of forces for a push through the Karbala Gap. Virtually every American army officer knew about the gap from war games and exercises at places as far afield as Fort Hood, Texas, and Grafenwöhr, Germany, because the city of Karbala represented the gateway to Baghdad. The area around the Euphrates where the division planned to cross the river was a nightmare of bogs and obstacles, all made more forbidding by the competent work of Iraqi military engineers. Immediately to the north of Karbala lay a huge reservoir. If the Iraqis managed to blow up the Hadithah Dam, the resulting flood would make an armored advance impossible. Even if they left the reservoir intact, the Iraqis would try to demolish the Karbala bridges.

Thus, several critical tasks confronted Wallace and Blount if 3rd Infantry Division were to cross the gap successfully. The first had to do with the terrain. The Hadithah Dam had to be captured. The original plan called for army rangers to secure the dam before moving on. That changed when Franks ordered the dam held until instructed otherwise. This resulted in a two-week battle, in which the rangers fended off determined Iraqi attacks and endured heavy shelling. They were eventually relieved by the 101st Airborne. The second critical task for the 3rd Infantry Division was to seize a river crossing point and move brigade combat teams through the gap so quickly the Iraqis would have no opportunity to use chemical weapons. If Saddam were going to launch WMD, this was the place he would do it: American troops were concentrated and the gap was far enough distant from Baghdad to avoid collateral damage.

The steep banks and marshy ground along the Euphrates made the mission of capturing the bridges at Karbala difficult. The 1st and 2nd BCTs attacked on the afternoon of April 1. Division artillery targeted areas where Iraqi artillery might be hidden. By late afternoon the 2nd BCT reported that its lead units were within fifty yards of the bridge at Al Hindiyah but that enemy forces were resisting fiercely. This was the first time Blount's soldiers had run into Republican Guard units, and the enemy was displaying not only ferocity but some tactical skills as well, in sharp contrast with the fedayeen. But the Republican

Guard shared the fedayeen's callousness toward their own citizens. In one case, as a woman who had been used as a human shield attempted to escape across the bridge, a Republican Guard shot her. By throwing smoke grenades on the bridge to shield her from view, American soldiers managed a dramatic rescue.

The fight for Karbala and control of the river banks continued throughout the first two days of April and eventually consumed virtually all of the division's firepower. Apaches from the 4th BCT preceded the ground units through the gap to assess conditions on the road to Baghdad. Early on April 1, the 3rd BCT, attacking with two armored battalions, seized control of the eastern side of the city. The 1st BCT struck from the opposite direction to encircle Karbala from the west. Its mission was to capture the bridges and dams; once in control of them, the division would have a clear run at Baghdad. The fighting north of Karbala was particularly tough. The marshy terrain was ill-suited for armor, and only a few paved roads were capable of supporting tanks.

By the morning of April 2, the resistance on the far bank had subsided sufficiently to risk a crossing north of the city. Blount hoped that the speed of his movement and the violence of his assault on Karbala had disrupted the enemy sufficiently that his troops could seize at least one bridge. The presence of special forces in the Karbala area added to the enemy's confusion, while providing key information about the condition of the bridges. Meanwhile, helicopters circling overhead forced the Iraqis to keep their heads down. Despite these advantages, the crossing was risky. Late on the afternoon of April 2, Lieutenant Colonel J. R. Sanderson, commander of Task Force 3-69 Armor, received word that one of his platoons had managed to get three tanks across a bridge the Iraqis had wired for demolition.

After the American tanks arrived on the east bank, the Iraqi engineers regained sufficient composure to detonate their charges under the bridge. The huge structure shuddered but, like the Ludendorff Bridge at Remagen in 1945, it did not collapse. Combat engineers from the division's 10th Engineer Battalion immediately plunged their rubber boats into the stream to cut the wires leading to the remaining explosives, while other teams destroyed the bunkers from which the Iraqis might blow the charges. After a quick survey of the structure, engineers reported that, though damaged, the bridge could still bear the weight of heavy vehicles. Within an hour Task Force 3-69 Armor had pushed three companies of Bradleys and Abrams across the Euphrates. Nevertheless, Blount ordered his engineers to construct a medium-girder bridge across the damaged span and begin construction of a pontoon float bridge just to the north. Back at his headquarters, Wallace was elated. As he recounted after the war: "At that point, I was pretty confident that we had Saddam by the balls . . . I knew we were essentially home free."[2]

Blount had not expected the move through the Karbala Gap to go so quickly. He knew that once over the Euphrates, the route to Baghdad was clear. Immediately, he saw the opportunity to press the attack against the Medina Division and close on the capital. As the soldiers advanced, they passed unimaginable scenes of carnage inflicted by their air force brethren on the Iraqis. A sergeant who had served in the Gulf War said, "I hope we won't experience anything like that again . . . When I see that many bodies, I just don't want to be here anymore."[3]

After hasty consultation with Wallace, Blount ordered his cavalry to push toward the western outskirts of the capital, with A Troop—a company-sized unit now consisting of twenty fighting vehicles—leading the way. It became the first American ground unit to threaten the city. Late on the afternoon of April 3, A Troop arranged its Abrams and Bradleys in a perimeter around two intersections just west of Baghdad's international airport. For the next twenty-four hours the troop fought on alone—one of the most remarkable actions of the campaign. Unknown to the soldiers, what was left of the Iraqi high command considered the appearance of American troops at these two intersections to be a critical, if not fatal, breach of Baghdad's defenses. They set about throwing many of the capital's fedayeen defenders at A troop's position. Throughout the afternoon and evening of April 3, the attacks came in waves from north, east, and west. The fedayeen were mounted on any transportation available: motorcycles, cars, trucks, buses, even dump trucks. At times the enemy attempted to rush the American positions on foot, with RPGs and AK-47s. The soldiers of A Troop called in artillery and mortar fire to kill enemy soldiers hiding in buildings and behind overpasses and abutments. By early morning the bodies of nearly 500 fedayeen littered the ground in front of American positions.

The most critical moment in the fight came in the early morning hours of April 4, when two Bradleys and two Abrams protecting the Abu Ghraib Expressway were rushed by large numbers of Republican Guard vehicles. In less than five minutes the four American vehicles destroyed twelve enemy tanks. The Bradleys wrecked five T-72s by engaging them with their 25mm chain guns. Late in the afternoon seven tanks and two Bradleys pushed out from the expressway's perimeter to attack twenty-two T-72s reported by overhead aircraft to be hiding behind one of the underpasses. For nearly an hour, fighter bombers plastered the area, but as the Abrams pushed forward they discovered that the strikes had destroyed only six of the Iraqi tanks. A fierce fire fight then broke out between the two groups of opposing tanks at the relatively short range of 800 to 1,300 meters—a range at which no competent tank gunner should miss. The Iraqis failed to hit anything; within ten minutes the Abrams had destroyed the remaining sixteen T-72s.

Encouraged by the success of his cavalry squadron, Blount believed that enemy defenses around Baghdad—such as existed—were on the point of collapse. The air and ground attacks in early April had rendered ineffective most of the Republican Guard units ringing the city. Intelligence estimated that the enemy now possessed only two Republican Guard brigades and approximately 15,000 fedayeen defenders. To accelerate the process of collapse, Blount ordered 3rd BCT to join up with the cavalry in completing a loose cordon around the outskirts of the city in the west. Once the cordon was in place, Blount ordered the capture of Saddam International Airport, the last major symbolic and military obstacle remaining before storming Baghdad.

Again the cavalry formed the tip of the spear, as 4th BCT pushed along Highway 1, approaching the airport from the south. By evening on April 4, the brigade was moving cautiously over the tarmac, searching for signs of enemy armor. Resistance came primarily from infantry attempting to rush the armored columns. By early morning the 1st BCT and the cavalry had secured the runways and the international terminal.

Iraqi forces were able to counterattack only after the 3rd Infantry Division had gained firm control of the airport. The same troopers who had won the fight at the Abu Ghraib Expressway found themselves again in a ferocious battle against enemy armor on the airport's outskirts. They destroyed twelve T-72s, two T-55s, and six other armored vehicles. By April 5, with the airport securely in American hands, the division caught its collective breath only long enough to cast an eager eye toward the administrative and political heart of Saddam's crumbling empire, the so-called regime district.

The question at hand was how to proceed with the risky business of taking Baghdad. Some advised caution, because of the dangers associated with urban combat. But to Franks and McKiernan, the campaign thus far had consistently rewarded audacity. They believed the Iraqis were incapable of dealing with an enemy who moved faster than their centralized regime could recognize or react. McKiernan ordered his V Corps subordinates to begin the "thunder runs."

THUNDER RUNS

I watched Ronny Johnson and the convoy roar pass us . . . It was an incredible sight! Drivers and tank commanders were firing as fast as they could, and they were *flying!* They must have been going fifty miles per hour when they passed me. I just cheered them on.

LIEUTENANT COLONEL STEVEN TWITTY, April 7, 2003

"Thunder run" was the nickname for the group forays that young soldiers launched into German and Korean bar districts on pay day. Blount's version of thunder run would be more threatening. His armor would conduct a sortie through Baghdad's center that traveled along a semicircular arc beginning in the southwest, momentarily brushing the west bank of the Tigris, then thrusting through the regime district's ministries, parks, and palaces, before exiting the city and rejoining the division at the newly renamed Baghdad International Airport.

Colonel Dave Perkins's 2nd BCT would conduct the first foray. Intelligence reported that after the Iraqis had failed to defend the airport, they had set up a series of roadblocks and other obstacles on the major routes leading into the city. Those regular army units still willing to fight had pushed armored vehicles back into perpendicular side streets. From such positions they could fire at the vulnerable side armor of American tanks as they drove by. Preceding Perkins's advance, the division's artillery launched a series of MLRS strikes at these enemy concentrations.

At first light on April 5, Task Force 1-64 Armor moved out. The

Iraqi forces were, as usual, surprised that the Americans could act so quickly. Early in the advance, the leading U.S. vehicles passed by enemy soldiers lounging about, some eating their breakfast with their weapons stacked nearby. Ten minutes down the road, the fedayeen had rallied sufficiently to inundate the rapidly moving armored force with dense, though ill-aimed, fire. Some attempted to run from buildings to their fighting positions. Others grabbed machine guns and RPGs and, without direction or logic, rushed the column, firing wildly until destroyed by tank or Bradley fire. The Iraqis turned out in hundreds, literally lining the route, seemingly waiting their turn to die as martyrs. The Americans obliged. Fighting became particularly surreal as the column approached the center of Baghdad: women and children stood along the streets or on rooftops, taking in the carnage before them with the seemingly casual interest of fans watching a soccer match on television. Equally surreal, General Wallace watched Perkins's attack first-hand on a Hunter UAV downlink piped into his command center. He remarked later that the experience reminded him of live-action television images of bank shoot-outs and car chases.

Overhead, A-10s provided close air support. Swooping down to rooftop level, the Warthogs continually strafed enemy positions or vehicles hidden in back streets. Attack helicopters added to the mayhem below. Once the armored column entered the city, the Iraqis scored a lucky hit with an RPG and damaged one Abrams. Seeing the tank on fire, the company commander ordered other tanks to form a protective shield around the stricken vehicle. Three of the four crew members immediately jumped off, but the driver remained buttoned up in his compartment as the 120mm tank rounds burned themselves up in a ferocious fire. When the flames were under control, the overhanging turret that had blocked the driver's hatch was moved, and the driver crawled out, somewhat shaken but unhurt. The crew caught a ride home on another vehicle after stripping their tank of everything the

Iraqis might find useful. Later that day an air force A-10 destroyed what remained of the damaged tank.

By early afternoon the first thunder run was over. Enemy fire had scarred virtually every vehicle in Task Force 1-64. Many had received multiple RPG hits. But except for the one Abrams that had caught fire, all the vehicles would be combat ready once they had been re-armed and refueled and minor damage repaired. The legendary toughness of the Abrams and the value of heavy armor had been proven once again, as in Kuwait twelve years before. Equally important was the demonstration that the Americans could drive an armored column through the middle of Saddam's capital city without suffering any casualties. They seemed to have nothing to fear from the regime's ragtag fedayeen and lackluster soldiers.

Curiously, one of the most intense engagements of the campaign was not in the center of Baghdad but over the northern exit routes. Called Objective Titans, this site consisted of a series of road intersections located along Highway 1. In retrospect, it is not surprising that the fight for Titans was intense. By April 6, the ruling elite wanted out of Baghdad. Highway 1 to the north was the only remaining route out of the capital and possible escape to Syria. The 3rd BCT was ordered to close it. The result was a ten-hour gun battle during which American soldiers fought off individuals and small teams as well as large convoys seeking to escape. A fight between the 7th Cavalry and a Republican Guard tank unit for the only bridge still unsecured left eight enemy tanks destroyed. By evening Iraqi leaders learned that the last exit from Baghdad had closed, and attacks against the 3rd BCT dropped to a trickle.

On the evening of April 6, Colonel Perkins knew intuitively that the culminating point in the campaign was close, but it still remained frustratingly out of reach. It seemed that the enemy just refused to acknowledge that the battle was over. While U.S. tanks rumbled by in the distance, the Iraqi information minister—"Baghdad Bob" to some, "Comical Ali" to others—was still proclaiming to the international press that the Americans had suffered defeat with massive casualties. Perkins passed on to Blount his thought that the surest way to dismantle the regime's propaganda machine would be to drive into Baghdad's center and stay there. Blount agreed. He was now convinced that the fight had gone out of the Iraqis in Baghdad. The time had come to conduct another thunder run, but this time the army would remain in the city. During a brief teleconference, Blount, Wallace, McKiernan, and Franks scheduled the attack for the next day. Perkins's unit got the go-ahead for a second, decisive thunder run. Ironically, though, as it turned out, the decisive event would not be the 2nd BCT's occupation of the presidential palace and its parks but rather the fight along three obscure overpasses into the city's center, positions the soldiers derisively nicknamed Curly, Larry, and Moe.

The morning of April 7 started badly. Perkins's mobile command post suffered a fluke hit from one of Saddam's surface-to-surface missiles. The rocket destroyed a dozen vehicles. Five soldiers lay dead, with several dozen wounded, many severely. One of them, the brigade sergeant major, rushed from his damaged track, burned flesh hanging from his arm. He frantically searched for his driver, who had been standing in the path of the explosion. In spite of wounds, shock, and destroyed vehicles and equipment, those who remained in the command post took only an hour to reestablish contact with units moving forward and thus regain control of the operation. The soldiers' instinct, training, and leadership gave them the upper hand.

Perkins's plan was to push rapidly into the center of Baghdad with two heavily armored task forces consisting of seventy Abrams and sixty Bradleys. Task Force 1-64 led the charge. After only a few moments the lead tanks found themselves engaged in a running gun battle with fedayeen and other irregulars, just as they had during the first thunder run. This time, the enemy fought more intelligently and with greater determination. Obviously, the Coalition's first drive-by shooting of downtown Baghdad had taught the Iraqis a few lessons. They had spent the next two days improvising obstacles and ambushes. Tanks from Task Force 1-64 fought their way through roadblocks created from overturned semitrailers, bulldozers, and other construction equipment, as well as an odd assortment of buses, trucks, and damaged military vehicles. Wallace sat in his command post and, through his blue force-tracker screen, watched Perkins's electronic icons roll into Baghdad. He saw Perkins and his tanks clear the second intermediate underpass and pause. The road ahead was clear. Without asking permission, he gunned his tanks and headed toward the city center. "Looks like Perkins is going downtown," Wallace radioed Blount.

The fast-moving convoy needed approximately an hour to reach the regime district. There, the commander of Task Force 1-64 met a special ops team that had infiltrated the area almost two weeks earlier. The team leader briefed the colonel on the large number of fedayeen in the city center who were prepared to launch human-wave assaults. Perkins radioed to Blount that downtown, with its open boulevards and parks, offered excellent defensive terrain. He requested permission to stay. Without hesitation, Blount agreed, but only if resupply convoys could reach Perkins before dark. Both task forces immediately fanned out to form a perimeter around the convention center and the Al Rasheed Hotel. Just as predicted, large numbers of fedayeen began to mass under an overpass to the north. Tanks and Bradleys opened fire, killing hundreds. Those who hid in buildings or in defilade positions were hit by American mortar fire and eventually—after much discussion with pilots in the air—by JDAMs delivered directly into the city center.

Task Force 4-64 drew the mission of securing the two palaces near the sharp bend in the Tigris that bounded the cluster of structures belonging exclusively to Saddam and his sons. Irregulars on foot and in the usual assortment of bizarre vehicles attacked the task force from the bridge that crossed the southern bend in the river. Again, cannon and machine gun fire killed hundreds of fedayeen. By nightfall the 3rd Infantry Division controlled Saddam's lair. Blount and Perkins were certain the task force could hold the city center in relative safety through the night and into the next day, if it could be resupplied. But resupply had become a problem. After two weeks of focusing on the tip of the spear, the Iraqis had belatedly changed their tactics to attack the lines of supply along Highway 8 that supported the forward task force.

Responsibility for protecting the lifeline into Baghdad belonged to infantry-heavy Task Force 3-15, commanded by Lieutenant Colonel Steven Twitty. Only the day before, April 6, Twitty's battalion had taken part in a fight for the Euphrates crossing at Objective Peaches. He was still collecting his remaining vehicles when Perkins assigned him the mission to support the attack into Baghdad. Late into the night, Twitty's soldiers worked frantically to refuel and rearm their vehicles. The battle began at first light.

Twitty planned to protect the brigade's supply line by establishing three defensive strongpoints, each surrounding a vulnerable underpass where the enemy would most likely choose to ambush convoys. Two of these strongpoints, Larry and Moe, separated by approximately a mile, would each be defended by companies of Abrams and Bradleys from his battalion. The defense of the third strongpoint, Curly—located approximately two miles from Larry—fell to an ad hoc collection of disparate units created specially for the mission and commanded by Captain Zan Hornbuckle, a staff officer in the battalion. Hornbuckle's defensive force consisted of one platoon of four Bradleys, a platoon of mortars mounted in M-113 armored personnel carriers, and an engineer platoon with two armored earthmovers and four

M-113 armored personnel carriers. What should have been a company of strangers fought together as a band of brothers—perhaps because they all knew and trusted Hornbuckle as the most experienced and mature of the battalion's captains.

The Iraqis engaged all three teams from the moment they crossed into Baghdad. After reaching their respective underpasses, the three teams deployed in roughly circular perimeters, with guns pointing outward. Within minutes the fedayeen were too close for A-10s overhead to attack them. Twitty's soldiers would have to fight this battle with the ammunition and weapons they carried in. The team at Curly took the brunt of the attacks. The enemy was far more skilled than any encountered at An Najaf and As Samawah. Hornbuckle was later to learn that most of the attacking fedayeen were not Iraqis but Syrian jihadists who had made the trip to Baghdad specifically to kill Americans; out of the thirty POWs captured on Curly, twenty-eight were Syrians. As for what the locals thought about their Arab "brothers": when the battle was over, all the dead Iraqis were buried, but the Syrians were left to rot—a gesture of contempt for fellow Muslims.

The enemy had dug a series of trenches and foxholes around the Curly cloverleaf. All through the day they charged furiously at Hornbuckle's line of vehicles. As soon as his soldiers killed one wave, another would appear. The fedayeen attacked on foot and in commandeered taxis, cars, and pickup trucks mounted with machine guns on pedestals. The Syrians displayed some degree of tactical proficiency, firing RPGs in two- or three-round volleys, often lobbing the rockets from long range to fall in the midst of the Americans. They employed artillery and mortars in two- or three-round volleys as well. Fortunately, the fedayeen had no time to adjust their fire, but the shelling was continuous and dangerous nevertheless.

The enemy were too numerous and suicidal to be handled by infantry alone. Soon every soldier, regardless of occupational specialty, became an infantryman, firing frantically from their tracks at the tenacious and ubiquitous enemy. Mortar crews at all three overpasses lobbed rounds at one moment and mounted their heavy machine guns at another to shoot down the attacking fedayeen. Robert Gallagher, the battalion sergeant major, fought on Curly. The embedded media had tagged him "Black Hawk Bob" because he had been seriously wounded in Mogadishu in 1993. He was out of luck again at Curly. Shot in the leg, he wrapped his wound with a bandage and then, standing on one leg and leaning against his Bradley for support, he continued to fire his M-4 carbine at the enemy. Convinced they were about to die, Hornbuckle's medics armed themselves and the wounded as well to take out as many of the enemy as possible before they were overrun. Even the chaplain picked up a rifle for what he thought would be the destruction of strongpoint Curly.

When queried by Twitty during the fray, Hornbuckle was reluctant to ask for reinforcements. But Gallagher was not at all reticent. "We need help and we need it now!" he barked at the battalion commander. Help came in the form of Twitty's B Company commanded by Captain Ronny Johnson, who had only minutes to scrape together every fighting vehicle he could find. B Company roared northeast at speeds over fifty miles per hour. With hatches open, every soldier in the column fired continuously from every hatch and gun port. Tucked into the convoy were twenty resupply trucks. Fuel- and ammunition-section soldiers stood erect in their gun ring mounts and fired continuously as they careened through charred, twisted vehicles, mines, and other obstacles on the way to Curly.

Like a scene from a western movie, the cavalry in the form of B Company roared into the middle of Hornbuckle's defenses and immediately joined the fight. Under intense fire, soldiers rushed to the supply trucks to grab armfuls of machine gun and mortar ammunition. The enemy quickly recognized the vulnerability of these vehicles and

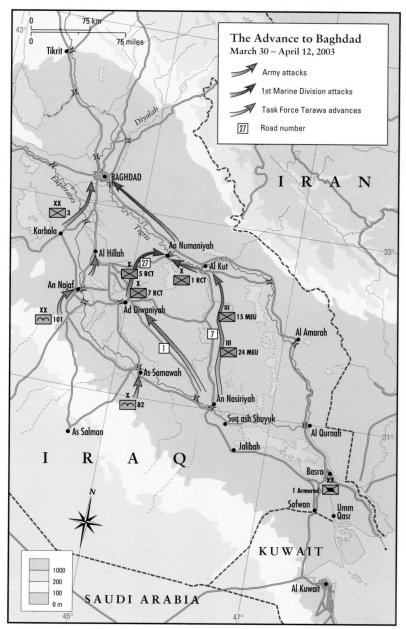

The Advance to Baghdad
March 30 – April 12, 2003

Army attacks

1st Marine Division attacks

Task Force Tarawa advances

27 Road number

Cartographica Ltd

Top: The 3rd Infantry Division opens the gate to Baghdad by capturing the bridge over the Euphrates at Al Hindiyah on March 31. An enemy vehicle burns on the bridge after being destroyed by the Bradleys of Task Force 4-64 Armor. Bottom: A "human shield" who was shot while attempting to escape her Iraqi captors is rescued by American infantry at the Al Hindiyah Bridge.

Top: Soldiers of the 3rd Battalion, 187th Infantry, the Rakkasans, join in the effort to secure Saddam International Airport (soon to be renamed) on April 6. Bottom: On April 7, Bradleys of Colonel Dave Perkins's 2nd Brigade Combat Team charge along the banks of the Tigris River, in the second "thunder run"—this time into the heart of Saddam's so-called regime district in downtown Baghdad.

US Army

US Army

Top: At Objective Curly, fear and determination grip the soldiers of Task Force 3-15 Infantry as they fight desperately to kill their fedayeen attackers before the fedayeen kill them. Bottom: The battle at Curly becomes more intense as soldiers push back a series of assaults.

The tensions of close combat are etched on the face of Captain Zan Hornbuckle, commander of the defense at Curly.

US Army

Right: Sergeant Major Robert Gallagher, nicknamed "Black Hawk Bob" because he was wounded in Somalia in 1993, is again wounded at Curly while fighting to defend the overpass. Below: A U.S. soldier searching for live enemy inspects a dead Syrian fedayeen.

US Army

US Army

Top: A squad of 3rd Infantry Division soldiers clears a house in Baghdad after coming under fire. Bottom: Soviet-built T-72 tanks were death traps. A single round fired from an Abrams could turn the Iraqi tank into a funeral pyre.

A Bradley from the 3rd Infantry Division drives under the massive arch of swords at Saddam's military parade ground.

Top: Marine artillerymen from 3rd Battalion, 11th Regiment, fire at Iraqi positions near Ad Diwaniyah on April 1. Most of the 5th and 7th Regimental Combat Teams had already started to move along Highway 27 toward An Numaniyah. Bottom: Brigadier General Rich Natonski, commander of Task Force Tarawa, inspects a hospital in An Nasiriyah on April 2. Restoring civilian facilities in Coalition-occupied cities and towns was already a major concern.

USMC/Erik S. Hansen

AP Photo/Laura Rauch

Top: Scouts cover the movement of their fellow marines from 3rd Battalion, 4th Regiment, outside An Numaniyah, as Cobra helicopters fly overhead. Bottom: Marines from 3rd Battalion, 7th Regiment, secure an Iraqi training facility near An Numaniyah on April 2.

Top: Marine amtracks from the 7th Regimental Combat Team cross the Tigris at An Numaniyah on April 3, passing by smashed Iraqi equipment. Bottom: Marines from 3rd Battalion, 4th Regiment, fire mortar shells in the neighborhood of Al Kut on April 3. Most of the 1st Regimental Combat Team had already turned toward An Numaniyah to meet up with the rest of the 1st Marine Division on the banks of the Tigris.

Top: Marines from 3rd Battalion, 4th Regiment, carry the body of a fallen comrade. Fighting on April 7 enabled the 1st Marine Division to move up the Diyalah River. Bottom: Marines, with the support of army engineers attached to the 1st Marine Division, build a bridge across the Diyalah in an eastern suburb of Baghdad.

Top: Marines clear a Republican Guard training camp on the way to Baghdad. Right: On April 8, a weary Major General James Mattis, standing outside the city, answers the questions of correspondents.

Top: Marines advance into Baghdad early on April 9, as a statue of Saddam Hussein appears to greet them. In the afternoon, that statue would be pulled down by cheering Iraqis, with help from marines. Bottom: India Company, 3rd Battalion, 7th Regiment, engages in heavy fighting with the last of the fedayeen on April 9.

Top: An Iraqi woman weeps as she passes the wreckage on her Baghdad street. Bottom: Locals set a bonfire at the base of a bust of Saddam Hussein, dressed in medieval armor.

On April 22, Shiites pray at Imam Hussein's shrine in Karbala for the first time in decades.

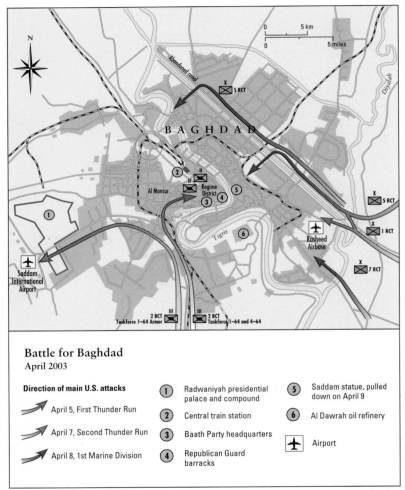

Battle for Baghdad
April 2003

Direction of main U.S. attacks

April 5, First Thunder Run

April 7, Second Thunder Run

April 8, 1st Marine Division

(1) Radwaniyah presidential palace and compound

(2) Central train station

(3) Baath Party headquarters

(4) Republican Guard barracks

(5) Saddam statue, pulled down on April 9

(6) Al Dawrah oil refinery

Airport

Cartographica Ltd

succeeded at setting one on fire with an RPG. In spite of desperate efforts to contain it, the fire spread to four other vehicles. Still, fifteen vehicles with nearly full loads of fuel and ammunition remained.

Meanwhile, heavy fighting had been going on around Moe and Larry. The companies protecting these underpasses had fought off a series of individual and group suicide attacks for over six hours. Many vehicles were stuffed with explosives. At Larry, one determined Iraqi managed to evade the withering fusillade of fire and drive his car directly toward Twitty's command vehicle. Fortunately, only moments before, the engineer with Twitty's convoy had used his earthmover to construct a berm in front of the command post. The Iraqi managed to get within a few yards of Twitty's position before hitting the berm at high speed. The driver ejected from the vehicle to land in a lifeless lump at the feet of Twitty and his soldiers. A few rounds from a Bradley aimed at the wrecked automobile caused an enormous explosion that rocked nearly every vehicle in the vicinity.

The fighting on Moe followed a similar pattern. Under constant threat from all directions but particularly from the north, the commander organized a spoiling attack aimed directly at the strongest Iraqi elements coming from the city center. His move caught the enemy by surprise and caused the Iraqis to fall back before the armored phalanx driving straight at them. Again the engineers on Moe proved their worth by cutting down light poles and bulldozing berms to stop suicide vehicles from approaching the strongpoint. After six hours of fighting, the team at Moe had destroyed over sixty vehicles and killed hundreds of fedayeen.

By late afternoon the other two strongpoints were running short of ammunition. Meanwhile, the two task forces in the city center were facing the prospect of not having enough fuel to return to the brigade's base. Perkins ordered his gas-guzzling tanks to shut down for two hours, while only the more fuel-efficient Bradleys remained in action. Both Perkins and Blount knew that the success of the operation rested on the ability of the task forces in the city to be refueled and resupplied. If the fifteen supply trucks on Curly could reach Perkins, the task forces could hold. If they failed, thunder run would terminate, and the enemy would gain confidence in his ability to turn the Americans back.

The man on the spot was, again, Captain Ronny Johnson. Blount ordered him to run his soft-skinned vehicles through the Iraqi gauntlet into the heart of Baghdad. Hornbuckle's team would add additional force as Johnson's escort. Blount ordered Lieutenant Scott Rudder's Task Force 2-7 Infantry from the 1st BCT to rush north and relieve Hornbuckle at Curly. Thus, Blount cast the die in favor of audacity. Instead of retreating, two more units would make the run into Baghdad just as night was falling.

Johnson's race started as his two dozen armored vehicles and fifteen heavily laden trucks roared up Highway 8. Drivers and tank commanders fired left and right as fast as they could load, aim, and fire. Twitty was standing in his command post at Larry as Johnson drove by and saw him halt only long enough to resupply the forces at Moe before continuing north to the center of Baghdad. Not for the first time, the Iraqis were caught completely flat-footed by the American soldiers' boldness.

The successful occupation of downtown Baghdad over the night of April 7–8 essentially broke the back of Iraqi resistance. A few luckless fedayeen, unaware of the capability of American thermal sights, came out after dark to attack the task forces, only to be shot down immediately by vehicles and soldiers they never saw. By morning, sporadic suicide attacks were all that remained of Iraqi resistance. Even civilians who had been in hiding began to emerge to reclaim the dead. The city's long nightmare of terror was over, but the future looked none too bright to a people who had known nothing but tyranny and darkness for thirty-five years.

THE MARINE ADVANCE

Still taking occasional small-arms and mortar fire yet unable to find a single shooter, the marines dismount and clear hamlets, moving house to house . . . Mortar rounds begin to hit extremely close by—when they come within fifty meters, the explosions cause a temporary surge in the surrounding air pressure, which makes the hair on your body feel like it's standing on end, as if you've been zapped with a mild electric jolt. An old woman in black begins screaming and shaking her fists at the marine guarding her. "This brings me back to my repo days," Espera says. "Women are always the fiercest . . . They always come at you screaming."

EVAN WRIGHT, "From Hell to Baghdad," *Rolling Stone,* July 2003

As with V Corps and the 3rd Infantry Division, General Mattis's 1st Marine Division gathered its strength at the end of March for the showdown at Baghdad. The main difference was that the soldiers of the 3rd Infantry Division still had to face a major fight at the Karbala Gap. The 1st Marine Division was already past its primary obstacle, An Nasiriyah, and had moved deep into the central Mesopotamian Valley. If it could cross the Tigris without another pitched battle, it would have a clear run at Baghdad from the east.

That was precisely what Conway, commander of I MEF, and Mattis intended to do. But the Iraqis would have to cooperate. Consequently, marine operations at the end of March aimed at persuading the enemy that the 1st Marine Division's objectives were something else entirely. It would not be clear until the end of the month whether the ruse had worked.

In the meantime, the 3rd Marine Aircraft Wing (MAW) would continue around-the-clock operations to wear down the Baghdad and

Al Nida Republican Guard divisions so they would no longer pose a significant threat to the advance on Baghdad. And Task Force Tarawa, after completing the nasty business of cleaning up the fedayeen in An Nasiriyah, would take on the job of protecting the ever-lengthening supply lines as Mattis pushed on toward the north and northwest.

During this period, marine forces needed less of a pause than their army counterparts. Their ammunition had been used heavily only by Task Force Tarawa at An Nasiriyah. Nevertheless, Lieutenant General McKiernan, as commander of the Combined Forces Land Component, ordered an operational pause from March 28 to 30 for both V Corps and I MEF. Conway later suggested that his marines could have continued their advance, but most of the grunts were delighted at the opportunity to rest and refit. By the end of March the marines had built up enough supplies and sufficiently cleaned up most of the areas around their lines of communications to resume operations against Baghdad.

The pause did not halt combat. Since the marines were in the heart of Iraq—unlike their army comrades, who were largely located in the deserts to the west of the Euphrates—they needed to patrol the rear areas and defend against raids and ambushes. Throughout this period, 5th RCT continuously suffered hit-and-run night attacks from enemy mortars and artillery. As a result, it had to send out patrols into the countryside to hunt fedayeen and Iraqi soldiers along Highway 1. Besides killing Iraqis, the marines ran into one of the quirks of this war: ammunition dumps and supply points scattered in large numbers throughout Iraq, either stored deliberately for fedayeen use or reflecting the regime's insatiable desire to place its weapons of internal control (as in RPGs and machine guns) throughout the countryside.

Ambushes were a fact of life along both Highway 1 and Highway 7. The marines of Bravo Company, 1st Marine Reconnaissance Battalion, moving along Highway 7, ran into one such ambush and might well have died had they been up against trained soldiers. The company's embedded reporter, Evan Wright of *Rolling Stone*, in perhaps the finest war reporting since Michael Herr's *Dispatches* on marines in the Vietnam War, described the situation this way:

> There's a blown-up truck turned sideways at the entrance to the bridge. We stop about twenty meters in front of it. To the left is a stand of eucalyptus trees about five meters from the edge of the road. Behind us there's a large segment of drain pipe. Person drove around the pipes a moment ago, believing it to be a piece of random debris, but now it's becoming clear that the pipe and the ruined truck in front were deliberately placed to channel the vehicle into what is known in military terms as a "kill zone." We are sitting in the middle of an ambush box. Everyone on the Humvee—except me—has figured this out. They remain extremely calm. "Turn the vehicle around," Colbert says softly. The problem is the rest of the convoy has continued pushing into the killing zone. All five Humvees in the platoon are bunched together with twenty more pressing from behind.[4]

In the end, the marines sprang the ambush themselves, shooting five Iraqis down out of the trees; the rest ran away. The Humvees backed out of the ambush site, and the ambushed convoy suffered only two wounded, one in the foot and one in the leg. Both men tied tourniquets around their legs and continued firing at the Iraqis. The coolness of the marines under fire as well as the exceptional behavior of their platoon commander, Lieutenant Nathaniel Fick—a Dartmouth graduate and one of the few Ivy Leaguers in the marine corps—prevented the ambush from turning into a disaster.

One of the ambushers, Ahmed Shahada, was wounded and fell into marine hands as a POW. In searching him, the marines discovered a Syrian passport with a date of entry into Iraq of March 23. His place of residence during his visit was listed as the Palestine Hotel, where many international correspondents were staying. The purpose of the visit was described in the entry visa as simply "Jihad." And so with no discernible preparation for his jihad, Ahmed had been wounded for the "Arab cause," whatever that involved. But in so doing he had inflicted virtually no damage on the Americans; his actions only brought more destruction down on innocent Iraqis huddling in their village on the other side of a nameless bridge. Foreign as well as Iraqi fedayeen and their sponsors had probably never heard, much less heeded, George Patton's comment that "untutored courage is useless in the face of educated bullets."[5]

What was it about Iraq that attracted so many volunteers from the rest of the Arab world? Undoubtedly, most were deeply committed to fundamentalist politics and a rejection of Western values. But Saddam also provided inducements in the form of cash and other rewards once the Americans were defeated. The hollowness of these promises and the military weakness of Saddam's regime had not registered in the Arab world beyond Iraq's borders—a region where political dreams rarely coincide with reality.

Marine efforts to secure their rear areas involved constant patrolling and the maintenance of road blocks to monitor and control the movement of vehicles. Inevitably such actions resulted in tragedies. In one case, marines of 3rd Battalion, 1st Marine Regiment, manning a roadblock on Highway 7, ordered two vehicles approaching at high speed to stop. The lead vehicle, a sedan, came to a screeching halt, while the second, a small truck, plowed into the car. A man, a woman, and two small children exited the sedan, as two Iraqi soldiers jumped out of the second vehicle. The soldiers immediately shot and killed the woman; in the ensuing fire fight, the marines killed the two soldiers, but the man and his children were wounded.

THE OPERATIONAL FRAMEWORK

Knowing that to succeed we must have been wise in planning to a large extent, but to a still larger extent must have good fortune—a difficult thing, as we are but men—I wish, when I set sail, to have committed myself as little as possible to fortune, but so far as preparation is concerned to be, in all human probability, safe.

NICIAS, speaking to the Athenian Assembly,
Thucydides, *History of the Peloponnesian War,* fifth century BC

By the end of March the marines had not yet reached Baghdad's outer defenses or—with the exception of the 3rd MAW's strikes at Republican Guard units—come into contact with the main elements of the enemy's ground strength. Nevertheless, there was method in the marines' seeming madness in sending two divergent drives through the Tigris and Euphrates Valley—one along Highway 1 and the other along Highway 7. On the left, the 5th and 7th RCTs, moving on Highway 1, threatened Ad Diwaniyah and in so doing appeared to seize a jumping-off position for a thrust at Baghdad. The 5th and 7th RCTs also seemed to be driving to join up with soldiers pushing from the Euphrates. This convergence of soldiers and marines would focus Iraqi attention on the area and away from the Karbala Gap.

The deception plans of V Corps and I MEF had not originally intended to suggest to the Iraqi high command a combined army-marine drive on Baghdad from the area to the east of the Euphrates. However, that is precisely what the two deception efforts achieved. Each plan was arrived at independently, but together they created the impression that the Americans were planning to attack from well south of the Karbala Gap and west of the Tigris, for a joint advance on the Iraqi capital. The Iraqis reacted by concentrating their forces to the south to meet this emerging threat. In so doing, they created even larger numbers of targets for Coalition air power to destroy before the battle of Baghdad began—a bonus on top of the other dividends that the deception effort paid further north.

The drive of 1st RCT toward Al Kut along Highway 7 suggested that the marines would cross the Tigris at that point and not farther up the river. In fact, Mattis had no intention of getting the 1st RCT tied up in a vicious urban brawl in Al Kut, especially after the marines' sour experiences in An Nasiriyah. The aim of the movement up Highway 7 was to freeze Iraqi military forces around Al Kut, so that the marines could bypass them entirely and cross the Tigris at An Numaniyah. The plan called for the 5th and 7th RCTs to create a gap at An Numaniyah by luring Iraqi reserves to the southwest to meet the apparent threat at Ad Diwaniyah. Information from UAVs and JSTARS would tell ground commanders when the gap opened up, and at that moment the 5th and 7th would dash for the bridges. As soon as they were across the river, the 1st RCT, having shielded Al Kut so that Iraqi troops in the area could play no further role, would move up the right bank of the Tigris and follow its sister formations across the river. If successful, the two pincers, as they closed on An Numaniyah, would also form what the Germans called a *Kesselschlacht*—an encirclement battle. In this case, however, Conway and Mattis expected that Iraqi troops, realizing they were surrounded and cut off from Baghdad, would desert and melt back into their towns and villages.

On March 31, Mattis and his marines struck. The Iraqis had committed themselves to the south, and the 1st RCT appeared to be on the brink of an attack on Al Kut. The bridges at and above An Numaniyah were largely uncovered. The 5th RCT took a right turn off Highway 1 onto Highway 27, the junction located almost directly north of Ad Diwaniyah. Highway 27 heads straight from that point to the bridges at An Numaniyah.

The division's first objective was the Iraqi airbase at Hantush. Seizure of Hantush would enable marine C-130s to bring in critical fuel, supplies, and ammunition needed by Mattis's division and allow the 3rd MAW to base its Cobras and Harriers closer to the ground battle. Within hours of the field's being secured, the MAW's commander, Major General Jim Amos, inspected the runways and judged the airfield satisfactory for C-130 operations. Within twenty-four hours the first resupply aircraft had landed.

The 5th RCT continued its advance. By the next day, after destroying a dug-in company, it captured the bridge over the Saddam Canal, which winds its way from the Tigris at Baghdad all the way down to the Euphrates near An Nasiriyah. On April 2 the 5th RCT reached the Tigris at An Numaniyah and immediately set about capturing the bridge.

It ran into strong resistance, sufficient to destroy one of its Abrams tanks. But there were not nearly enough Iraqis to prevent the marines from seizing the bridge. Many Iraqis fled; with the marines approaching Baghdad, morale even among Republican Guard troops was beginning to crack. As one marine commented: "When they ran, it wasn't for lack of ammo. They've got enough."[6] Almost immediately the regiment's combat engineers were at work establishing a second crossing site to speed the advance on the left bank of the Tigris. By morning of April 3, the marines of the 7th RCT were crossing, and two thirds of Mattis's division was on the opposite bank, ready to make a run at the capital. Moreover, the 1st RCT was beginning to turn away from Al Kut and sprint up to An Numaniyah. A screening force remained in place to prevent the Iraqis from attacking the division's rear.

The marines were forced to use considerable firepower to suppress the fedayeen during the fight for the bridge. Despite the destruction, the local population of An Numaniyah, mostly Shia, were delighted that the fight was going the Americans' way. An embedded reporter noted their reaction:

> At about 9 a.m. [the marines of Baker Company 1st Battalion, 7th Marine Regiment] entered the town of Numaniyah, which had been under marine control since Wednesday. The town at first appeared deserted, its streets abandoned and bombed-out buildings and shuttered vending stalls unoccupied. But as they turned down a main street, the marines were greeted by hundreds, if not thousands, of Iraqi men, women, and children clapping their hands, waving and giving them the thumbs-up sign. One young boy in a baseball cap blew kisses with both hands. Four others jumped up and down as the troops passed . . . "They had told us we would be cheered when we invaded, but we haven't really seen it until today," said Lance Cpl Brian Whelan, 21, of St. Francis, Wisc., an Amtrack driver. "It makes it all seem worthwhile."[7]

Mattis's and Conway's instinct about the cohesion of regular Iraqi military units under difficult circumstances proved to be, as the British say, spot on. Many Iraqi troops, realizing they were encircled and cut off from Baghdad, deserted and quietly melted back into their local villages. A British observer at Centcom who watched the marine operation unfold characterized it as the "most brilliant" military movement of the campaign—"one that should be taught in staff colleges for years to come." There is an old saying, usually attributed to the great German field marshal Helmut Moltke, that "no military plan survives first contact with the enemy." In the case of both the marine

crossing at An Numaniyah and the 3rd Infantry Division's breakthrough of the Karbala Gap, one could say that "the Iraqis did not
survive first contact with the plan."

After the war, Mattis commented on the inclination of the Iraqis to
believe that the marines would fight their way through Al Kut: "The
Iraqis expected us to go all the way to Al Kut—that the 'dumb marines' would fight their way through the worst terrain to Baghdad."
Deprecating his own efforts, he added, "I'm not a great general. I was
just up against other generals who don't know shit."[8] Mattis was being
less than fair to himself. He and Conway had evaluated the enemy
with considerable care and then offered the Iraqis a deception that fit
within their own misconceptions about the psychology of American
fighters. The equivalent in football might be a head fake or a flea-
flicker pass. Once the Iraqis had committed, the game was essentially
over. The 1st Marine Division moved behind the main Iraqi defenses,
and by April 3 5th RCT was moving up Highway 6, which led
straight to Baghdad.

BAGHDAD AND BEYOND

It was like that game, you know, where the critter sticks his head
up from one hole and you try to wack it before it sticks up from
another one . . . There were guys with RPGs on their shoulders
everywhere.

Unidentified marine, quoted in Jim Landers, "Ambush costly
for Marine Battalion," *The Dallas Morning News,* April 9, 2003

The advance on Baghdad ran into a considerable fight, however, near
Al Aziziyah. The 5th RCT's "Narrative Summary" of events reported
that "enemy resistance was significant and fierce fighting continued
for several hours in the town. The enemy order of battle included T-

55s, T-62s, mechanized vehicles, air defense artillery, long-range artillery, and mortars of the Republican Guard. This was the most significant battle against enemy conventional forces during the war. The enemy fought from defensive positions along the highway and defended with two dismounted companies from within the confines of the city."⁹ The drive continued unabated by these outbursts of Iraqi resistance. Ambushes and attacks by small numbers of fedayeen were just a fact of life for marines.

On April 4, 5th RCT ran into several hundred fedayeen from Syria, Jordan, Egypt, and other parts of the Middle East and Africa. The result was wholesale slaughter, but the cost was considerable: two Abrams tanks were destroyed by the attackers, while numerous vehicles sustained damage from RPG fire. The marines killed a senior general from the Republican Guard, a corps commander, by riddling his vehicle with .50 caliber machine gun fire as he and his driver attempted to run one of the U.S. blocking positions. In addition, marine tankers destroyed twelve to fifteen T-72s and T-55s as well as numerous 37mm anti-aircraft guns, which the Iraqis attempted to use against advancing marines.

By April 6, the 5th RCT was scouting the Diyalah River, which runs through the eastern suburbs of the capital city. The marines had arrived at Baghdad's back door—the sections on the left bank of the Tigris that are populated mostly by Shia. Immediately behind the 5th RCT was its sister formation, the 7th RCT. The problem confronting the marines was how to traverse the river, because for once the Iraqis had damaged the bridges sufficiently to prevent heavy armor from crossing. Thus, for the second time in its history (the first being at the Han River during the Korean War), the marine corps confronted the task of conducting a river crossing in the face of substantial enemy defenses—in military terminology, "an opposed river crossing."

By April 7, all three regimental combat teams had assembled near the Diyalah. Mattis's main effort would come early the next morning with the 7th RCT on his left. In that sector, the Iraqis had blown both bridges as well as a footbridge. Meanwhile, 1st RCT would cross on the right, and 5th RCT would follow its sister RCTs. Up front in the fight for the crossing of the bridge closest to the Tigris were ten Abrams tanks of the 3rd Battalion, 4th Marines—part of the 7th RCT. Their job was to provide covering fire for infantry charged with driving the Iraqis back. The marines soon managed to span the damaged footbridge sufficiently to get two infantry companies across.

As the fight unfurled, the 3/4's battalion commander, Lieutenant Colonel Bryan McCoy, with that penchant marines have for saying things that upset reporters, commented: "Lordy, heck of a day. Good kills." McCoy's job, according to the reporter embedded with the battalion,

> was to kill or drive away enough of the forces on the north side of the river to let him move his men and equipment across. He had no doubt that he would succeed. He was sitting in the front seat of his Humvee, with an encrypted radio phone to his ear . . . Two Abrams tanks lumbered past us—vehicles that weigh 67 tons apiece do not move softly—and the earth shook, though not as much as it was shaking on the other side of the river, where American mortars were exploding, 150 yards away. The dark plumes of smoke that created a twilight effect at noon, the broken glass and crumpled metal on the road, the flak-jacketed marines crouching and firing their weapons—it was a day for connoisseurs of close combat, like the colonel.[10]

With a bridgehead across the Diyalah and the support of 3/4's tanks, an army multirole bridging company repaired the 150-yard span. The army's engineers also ferried marine Abrams across the river. Meanwhile, 1st RCT had used some of its amphibious assault vehicles to create a bridgehead just east of an abandoned canal. By now the army engineers had repaired a second bridge across the Diyalah, and with that task complete, the 1st Marine Division's regimental combat teams could flood into the war-torn city.

As the marines rolled slowly toward downtown Baghdad, their army comrades on the western side of the Tigris had already crushed the Iraqi resistance in that area. The landscape through which 7th RCT passed resembled a scene out of Stanley Kubrick's *Full Metal Jacket*. An embedded reporter commented that the neighborhood "fit every Hollywood stereotype of a war zone, complete with bullet-riddled buildings, streets covered in garbage, and the booms of impacting artillery shaking the ground every few minutes."[11]

The 5th RCT, the last to cross the Diyalah, drove all the way through eastern Baghdad and then swung up the Tigris to link with the soldiers of the 3rd Infantry Division. The city was now completely surrounded. Some remnants of fedayeen were still fighting, as Saddam's sons deployed them hither and thither, but the constant pounding from the air and on the ground had wrecked whatever military effectiveness they had once possessed. Their morale was not helped by the air attack on Saddam himself on April 7. It seems to have had an impact similar to what happened in Basra when it was reported that a JDAM had killed Chemical Ali. Saddam, as it turned out, was not dead, but the perception that he was seems to have sped up the regime's deterioration.

In the early morning of April 9, marine commanders considered sending in their equivalent to the 3rd Infantry Division's thunder runs. But by afternoon it was clear that the whole Baath power structure had collapsed. As Conway put it, the plans for the day were "OBE" (overtaken by events). The marines simply rolled into downtown Baghdad, greeted more often than not by huge crowds of cheering Shiites—a reception that was broadcast throughout the Islamic world. Mountains of Iraqi equipment fell into the hands of soldiers and marines. Included were over 100 tanks parked in a tank park and never used. Perhaps some Baath bureaucrat had simply forgotten they existed.

While the 1st Marine Division was closing in on the Tigris and then on Baghdad, Task Force Tarawa had the mundane but thoroughly dangerous job of keeping open the lines of supply on Highways 1 and 7 leading out of An Nasiriyah all the way to Highway 27 and the An Numaniyah bridges. Here, the marines controlled a considerable expanse of built-up areas and farmland between the Tigris and Euphrates. Task Force Tarawa had also inherited the complex civil duties associated with controlling occupied territories. The original core of the task force, the 2nd Marine Regiment, deployed along Highways 1 and 27, while the 15th and 24th MEUs were responsible for Highway 7.

If these duties were not enough, policy makers somewhere in Washington became alarmed at the Iraqi divisions stationed along the border with Iran. These divisions had been in that area long before the war, and a Coalition leaflet campaign had suggested that if they stayed in place, they would not be bombed—a promise not kept when hostilities began, as it turned out. Still, the divisions behaved themselves. Throughout March and into April, as the war continued, however, the icons representing the Iraqi divisions glared from computer screens for all to see, including senior policy makers. And so now, with the war virtually over, Task Force Tarawa was ordered to remove the icons that were so bothersome to someone in Washington. Weary to the bone from weeks of tense fighting, marines rolled across central Iraq to the dismal town of Al Amarah, where the Iraqi corps headquarters was located. There, they discovered that the officers and conscripts they were supposed to dispatch had disappeared—sensibly, the deserters had returned to their towns and villages without a peep. The marines reported their findings to their superiors, the icons went into the appropriate computer trash bin, and policy makers in Washington were happy once again.

In the days after the fall of Baghdad, the marines were called upon to put together another task force to move north and finish off whatever resistance might exist in Saddam's hometown of Tikrit. Task Force Tripoli received the assignment. It consisted of three LAV battalions, reinforced by Abrams tanks and marine air power. For slightly more than a week it moved north and occupied Tikrit, encountering some minor opposition on the way. It also found the American POWs the Iraqis had captured in the ambush of the 507th Maintenance Company, as well as the two Apache pilots downed earlier in the war. For them, the war was over; for many others it would not end.

CONCLUSION

Collateral damage is far easier to bear for those who are responsible for it from afar—from the cockpit of a B-1 bomber, from the command center of a naval destroyer, from the rear positions of artillery crews. These warriors do not see the faces of the mothers and fathers they have killed. They do not see the blood and hear the screams and live with those memories for the rest of their lives. The grunts suffer this . . . The civilians who were killed—a precise number is not and probably never will be available for the toll at Diyala bridge, or in the rest of Iraq—paid the ultimate price. But a price was paid, too, by the men who were responsible for killing them. For these men, this was not a clean war of smart bombs and surgical strikes. It was war as it has always been, war at close range, war as Sherman described it, bloody and cruel.

PETER MAASS, "Good Kills,"
The New York Times Magazine, April 20, 2003

In a campaign that lasted barely three weeks, U.S. and Coalition military forces erased the evil regime of Saddam Hussein—a notable achievement. The operation represented more than just the triumph of superior military technology. Success came from superior military intellect—the tough mental as well as physical leadership of generals like Franks, McKiernan, Wallace, Conway, Moseley, Mattis, Blount, Amos, and Petraeus.

And yet, for all the generals' brilliance, the war was won on the sharp end by the individual marines, soldiers, airmen, and sailors who risked their lives for their country and their friends. And they are the men and women who will have to bear the burden of memories and nightmares, while the rest of their countrymen live in peace and freedom, far from the terrors of the tyrannies under which so much of the world struggles.

7

Military and Political Implications

[These men, the Athenian dead] have blotted out evil with good, and done more service to the commonwealth than they ever did harm in their private lives. No one of these men weakened because he wanted to go on enjoying his wealth; no one put off the awful day in the hope that he might live to escape his poverty and grow rich . . . In the fighting, they thought it more honorable to stand their ground and suffer death than to give in and save their lives. So they fled from the reproaches of men, abiding with life and limb the brunt of battle; and, in a small moment of time, the climax of their lives, a culmination of glory, not of fear, were swept away from us.

PERICLES, funeral oration, quoted in
Thucydides, *History of the Peloponnesian War,* fifth century BC

The tip came late Monday evening on July 21. The young sergeant, an intelligence specialist with the 101st, had spent the day interviewing a string of Iraqis. They had filtered into his command post with bits and pieces of information, most of little consequence. This particular Iraqi, however, seemed different and triggered the sergeant's training and instincts. As the Iraqi's eyes flicked nervously about the room, he whispered that he knew where Saddam's sons were hiding—in plain sight at a distant cousin's house right in the middle of Mosul. The sergeant believed him.

His report set in motion an assault on the building the next day. A company's worth of soldiers surrounded the dwelling at 10 a.m. An Iraqi interpreter, using a bullhorn, ordered the inhabitants to come out. After ten minutes and no response, a small team from Task Force 20, part of the army's elite counterterrorist organization, knocked and entered cautiously. They searched the first floor and found it empty. As they inched up to the second floor, a fusillade of AK-47 fire erupted, and three soldiers fell wounded.

The commander on the scene was Brigadier General Frank Helmick. Like his boss, General Petraeus, he was a lean, athletic infantryman, famous even within the airborne community for his stamina as a runner. On Helmick's orders, the soldiers surrounding the building initiated a "shoot-pause-enter" operation. They sought to escalate the level of violence directed at the inhabitants on the second floor until they either surrendered or died. Helmick began with small arms, followed by Mark 19 automatic grenade launcher and machine gun fire. The fusillade was directed into the structure with great precision to avoid hurting Iraqi citizens huddling for cover next door.

An explosive strike followed in the form of AT-4 antitank rockets, along with machine gun and rocket fire from Kiowa helicopters. At noon, another attempt to enter was met with a return volley. The air force offered the finality of a few JDAMs, but Helmick refused, preferring to capture the brothers alive if possible. Instead, he ordered ten TOW antitank missiles to be fired into the structure. When the noise of that attack subsided, only one Iraqi remained alive to return fire, and he was dispatched with ease. Qusay, Uday, a bodyguard, and Qusay's son were taken from the building, dead.

The assault in Mosul is emblematic of a new phase in the Iraq War. The first was conventional: the superiority of American weapons created a killing machine that the Iraqis could never match. But the ghost of Carl von Clausewitz returned after the fall of Baghdad to teach a timeless lesson: no matter how unmatched opponents may be, wars are always two-sided affairs. The object is to break the will of the other side by striking at his vital center of gravity. Saddam's center was his ruling elite, the Baathist regime that was built ideologically and physically around the unholy trinity of Saddam and his two sons. After the fall of Baghdad, that center was shaken to its foundations, but it did not completely collapse.

Watching the retreat from Mogadishu in 1994, Saddam believed that the American center of gravity was dead soldiers. Spontaneously and with seemingly little direction, the Baathists who survived the Coalition's drive on Baghdad adapted. Failing to win the conventional war, they began an unconventional war focused on dueling civilizations. If they could kill enough Americans in the name of religion and culture, then perhaps they would regain the support of the Iraqi people and others in the Islamic world, and the Americans would become discouraged by the human cost and withdraw.

Technology is useful in unconventional warfare, as the events in Mosul make clear. But machines alone will never be decisive in this new phase of the Iraq War. This will be a struggle for the allegiance of the Iraqi people, who must choose among three conflicting sides: the first represented by the promise of freedom and democracy imposed by an occupying infidel, the second by a return to the tyranny and terror of the old regime, and the third by Islamic fundamentalists. The tools most useful in this new war are low-tech and manpower-intensive. Instead of JSTARS, JDAMs, ATACMS, and Global Hawk, the American command will employ night raids, ambushes, roving patrols mounted and dismounted, as well as reconstruction, civic action, and medical teams. The enemy will be located not by satellites and UAVs but by patient intelligence work, back-alley payoffs, information collected from captured documents, and threats of one-way vacations to Cuba.

The new Centcom commander, General John Abizaid, must match the enemy's ability to adapt with adaptations of his own. Small units trained for urban offensive tactics like those used to kill Saddam's sons are replacing the armored fighting formations of the conventional phase. The hunt no longer focuses on the remnants of the old regime's leadership but on the fedayeen's middle management—the violent, fanatical believers. Success in this new war will not be gauged by how many Republican Guard tanks are destroyed but by the less tangible and quantifiable measurement of people's acceptance of a new Iraqi leadership. Attitudes will be influenced less by demonstrations of fighting strength than by the emotional security that comes from safe streets, employment, electricity, and fresh water. In a sense, this phase reminds us all that the nature of war is immutable. Technology may alter how wars are fought, but it will never change the fact that wars are conducted by human beings for political ends.

THE UNCHANGING NATURE OF WAR

> Those . . . events which happened in the past . . . (human nature being what it is) will at some time or other and in much the same ways, be repeated in the future.
>
> Thucydides, *History of the Peloponnesian War,* fifth century BC

THUCYDIDES, the great historian of war, and Carl von Clausewitz, the great theorist of war, understood that some factors in the conduct of war will never change, no matter how much the political landscape alters and technologies advance. What, then, can history, particularly experience in Iraq, teach the Coalition about war in the twenty-first century?

Surveying twenty-five hundred years of recorded history, Clausewitz used the concept of "general friction" to explain why "everything in war is very simple, but the simplest thing is difficult. The difficulties accumulate and end by producing a kind of friction that is inconceivable unless one has experienced war." General friction "more or less corresponds to the factors that distinguish real war from war on paper"—uncertainty, ambiguity, miscalculations, incompetence, and above all chance.[1] Friction was a fact of life—and death—in Iraq, as it has been in military conflicts since the beginning of recorded time.

U.S. forces brought twenty-first-century technology to the battlefield and achieved "information dominance," but they never escaped the dangerous reality that their enemies were trying to kill them. To quote Clausewitz again: "In the dreadful presence of suffering and danger, emotion can easily overwhelm intellectual conviction, and in this psychological fog it is . . . hard to form clear and complete insights . . . It is the exceptional man [or woman] who keeps his powers of quick decision intact" under the conditions of combat.[2] The dangers of war in Iraq were accompanied by extreme physical exertion and fatigue. A recurring theme in soldiers' and marines' accounts of their experiences was the bone-deep weariness of day-after-day tension during the movement forward to contact the enemy. Fatigue and fear, along with sleep deprivation, hunger, no ability to wash or shave, MREs that provided calories but little more, a fierce and unforgiving climate, an alien landscape, and the terrifying sight of the dead and the wounded inevitably led to miscalculations, mistakes in judgment, and accidents.

In the Iraq War, those in command of Coalition forces had to make decisions of life and death under split-second pressure and an unprecedented barrage of information that was often ambiguous, uncertain, contradictory, or quite often wrong. Added to this information overload were unremitting demands from Washington for answers to difficult, simple, and simple-minded questions. Commanders and their staffs in the Gulf were expected to participate in video-teleconferencing sessions with civilian and military leaders half a world away who were operating on entirely different biorhythms. They also had to feed the insatiable appetite of twenty-four-hour news networks, all seeking up-to-the-minute information. In the midst of those pressures, commanders had to run a war. They had to make strategic decisions around the clock, thinking as much in terms of what was going to happen as what was actually happening.

Commanders today can see and sense the battlefield with extraordinary clarity. But in an information-rich environment, what one needs to know is often buried in a blanket of white noise, and individuals at every level reach limits in what they can absorb and pass along. Many factors of critical importance become inaccessible due to lack of patience or discrimination, no matter what the reach of sensors and the power of computers. Being human, commanders often seize on that fraction of information that agrees with their own preconceptions.

Some futurists claim that new information and computing technologies will allow U.S. military forces to "lift the fog of war."[3] According to this view, a vast array of sensors and computers, tied together, can work symbiotically to see and comprehend the entire battle space and remove ambiguity, uncertainty, contradiction, and error from the military equation. Technology will triumph over the general friction of war, they claim. This view leads to the belief that all the American military needs to do to remain preeminent is to focus on acquiring more sophisticated technology. The arguments in support of technological monism echo down the halls of the Pentagon, precisely because they involve the expenditure of huge sums of money. In some cases, law makers may reduce spending on relatively inexpensive but critical items such as body armor, believing that technology has precluded its use. Such policies, however, rest on a profound ahistoricism that misses the lessons of the past, much less even a reasonable examination of recent events.

Crucial to success in combat is an understanding of one's opponent as he is, rather than as Americans would like him to be. This is intelligence in the largest sense. It does not rest on satellites, UAVs, reconnaissance aircraft, and electronic surveillance. Since the Vietnam War, U.S. intelligence agencies have increasingly depended on such technological means, and the information gathered in this way has been of considerable use, particularly to commanders engaged in combat. But it provides little that is of value in understanding the enemy's intentions, his motivation to fight, and the strength of his will—factors that matter most in war. It is well to talk about destroying the enemy's combat power by 50 percent in order to precipitate his collapse, but those with experience in Vietnam know that in some cases attrition of 90 percent was not sufficient to stop a North Vietnamese unit from fighting as a cohesive, effective force. Iraqi regular units in the north at nearly full strength fought not at all, while some fedeyeen attacked until their strength was nearly zero. At the level of command and control, where political as well as strategic decisions occur, good intelligence gathered by thinking human beings can make the difference in victory or defeat.

In this recent war, many senior leaders expected the opening moves of the Coalition's air and ground offensive to cause Saddam's regime to collapse from within. Thus, for the second straight war against Iraq, the revealed wisdom was that the Baath regime rested on a weak political foundation and that the Iraqi people would quickly rally to their liberators. Nothing could have been further from the truth. The great majority of Iraqis, especially the Kurds and Shiites, despised the Baath, but after witnessing American perfidy in the spring of 1991, few people in Iraq, no matter how much they hated Saddam, were going to act against the Baath until it was clear that Saddam was gone and the Coalition was there to stay. Flawed political intelligence like this had little impact on the conventional phase of the Iraq War. But in Vietnam, political and strategic misjudgments resulted in military disaster. This is a clear warning that applies to the unconventional phase of the war in Iraq. This war is one in which culture and politics matter as much as technology. Political and cultural knowledge require immersion in the languages, history, and contemporary life of a region.

Like it or not, the political context within which wars always occur will demand that the United States—at times not necessarily of its own choosing—commit military forces to achieve its aims. And for political reasons, those forces will not be able to use all of their sophisticated capabilities even against significant targets. Under many such circumstances, a "decisive" military outcome will be difficult to achieve. If Americans wish to gain political results from their military actions in the future, they must pay particular attention to how their low-tech enemies define victory and defeat. That calculus may prove very different from their own. This is already becoming evident in Iraq.

THE CHANGING MILITARY ENVIRONMENT

The owl of history is an evening bird. The past is unknowable; only at the end of the day do some of its outlines dimly emerge. The future cannot be known at all, and the past suggests that change is often radical and unforeseeable rather than incremental and predictable. Yet despite its many ambiguities, historical

experience remains the only available guide both to the present
and to the range of alternatives inherent in the future.

MacGregor Knox, "What History Can Tell Us about
the New Strategic Environment," 1995

For all that appears familiar in this conflict, a number of signposts to
the future have emerged from the fog of the Iraq War.

Interdependence

The inability to perform adequately as a joint force in Grenada
sparked major reforms in the American military that are still reverber-
ating through the force. The Iraq War underlines how much progress
has occurred, despite the continued existence of interservice rivalries.
In recent years, combined arms have expanded from integration of
ground forces—infantry, armor, artillery—to the incorporation of direct and indirect air power. Beginning in Afghanistan and even more
so in Iraq, close air support with precision weapons has brought a new
dimension of lethality to combined arms. In Kosovo, where NATO
did not deploy ground forces, the Serbs were able to keep their army
dispersed and hidden, so that air strikes did little damage against Ser-
bian armor. In the Iraq War, however, the Coalition's speedy advance
forced the Iraqis to react and thus provide ideal targets for precision
air power. At the Karbala Gap, 3/7 Cavalry Squadron maneuvered deliberately to draw out Iraqi armor so that aerial firepower could destroy them.

The degree that the American military has achieved interdependence between ground and air forces was eloquently described by a senior ground commander who confessed that in the heat of battle he
had no idea of the source of the destructive power in front of him. "It
could have been air force, navy, or marine. All I cared about was that
the stuff was killing the enemy." But the fighting in Iraq also suggests

that America's land forces need to tailor and combine the various combat branches at lower levels of organization than is currently the practice. What the United States needs in the future are smaller, leaner, brigade-sized units that can deploy more quickly and fight independently.

Convergence

The end of the Cold War simplified the roles and functions of all the services, and the experience in Iraq suggests that the respective roles of the ground forces are beginning to converge. Neither the air force nor the navy confront an enemy with technologically sophisticated forces at sea or in the air. Consequently, the function of those services is now mostly to project and deliver ground forces to a particular theater and then support those forces with precision killing power. As the army has become more strategically transportable and expeditionary, the marines have begun to employ larger, heavier formations capable of taking on enemy armor. This is not to say that the two services possess similar missions and cultures, but the convergence suggests that they need to work more closely in the future.

Ad Hocery

In the Iraq War, army and marine units set up ad hoc formations on the basis of the tactical context and the demands of combat. Their success suggests that such an approach (in many ways similar to the German *Kampfgruppe* of World War II) needs to be regularized in training and procedures. Light infantry, mechanized infantry, armor, and artillery should all train more regularly together in tactical scenarios that test the adaptability and flexibility of commanders as well as troops. Here the marines have a considerable advantage, because the organization of MEUs brings combined arms to a lower level.

What died on the battlefields of Iraq was the vision, held by many, of a homogenized army—one in which units would largely resemble one another. Instead, the army of the future will require a large kit bag of capabilities that it can deploy and fit together, sometimes in the middle of battle, to meet the many exigencies of this new era in warfare. For example, on the open battlefield, lighter forces equipped with new information systems proved highly effective at engaging and destroying the Iraqis. But speed and information superiority became less decisive when combat occurred at closer range, in the complex urban terrain of Basra and Baghdad. There, older weapons systems such as the Abrams and Bradley, with their advantages in protection, mass, and explosive power, proved to be particularly effective. This traditional machine-age equipment is likely to remain a part of ground forces in the future.

Special Operations

Drawing on the experiences of Afghanistan, the Coalition employed special operations forces to great advantage. Here, the contrast could not be more different from the use of special forces in the Gulf War. In the future, special operations forces will play an increasingly important role in the projection of American military power against the nation's enemies, while the operations of those forces will be ever more closely integrated with those of conventional forces.

Also, the unconventional phase of this war highlights the truism that regular army and marine infantry units are increasingly finding themselves in close combat situations that resemble those of their special operations colleagues. Regular infantry units have much to learn from special forces and should begin soon to adopt many of their techniques for selection, training, and leadership development.

Speed

In war, speed kills, especially if military forces move fast enough to disrupt the enemy's ability to make decisions. Franks and his planners maintained the speed of movement by making the tip of the spear as supple, mobile, and flexible as possible. They had clearly learned the lesson of the Gulf War that a fundamental law of Newtonian physics applies also to military maneuver: one can achieve overwhelming force by substituting velocity for mass. In this campaign, Coalition ground forces moved with such swiftness that virtually every decision the Iraqi high command made was already overtaken by events. Pressure from marine and army commanders at every level to maintain the pace of the offensive ensured that the Iraqis could never recover. The unexpected appearance of Coalition forces far in advance of where the Iraqis expected them to be simply overwhelmed the capacity of the enemy to respond.

Speed of movement resulted from a willingness to adapt to the actual conditions of the battlefield. Franks and his immediate subordinate commanders, McKiernan, Conway, and Wallace, encouraged their officers to take risks. Throughout the campaign the Coalition focused on getting to Baghdad as fast as possible, even if it caused some dislocations in the logistic flow. Subordinates willingly bypassed enemy defenses with the assurance that speed, supporting firepower, and the competence of follow-on forces would protect rear areas. Air power reduced the risks by addressing threats as they arose, amplifying and extending the impact of ground maneuver. Speed of ground movement flushed the enemy; air power killed him while he was exposed, massed and in the open.

Still, in the short term, speed came with a cost. As a number of accounts of the fighting make clear, Coalition forces were at times caught in ambushes. The more fluid and fast-moving the situation, the more vulnerable the rear echelon was to attack. In the future, only training can ensure survival. The army needs to be far more vigorous in preparing rear area troops to defend themselves in close combat. As American ground forces move to a more distributed rather than linear use of the battle space, close combat training for service troops will become even more crucial.

Knowledge

Coalition forces would never have been able to achieve the tempo of their operations without the confidence drawn from a deep understanding of Iraqi military forces. Particularly important was knowledge gained from watching the Iraqis operate in the period between the two Gulf wars. Once the war began, commanders and decision makers in the field were able to take advantage of surveillance technologies that allowed them to adapt and modify their plans and movements in accordance with the developing situation, while at the same time denying the enemy any sense of what was happening.

Yet the campaign also reinforced the lessons learned repeatedly and consistently in previous wars: no matter how sophisticated the technical means of information-gathering, a real picture does not begin to emerge until there are human eyes on the target. Counting vehicles from the air does not tell a commander what the enemy intends to do with them. Time and again, army and marine scouts and special forces' reconnaissance units were able to spot, track, and anticipate Iraqi movements and to turn raw intelligence into what soldiers call "ground truth"—a real picture of what was occurring on the battlefield.

Precision

As in Afghanistan, this campaign highlighted the extent to which precision capabilities had improved over the course of the last decade. Likewise, advances in the capacity (and willingness) of the air force to connect with ground forces and concentrate its precision killing power on Iraqi army targets had a dramatic impact on the ability of soldiers to close with and destroy the enemy.

However, the campaign served to elicit the same cautions that had occurred in Kosovo and Afghanistan: precision of weapons alone is not enough to ensure precision of effects. Precision killing comes only with the ability to locate the target precisely—to hit the right target and avoid accidentally striking friendly troops—and quickly, in order to strike before the enemy moves. The appearance of the fedayeen in this war is a reminder that as American weapons become more precise, the enemy will find ways to become harder to hit and kill. Putting together information about where the enemy is and discovering what the really important targets are still represent daunting challenges in a complex, ambiguous environment. Battle damage assessment, even in the case of precision weapons, remains an intractable problem for both air and ground forces.

The Iraq conflict also underlined that at present only aerial systems possess a full complement of precision weapons. With few exceptions, ground munitions, particularly artillery systems, are still area-fire weapons incapable of attacking point targets. This was a problem in close combat, where the explosive radius of precision bombs made them too dangerous to drop in front of friendly troops, while the imprecision of artillery and mortars limited their effectiveness close-in. The lesson is clear: in the future the U.S. military needs more precision in weapons designed for the close fight, and these weapons must be made available to every maneuver unit on the battlefield.

Simultaneity

The war plan developed by Centcom adopted the principle of simultaneity first practiced so successfully during the invasion of Panama. In both cases, the secret to winning quickly was to strike the enemy across the entire extent of his territory in many dimensions—air, land, and sea—in the shortest period of time. The objective of simultaneity was as much psychological as physical. The pattern of assaults against the Iraqis aimed at paralyzing a command structure that moved at a glacial pace, given Saddam's penchant for total control. Coalition air and ground forces may not have achieved real simultaneity in every instance, but the evidence suggests that the Iraqi high command perceived from the beginning that they were under attack everywhere.

Dispersion

The battle for Iraq has again reinforced the observation that the modern battlefield continues to empty and expand. Future enemies will seek—as did the Iraqis, albeit ineffectively—to disperse, dig in, and go to ground to avoid the impact of American precision weapons. At the same time, American forces will disperse over greater distances as the battlefield becomes more opaque and as the range of weapons increases. But as we have seen in this campaign, an empty battlefield is a lonely place where a soldier's instinct is to take counsel of his fears. Soldiers and their leaders must be superbly trained and psychologically prepared for such frightening circumstances.

Adaptability

This war, like all those fought by the United States since the end of the Cold War, demonstrated dramatically the truism that competent militaries are those capable of adapting rapidly to the unexpected.

Great militaries fight the enemy, not the plan. Speed of decision making and the ability to move within the enemy's decision cycle ultimately help determine who wins. Quick thinking allows commanders to make up for deficiencies in planning and to react to the unexpected. What was particularly impressive in this conflict was the ability of soldiers and marines to cobble together ad hoc units to meet unforeseen circumstances and for even the smallest units to be creative tactically and to act against the enemy without seeking permission. Equally impressive was the ability of ground units to alter behavior as the character of the war changed from open mechanized warfare to stability operations centered in towns and cities. Only soldiers and marines who are well trained and accustomed to dealing with uncertainty could have adapted to such radically different circumstances so quickly and effectively.

Quality

The Iraqi campaign reinforced the lessons of Afghanistan that quality trumps quantity on most modern battlefields. From the Civil War through Vietnam, the American military relied primarily on mass and industrial might to smother its enemies in men and materiel. Since then, largely influenced by an all-volunteer military, the services have increasingly emphasized smaller, higher-quality aggregations of men armed with sophisticated weapons. Limited wars fought for limited strategic ends in this new American age of warfare have obliged commanders to win with fewer casualties. The emphasis on precision firepower and sophisticated weapons has resulted in fewer soldiers having to be placed in harm's way.

But smaller numbers on the battlefield place a premium on leadership. Small-unit leaders must assume responsibilities once the purview of officers with higher rank. Close combat soldiers and marines will invariably find themselves involved in fast-paced operations that demand rapid decision making. The wrong decision might well result in an incident with global media exposure and international repercussions. The requirements for initiative and leadership have now moved down to the lowest levels of command, which has enormous implications for how junior officers and NCOs are recruited, trained, and selected.

Training, Leadership, and Education

In March and April of 2003, both Coalition and Iraqi forces lived in an environment where fear, ambiguity, uncertainty, danger, and chance inhibited their ability to fight. Yet such factors had a much greater impact on the Iraqis. The essential difference lay in the willingness of the Coalition's men and women to train long and hard in preparing for combat.

Good human material turns into outstanding marines, soldiers, airmen, and sailors only through realistic, tough training. Much of the exceptional performance of ground forces in Iraq resulted from three decades of experiences at training centers in California, Nevada, Louisiana, and Germany. But training is expensive. It uses up considerable resources. It places enormous strain on officers and NCOs as well as the individual soldier and his family. Scientists can predict with some precision how technological improvements in weaponry will pay off on the battlefield. The payback for training cannot easily be predicted; it can be accurately measured only in combat. In both the Gulf War and the Iraq War, the Iraqis possessed modern weapons. They simply did not know how to employ them. Technology will do little for the badly trained. In the end, technology is a tool. Only training can enable the soldier or marine to use the tools of war effectively.

The performance of America's military institutions from 1991 to

2003 represents the triumph of a systematic approach to training and education that the services put in place during the Cold War. Yet the strategic environment today is far more complex than a generation ago. The military today must not only understand technology but also the cultural environment in which that technology will be employed.

Key leaders in the Iraq campaign came from many different backgrounds and services, but virtually all of them shared a common characteristic: a commitment to the study of their profession and a desire to understand the nature and character of human conflict. But this new era of warfare demands much more of a combatant. Constant deployments and the pressures of practical service might in time diminish opportunities for our young leaders to study and reflect on their profession. The personnel systems of the services by their nature will slight education and study in favor of endless back-to-back deployments. This tendency leads down a dangerous path. The services must give their officers time to learn. The same intellectual qualities that marked the commanders in this war must be passed on to future generations of the American military.

THE CHANGING POLITICAL ENVIRONMENT

War should never be thought of as something autonomous, but always as an instrument of policy.

CARL VON CLAUSEWITZ, *On War,* nineteenth century

At the end of the day, the Iraq War of 2003 was not just about oil or the stability of the Middle East, though these were important factors, to be sure. Nor was it primarily about the liberation of the Iraqi people or even about the need to rid the world of weapons of mass destruction. Rather, like the operation in Afghanistan, the Iraq War was a clear demonstration to the entire world that the United States, in the wake of September 11, has the capacity and will to defeat rogue states and confront those who threaten the vital interests of the American people.

Yet, as we put this book to bed in mid-August 2003, it is not entirely clear whether the conflict that began in mid-March has actually ended. Conventional operations came to a halt shortly after soldiers and marines stormed Baghdad and occupied Saddam's hometown of Tikrit. But attacks on American soldiers and marines continue, particularly in Iraq's Sunni Triangle—the region where the Baathists drew their support. These attacks have been precipitated by criminal gangs, Baath Party members, foreign fedayeen, and, in one case, even a twelve-year-old girl. The number of Americans killed in Iraq has already surpassed the number killed in the Gulf War, and the end is not in sight. Whether such violence represents the death throes of an evil and pernicious regime or the first phase of a protracted guerrilla insurgency is impossible to say. At a Pentagon briefing in July, Centcom commander General Abizaid said of the situation in central Iraq, "Guerrilla tactics is a proper way to describe it in strictly military terms."

The current U.S. administration and its military advisers could have been better prepared to handle the intractable problems raised by victory. To a great extent, that failure reflected a reluctance to involve America's military in nation building and peacekeeping. Insistence on this point closely mirrored the inclination of some in the military services to believe that they should avoid the messy business that lies beyond clear-cut, decisive military operations.

The United States' record of nation building has not been a high point of military or civilian competence over the past forty years. General William Westmoreland, commander in Vietnam from 1964 to 1968, neglected the tasks that lay beyond defeating the Viet Cong and the North Vietnamese in battle. His successor, General Creighton

Abrams, did care, but by the time he took over it was too late to win the war, much less the peace. With the end of the Cold War, when the Clinton administration voiced the intention of using the U.S. military to bring stability to some of the world's trouble spots, members of Congress, Democratic as well as Republican, were rarely supportive. Clinton himself did not want to pay the political price that the inevitable casualties would demand.

The argument that the American people are unwilling to suffer casualties misses a larger point. Whenever political leaders have taken the trouble to explain in clear, honest terms why military commitments were essential to the nation's interests and ideals, Americans, throughout their history, have willingly and consistently paid the price. The greatest benefits that a commander-in-chief can bequeath to soldiers and marines engaged in combat are clarity in defining the mission and resolve to see it through.

The events of September 11 profoundly altered the view that the United States is immune from the troubles besetting the rest of the world. American operations in Afghanistan represented a realization that both air and ground forces must be enlisted in the fight—a departure from the "distant punishment" approach of the Clinton administration. While it was all very fine to overthrow the Taliban and clean out the nest of Al Qaeda terrorists, the question then arose: what were U.S. forces to do in Afghanistan once they had accomplished their purely military mission? The United States could not simply leave the country and risk a resurgence of the Taliban. Something had to be put in its place, and like it or not that something required a commitment to nation building. A failed effort in Afghanistan would not have had an enormous impact on the delicate balance among the nuclear powers India and Pakistan and the soon-to-be-nuclear power Iran. In Iraq, by contrast, an American failure to provide something substantially better than Saddam's regime could well have a catastrophic impact on the continued flow of the world's oil supply, the activities of international terrorists, and the chances for an end to hostilities between warring factions throughout the region. Postwar failure in Iraq would suggest to much of the Islamic world that their only viable path to the future must lie with the fundamentalists rather than with those who wish to bring stability and modernity.

Hard as it may be to believe, Saddam's regime could claim some genuinely devoted supporters, some of whom went on to participate in organized guerrilla attacks against American soldiers after the war. While a portion of Saddam's followers were simply hangers-on, loyal to the regime because of what it could do for them, others were true believers in the Baath ideology who now seem willing to do everything in their power to prevent consolidation of the Coalition's hold over what they regard as their country alone. Members of the Sunni Arab tribes in Iraq's center, who have dominated the Kurds and Shiites since 1932, do not view the kind of democracy promised by the Coalition as being to their advantage. Added to these internal pressures are foreign complexities. The Turks strongly oppose independence for Iraqi Kurds, while the Iranian clerics already are meddling among the Iraqi Shia. Baathists in Syria and fundamentalists in Iran support like-minded groups in Iraq.

These cultural and geopolitical complexities will make the securing of Iraq far more of a challenge than virtually anyone had foreseen before the conflict began. And this task will, as always, fall on the military to accomplish. The great justification for the resources that America lavishes on its military forces lies in the ability of those forces not just to smash and destroy the enemies of the United States but to participate in rebuilding shattered and broken societies. The United States cannot deal with every failed state in the twenty-first century, but it can, under certain circumstances where morality and self-interest converge, make a difference, through combined military and stability operations.

The strategic circumstances in Iraq today reflect the fact that the gods of war have a sense of irony. For the most part, the ships have sailed back to port and the bombers and fighters are secure at home bases. Much of the steel phalanx that rolled over the Iraqi military has been evacuated out of theater or sits idled in motor pools. The 4th Infantry Division, the army's most technologically sophisticated unit, now has responsibility for searching the streets and alleyways of Tikrit for Saddam Hussein. Today, these mechanized "laptop warriors" are foot soldiers performing grunt tasks no different from the British army in Palestine in the 1930s and Northern Ireland in the 1970s and 1980s, or, for that matter, the Roman army in first-century Judea. While the stability mission in Iraq is manpower-intensive, the forces responsible for performing this mission form a very thin line indeed. Infantrymen bear most of the burden. Yet army and marine grunts make up less than four percent of America's military, a force only slightly larger than the New York City Police Department.

The tasks these soldiers perform are timeless, to be sure—and dangerous. By day, Iraqi streets bustle with commerce much as they did before Saddam. But at night inside the Sunni Triangle these same streets turn into free-fire zones where the thugs, criminals, and foreign fanatics come out to kill Americans. Those who have seen war firsthand and close-up know the debilitation that comes with facing the constant fear of violent death. Unlike firemen and cops on the beat, marines and soldiers go out on patrol every night expecting to kill.

In the afternoon, they undergo the necessary routine of briefings, inspections, and rehearsals. At dusk, they don heavy body armor, helmets, weapons, night vision goggles, radios, and all the other impedimenta that makes up a soldier's and marine's burden. At dark, they move out into a miserably hot, humid, and dusty night to do the job. Only a soldier or marine can describe the gut-churning fear that accompanies the moment when the "search-and-clear" team kicks in a door to confront whatever is inside. Within the confines of a tiny room, the soldier looks through the two-dimensional, grainy-green image of his goggles to determine if his welcome will come from a fedeyeen or a child huddling with its mother in fear. Dripping with sweat, gripped with anxiety, the soldier or marine has only an instant to determine whether to shift his finger into the trigger well or reassure the occupants inside.

Today, this scene is repeated daily in Afghanistan and Iraq, as well as other places too secret to recount. These young soldiers and marines endure privation, fear, and separation for a thousand dollars a month and the promise of a trip home to a nation that, they hope, will understand and appreciate the true meaning of their sacrifice.

WEAPONS OF WAR

NOTES

ACKNOWLEDGMENTS AND SOURCES

INDEX

WEAPONS OF WAR

Even with today's precision-guided munitions, the human factor—expressed in the organization, training, maintenance, morale, logistical support, and leadership of a combat unit—is still the single most important variable in the performance of a weapons system. That said, an imbalance in equipment can be significant as well. Before the first shot was fired in the Iraq War, twelve years of semi-isolation had taken their toll on the arsenal Saddam had amassed in the 1970s and 1980s from his European, Soviet, and Chinese suppliers. The Coalition's equipment was in many cases several generations ahead of Iraq's obsolete weaponry, especially with regard to aircraft and naval vessels. The United States and Britain also possessed types of equipment that did not exist at all in the Iraqi inventory, such as airborne command and control aircraft and aircraft carriers.

But the most notable advances had occurred in precision munitions and the capacity to find targets for those munitions. The lethality and routing options of Tomahawk and CALCM (Conventional Air Launched Cruise Missile) had expanded, while the JDAM (Joint Direct Attack Munition) and JSOW (Joint Standoff Weapon) introduced low-cost all-weather precision strike capacity. Predator and Global Hawk offered a glimpse of what unmanned aerial vehicles (UAVs) hold for the future of reconnaissance. The Patriot, with its new PAC-3 missile, provided history's first demonstration of an effective ballistic missile defense. The B-52 made a repeat appearance, though a far more effective one with precision munitions, and was joined by its heavy bomber teammates, the B-1 and B-2. B-1s had been in service in 1991, but they were dedicated exclusively to nuclear attack; their crews had no training with conventional munitions. All that had changed by 2003. The blending of newer precision munitions and heavy bombers proved to be a potent combination.

In the text and tables that follow, we will present only a sampling of the vast array of equipment fielded by both sides. Table 1 covers a range of vehicles with sufficient armor to withstand small arms fire. Table 2 on artillery systems favors Iraqi equipment because that was the one area where the Iraqis came closest to matching the Coalition. Table 3 contains mostly Iraqi air defense systems because their assets in this area saw far more action then those of the Coalition. Tables 4, 5, and 6 on combat aircraft, reconnaissance and support aircraft, and helicopters are skewed toward Coalition systems for much the same reason. Table 7 features Coalition naval vessels exclusively because the Iraqis had no real naval force. Table 8 on munitions shows the range of weapons, mostly precision-guided, that each side had at its disposal.

Armored Vehicles

Tanks

In the Iraq War as in previous wars, the primary role of the tank was to destroy other armored vehicles. For this task it needed a main gun capable of killing at long range, sensors to detect targets, and thick armor to keep it alive on a dangerous battlefield. Every tank design has to balance these competing capabilities of lethality, armor, and speed. Some do it better than others.

Coalition tanks had significant advantages in lethality over Iraqi tanks. The U.S. M1A1 Abrams and British Challenger II both used 120mm guns, though they differed slightly in that the Challenger gun was rifled while the Abrams was smoothbore. These guns were moderately more lethal than the best gun in the Iraqi inventory, the 125mm on the T-72 tank. A substantial part of that advantage came from the higher-quality ammunition used by the United States and Britain. Most of the Iraqi inventory, however, consisted of the T-62's 115mm gun and the T-55's 100mm gun, both of which were much less capable, especially at ranges beyond 1,500 meters. Even Iraq's best tank, the T-72, dated back to the Gulf War and could be destroyed by Coalition tanks at ranges exceeding 3,000 meters.

Where Coalition tanks realized the greatest lethality advantage was in their sensors. They could locate and accurately target Iraqi tanks well before enemy forces even knew the tanks were there. This sensor advantage was greatest at night or in the poor visibility of sandstorms or fog.

Coalition tanks also possessed far better armor than Iraqi tanks. Both the M1A1 and the Challenger II were so well armored as to be basically invulnerable from the front. The excellent Chobham type armor of British design used by both tanks faired well against conventional heavy tank gun rounds and the light-weight warheads used for antitank missiles and man-portable rockets (like the RPG). They were somewhat vulnerable on the sides and rear, where armor has traditionally been thinner. Infantry could disable these tanks with relatively simple weapons (satchel charges and grenades) if they could get next to them. Consequently, in addition to their main guns, tanks also carried several machine guns for dealing with infantry.

Two basic types of rounds used to kill tanks relied on either kinetic or chemical energy as the kill mechanism. Kinetic rounds relied on raw momentum to punch through armor. These rounds were often large darts of some superdense material, such as depleted uranium, that traveled at extreme speeds (up to 1,500 meters per second). To fire a large projectile that fast, however, required a heavy gun. If a "light" 20-ton vehicle tried to fire the Abram's 120mm gun, the recoil would probably roll the vehicle over.

The Germans, in WWII, were the first to figure out a way around this problem. Instead of relying on the momentum of an inert projectile, they developed specially shaped high-explosive rounds (HEAT: High Explosive Antitank) that produced narrow jets of hot gasses upon contact with the target. Those jets of gas could burn through thick armor plates and did not require the warhead itself to travel at high speed. That reduced requirement for speed (typically 200–300 m/s today) then allowed the weapons firing these HEAT rounds to be much lighter. Since WWII, the most famous of these lighter launchers was the rocket-propelled grenade (RPG). Defeating this lightweight threat vexed armor designers for many years. But by the Iraq War, Chobham armor, along with other solutions, was available.

In addition to their overall level of protection, both Coalition tanks, especially the M1A1, were well designed to protect the crew if the armor was penetrated. Iraqi tanks possessed no comparable level of armor protection or crew survival. A common sight from the war was a turret of an Iraqi tank lying some distance from its parent vehicle. "Catastrophic turret separation" was an event few if any crewmen survived.

Despite its considerable weight, the M1A1 was highly mobile, thanks to its powerful 1500hp engine and robust suspension. This is one area where the Challenger II fell short of the Abrams. While being slightly heavier, it used a less powerful 1200hp engine. (The M1A1's power-to-weight ratio was 27hp/ton while the Challenger II was 19.2hp/ton.) The Iraqi T-72 was a fairly agile vehicle, coming close to the Challenger II in mobility, owing to its substantially lighter weight. The other two primary Iraqi tanks (T-62 and T-55) were much inferior. But there was another area where the Challenger II enjoyed a substantial advantage. Because it was powered by a diesel engine rather than a turbine, it got far better mileage per gallon of fuel.

Armored Personnel Carriers

These vehicles were essentially light tanks that carried infantry. APCs provided protection, mobility, and firepower for infantry on a dangerous battlefield. They did not carry the large main guns of tanks, but they could take on tanks when fitted with long-range wire-guided antitank missiles (ATGMs): TOW, Milan, HOT, AT-3, and AT-4. They could also carry machine guns, and sometimes medium caliber cannon (20–40mm), to engage infantry and other lighter armored vehicles.

The Coalition's APCs were superior to their Iraqi counterparts primarily because of their sensors. They could usually detect and engage enemy vehicles long before the Iraqis could. The U.S. Bradley and British Warrior were the two APCs offering the best armor protection and most capable weapons. The Bradley also carried the excellent TOW ATGM, allowing it to effectively engage any Iraqi tank out to 3,750 meters. The marine corps' Light Armored Vehicle (LAV) used the same 25mm cannon as the Bradley. While lightly armored, the LAV had excellent on-road range and speed by virtue of its wheels. The marines also used the Amphibious Assault Vehicle (AAV), a large-capacity fully amphibious transport usually assigned to bring marines ashore from ships.

Iraqi APCs were less well protected. They tended to be an unhealthy place for infantry and crew when taking fire from anything heavier than a machine gun. The best Iraqi APC was the Russian-made BMP-2, with good mobility and weapons. At the other end of the spectrum was the BTR-60 and Chinese YW531. Both were old designs and the products of militaries favoring quantity over quality.

ARTILLERY SYSTEMS

Artillery's role in the Iraq War was to deliver large doses of firepower at long-range, usually beyond the horizon. Three general types of artillery systems were used: conventional tube artillery, rocket artillery, and mortars. All three types came in towed or self-propelled versions.

In tube systems, the projective was launched by an explosion in a single tube. A mortar was a lighter version of the same concept that fired over shorter distances and with a much higher trajectory. Rocket artillery was usually arrayed in banks of tubes where each round had its own launch tube. These tubes could be fired in rapid succession, followed by a lengthy reloading process. Rocket systems could put more firepower on target in a short amount of time, though the individual rounds were often less accurate. Rocket rounds also differed in that each round had its own motor. This allowed for a lighter launch vehicle because it did not have to withstand the shock of a severe launching explosion. There were tube artillery rounds that used some form of boosting motor in their base (for example, base bleed rounds or rocket assisted projectiles), but these rounds still derived the bulk of their range from the initial explosion in the launch tube.

Artillery was the one category of equipment where the Iraqis compared reasonably well with the Coalition forces. But again, much of Iraq's artillery capability ended up wasted by an inability to find targets. Longer-range detection systems like helicopters, aircraft, unmanned aerial vehicles (UAVs), and satellites were not available to the Iraqis. So Iraqi forces often did not know where Coalition units were until they were engaged by them. And then those contacts were fleeting because engaged Iraqi units usually died quickly, and Coalition forces rapidly moved on. In striking fleeting targets the Iraqis were also slower than the Coalition. Iraqi artillery systems that did manage to fire had rather short life spans. Coalition forces were well equipped with counter-battery radars that allowed the trajectory of rounds to be tracked in real-time back to their point of origin. In some cases the Coalition had rounds on the way to an Iraqi unit before that unit's first round landed.

The two premier tube systems for the Coalition were the U.S. 155mm Paladin (M109A6) and the British 155mm AS90. The AS90 was a relatively new design, while the Paladin was a heavily modified version of a 1960s design. Both were self-propelled, which was important for survivability and keeping up with the troops they were supporting. At first glance these two vehicles could be mistaken for tanks, given their armored shell, tracks, turrets, and guns. But unlike tanks, they rarely engaged close-in targets. While tanks dealt with targets inside of 4,000 meters, the Paladin and AS90 reached out to 30,000 meters. Consequently, their design included only a thin layer of armor, a larger gun, and a turret that sat at the back of the vehicle rather than over the center. Arguably the AS90 was the better of the two—unusual when U.S. and British equipment is compared. As many British soldiers have said, "Those Yanks get all the good kit."

Another prominent Coalition weapon was the Multiple Launch Rocket System (MLRS). While slightly less accurate than most tube artillery, this self-propelled artillery system made up for inaccuracy with firepower. An MLRS could fire all twelve of its rockets in about a minute, and each of the 227mm rockets could blanket a football field with 600+ small bomblets (like exploding baseballs). In the 1991 Gulf War the Iraqis called it steel rain.

Supporting these systems were two notable towed tube artillery systems. The M198 was a towed 155mm gun used by the marines. While lacking the armor protection or shoot-and-scoot capability of a self-propelled system, it was far lighter, at about one-third the weight. Both the British and the United States also used a light-weight towed 105mm gun. This British design made a name for itself in the 1982 Falklands War and has been used by parachute units in both nations. Its light weight allowed it to be dropped via parachute or moved short distances by muscle power alone.

Iraqi artillery was quite good by some measures. The Brazilian Astros rocket systems were comparable or better than the MLRS in range and firepower. The South African 155mm G5 was perhaps the best towed piece in service anywhere. Iraq also had a large number of Russian and Chinese towed pieces. The weak link here was, again, the inability to find targets. During the 1991 war,

Coalition commanders listed the Iraqi artillery as the number one priority for air strikes, even ahead of tanks.

AIR DEFENSE SYSTEMS

Since WWI, air defenses have evolved in parallel with the improved capabilities of military aircraft and munitions. As aircraft became more and more accurate at killing every class of ground target, it became more important to field systems that would keep those aircraft at bay, or at least kill enough of them to make their use uneconomical. The two sides in this war faced different air defense problems. The Coalition was not worried about the Iraqi Air Force, given its poor condition and inability to survive more than a few minutes in the air when going up against the Coalition's fighters. But what did worry them were the ballistic missiles in the Iraqi arsenal, most notably Scuds. Unlike Iraqi aircraft, which rarely traveled over Mach 2 (roughly 1,200 mph), Iraqi ballistic missiles could approach their target at Mach 4–7. To deal with such a fast incoming missile required a highly specialized air defense system, and that is where the new version of the Patriot came in.

In the Iraq War, the United States fielded several new missile variants of the Patriot, the same basic launch system that saw service in the Gulf War. One of the problems encountered with the 1991 version of the Patriot was that it still used conventional warheads that relied on blast and fragmentation to destroy targets. When the missile got close to the target, it exploded a warhead that sprayed out metal fragments. But Scuds moved so fast they could sometimes outrun those fragments. Instead of spraying out fragments from a warhead, the new Patriot missile rams the entire warhead into the target. While hitting a target that is closing at speeds around Mach 10 is certainly challenging for a guidance system, when it hits the Patriot is lethal. While no unclassified head-to-head comparisons are available, the latest Patriot variant used in the Iraq War was probably the best antimissile missile in service anywhere. Some systems from Russia, said to be capable against ballistic missiles, have never been combat-tested like the Patriot.

For the Iraqis the air defense problem was more conventional but also more difficult. They faced an opponent who relied on air power to do much of its damage, and that opponent fielded a large force of state-of-the-art aircraft and munitions. Additionally, that opponent was a world leader in having the tools and skills to defeat an air defense system. Adding to the Iraqi burden was the age of their equipment. Air defense was probably the one system where the Iraqis were hurt most by U.N. sanctions. They badly needed to upgrade and replace much of their equipment in this area, but the sanctions cut them off from a market of advanced hardware and willing vendors.

The equipment they did field in this war was mostly older Soviet-era systems. Most could not engage above 15,000 feet, where Coalition aircraft spent much of their time. The three systems that could engage at higher altitudes were the SA-2 (and its Chinese copy, the HQ-2), the SA-3, and the SA-6. The SA-2 could engage Coalition aircraft up to 80,000 feet, but this large system had to be set up at a fixed site. Against a sophisticated foe, those fixed sites had average life spans measured with a stopwatch. The SA-3 had been made mobile by the Iraqis but still was not much better than the SA-2. The SA-6 was the best of the bunch. It could hit aircraft up to about 40,000 feet, and more importantly it was a mobile system mounted on its own tracked chassis. By being mobile, it was much harder to find and kill. However, all three of these systems worked with old guidance systems that the United States and the British had plenty of practice defeating.

Even more so than in the other equipment categories, in air defense the ability to sense and track a target was paramount. The Iraqi low-altitude systems were a little better but not much. The Russian-built SA-8 and the French-built Roland were quite good. The Iraqis fielded a lot of what the military calls triple-A, or anti-aircraft artillery. These were the thousands of gun systems that made every night in Baghdad look like the 4th of July. While a few of them had the sensors and guns to be moderate threats under the right conditions, most were junk. While the larger guns were theoretically capable of shooting down a Coalition aircraft at 40,000 feet, the odds were akin to winning the lottery.

COMBAT AIRCRAFT

Combat aircraft were extremely effective in the Iraq War, but they are also expensive. For that reason, U.S. combat aircraft, and to a lesser extent British and Australian, were unmatched. A high-quality air force does not require huge numbers of personnel but it does require people with the skills to maintain sophisticated equipment. A relatively low-end U.S. aircraft such as the F-16 costs more than a dozen T-72s, while an F/A-18E Super Hornet costs more than 60 LAV-25s. The U.S.'s top-quality fleet of combat aircraft made several contributions to warfare. It attacked the enemy's military from long range, while putting only a handful of personnel in harm's way. It destroyed the foe's infrastructure, both economic and political, from afar. That same fleet also peered down on the enemy to see where he was and what he was doing, while denying him that same ability.

Combat aircraft fell into several categories, defined by how they were used. Single mission aircraft such as the U.S. F-15C did one specific job—in this case, hunting and destroying the enemy's airborne aircraft. Multirole aircraft were more flexible, having the ability to do several different missions depending on the circumstances. The downside was that they tended to be somewhat less capable in each area relative to top-of-the-line single-mission aircraft. Most multirole aircraft were reasonably good at striking both ground targets and hunting other airborne aircraft. The F-16, for example, could attack ground targets but could not do the air-to-air mission as well as the F-15C, which was outstanding in the air-to-air role but had no ground attack capability. The A-10—a single-role aircraft—specialized in a particular kind of ground attack called close air support (CAS), which involved attacking enemy forces closely engaged with friendly forces. CAS differed from the other primary ground attack mission, called strike, whose purpose was to attack ground targets that were not close to friendly ground units. CAS required precision so that friendly forces nearby were not hit, rapid reaction so that targets of opportunity could be hit in the whirl of a ground fight, and flexibility because the particulars of what to attack could not be preplanned.

In the Iraq War the Coalition fleet consisted mainly of multirole aircraft (F-16, F/A-18s, F-15Es, and so on), though a significant number were specialized. The best CAS aircraft were the A-10, AV-8B Harrier, and AC-130. The A-10 was built to survive ground fire when flying low, and the AC-130 was designed with firepower like a flying battleship. The Harrier could use bases close to the fight because of their vertical take off and landing capability. The best aircraft for striking targets deep within Iraq were the heavy bombers (B-1, B-2, B-52) because they had the range and payload needed. If the range was not too great, the U.S. F-15E and British Tornado also excelled at the strike mission. If the target was in an area especially well protected by Iraqi air defense, the best tools for the job were the stealthy F-117 and B-2. Carrier aircraft (F-14, F/A-18) enjoyed the advantage of bringing their own airbase with them.

The Iraqi air force was outmatched by every possible measure. It was outnumbered and outclassed in both personnel and equipment. The no-fly zones of the previous decade had curtailed its ability to train, as had the fiscal pressure imposed by U.N. sanctions. The Iraqis did have a handful of aircraft that could be considered of the current generation (MiG-29s). The bulk of their aircraft, however, were two or three generations behind the majority of the Coalition fleet. The French-made Mirage F1 and the Russian-made MiG-23—both moderately effective for air-to-air combat—were comparable to what the U.S. fielded in the early 1970s.

RECONNAISSANCE AND SUPPORT AIRCRAFT

While combat aircraft tend to get all the glory, many types of aircraft fill a lot of other important roles. Without them, combat missions in the Iraq War either would not have been done or would been done less well, and as a result the rest of the military would have been substantially less effective.

One of the key supporting missions vis-à-vis other aircraft was aerial refueling. The majority of Coalition aircraft needed to refuel in the air because they lacked the range to hit many targets and still return to their bases. Without tanker aircraft, these planes would have been forced to carry smaller payloads or spend far less time searching for targets. More distant targets would have been turned over to the heavy bombers. Because aerial refueling was in high demand, the Coalition deployed over 250 aerial tanker aircraft. The most common type was the U.S. KC-135, an old aircraft based on Boeing's 707 civilian jetliner from the late 1950s. With over 500 in its fleet, the U.S. Air Force's inventory of KC-135s is bigger than that of most airlines. A less numerous though larger tanker aircraft is the U.S. KC-10, based on the DC-10 civilian aircraft. While the United States only has 59 of these aircraft, they can carry substantially more fuel. The KC-130 is a smaller tanker based on the C-130 cargo aircraft. The VC-10 is a British tanker that is roughly equivalent to the KC-135.

Aerial tankers were put under great strain during the Iraq War. In recent years the U.S. military had been looking at ways to increase its supply of aerial tankers, but it had given little attention to the demand side of the issue. All the services had major plans to purchase new short-range (less than 1,000 mile radius) combat aircraft, which require aerial refueling, but at the time of the Iraq War not a single program existed for producing new long-range aircraft for striking ground targets. Ironically, just before the war, the air force mothballed a third of its B-1 fleet, an aircraft that had far less need for aerial tanking.

Another important mission for aircraft in the Iraq War was command, control, and communications (what the military calls C3)—essentially, a flying command post. The reason to make the command post airborne was to give its sensors a better view of the battlefield and to ease the communications burden. Because of the curvature of the earth, a sensor could observe more real estate from 30,000 feet than it could on the ground. Being airborne also allowed for more direct communications and required less message traffic to be routed through the limited supply of satellites. Because C3 aircraft tend to be large and packed with sophisticated electronics, they are very expensive, and as a result few nations can afford them. While these aircraft did not kill the enemy directly, they made all other combat aircraft more effective.

The two premier C3 aircraft used in Iraq were the U.S. AWACS and JSTARS, both based on the Boeing 707 airframe. The AWACS was distinguished by the large radar disc mounted on its back, while the JSTARS had a less pronounced radar housed in a thin bulge under the front half of its fuselage. The difference between these two aircraft was that the AWACS focused on the air fight, coordinating friendly aircraft, while JSTARS did the same thing for the ground battle. The E-2C Hawkeye, a U.S. Navy aircraft, was a much smaller two-engine propeller-driven aircraft based on carriers.

Some of the best C3 aircraft used in Iraq were also among the best reconnaissance aircraft. Both AWACS and JSTARS could survey several hundred miles in multiple directions simultaneously. Reconnaissance aircraft used a variety of sensors in addition to radar. Some could take visual-light or infrared images while others listened for signals emitted by the Iraqis, both to hear what they were saying and to locate them. None of these sensor categories were mutually exclusive; some aircraft mixed and matched several sensor types. One of the more famous reconnaissance aircraft was the high-flying U-2, which first flew over the Soviet Union in the 1950s. The version used in 2003 was much more capable, primarily because it carried state-of-the-art sensors. The RC-135 was another 707-based airframe that snooped for signals, the details of which are not openly discussed by the military.

Two fairly new players in the reconnaissance game were the Predator and Global Hawk unmanned aerial vehicles (UAVs). In reconnaissance, one of the primary performance parameters was duration of the mission. The longer an aircraft could stay up, the more information it could collect, and this was the area where UAVs excelled in the Iraq War. While other aircraft were limited by what their human crews could endure, UAVs could go until they had to return for fuel. The Predator, a medium altitude UAV, spent most of its time at or below 25,000 feet. The Global Hawk, which was larger, flew high-altitude missions (~65,000 feet) for durations longer than any other aircraft in the world. During flight testing, a Global Hawk flew from Southern California to Maine, stayed aloft for 24 hours, and then returned to California on one tank of gas without aerial refueling. Another important advantage of UAVs was that when they were shot down, no American servicemen and women were captured or killed. While UAVs are still in their infancy, as evidenced by their limited payloads, they have a bright future.

Another support category was jamming—interfering with the electronic communications or radar emissions of the enemy. Radar jamming aircraft blinded enemy air defenses that were trying to attack friendly aircraft and rendered those air defenses harmless and vulnerable to attack. Jamming is a "soft-kill" tool because it does not actually physically damage the target but renders it ineffective. The primary Coalition jammmer was the EA-6B Prowler, a carrier-based aircraft with four crewmembers.

The last category of support aircraft used in the Iraq War was airlifters. These aircraft hauled equipment and supplies, with a secondary mission of moving people. Hauling people was secondary because civilian airliners were easily contracted for that job most of the time. What civilian airlines could not do as well was haul specialized military equipment. The two largest airlifters were the U.S. C-5 and C-17. The C-5 Galaxy, sometimes called the Aluminum Overcast, had the greatest payload but also required a long, smooth runway. This huge aircraft could transport 130 tons of equipment and supplies over long distances. The newer C-17, used by both the United States and Britain, could carry about two thirds the payload but used shorter runways and even unpaved airstrips. These heavy lifters primarily hauled equipment into the theater of operations from distant places, like Europe and the States. Once the equipment and supplies got to the theater, the C-130 Hercules—a smaller turbo-prop aircraft that excelled at using shorter rough airstrips closer to troops in the field—moved the equipment and supplies around the theater. As capable as these airlifters were, the bulk of the supplies and equipment still arrived via ship. The heaviest equipment, like tanks and armored personnel carriers, rarely traveled by aircraft.

HELICOPTERS

Helicopters were the ground guy's air force in Iraq. While they generally cost less than fixed-wing aircraft, they fly more slowly, have less range, and carry less payload. Their big advantage is the ability to land without a runway. This allows them to stay close to troops that are in contact with the enemy and to respond quickly. Iraq had a considerable inventory of helicopters (several hundred), but they did the Iraqis no good because the Coalition owned the airspace over the battlefield. Any Iraqi aircraft that tried to get airborne was found and destroyed within minutes.

The two most common types of helicopters were attack and transport. Attack helicopters primarily hunted ground vehicles and infantry, with a secondary mission of attacking other helicopters. The transports hauled troops and equipment from point A to point B, with point B sometimes being an enemy location. While helicopters could not fly with the same speed and high altitude of fixed-wing aircraft, they did gain some protection from flying low (called "terrain masking"). When a helicopter is flying at 50 feet, many obstructions like small hills, trees, and buildings block people on the ground from seeing it. The downside to flying low is that obstacles to vision are easy to run into.

The premier attack helicopter in the war was the AH-64 Apache. This highly lethal machine could carry 70mm unguided rockets, long-range Hellfire anti-tank missiles, and a 30mm cannon under the nose. The Hellfire missile could take out any tank in the world out to 8 kilometers. The rockets and cannon worked well against lighter vehicles and infantry. This war was the debut for the latest version of the Apache, the AH-64D Longbow, with its distinctive radar dome fitted above the rotors. This new version of the Apache used a new radar to track targets, which improved poor-weather performance. The Apache was also well protected from ground fire, though not as well as an A-10. The United States also deployed the OH-58 Kiowa, a lighter attack helicopter that performed scouting missions. Special forces units used the AH-6, which combined light attack and light transport functions.

The most common transport helicopter was the UH-60 Black Hawk. Its many variants were used by different branches of the military (navy, coast guard, special forces); their names began with different letters (HH-60, SH-60, MH-60) but always ended -60. The basic army Black Hawk could haul ten to twelve soldiers roughly 100 miles and then return to base. It usually also had a machine gun or two out the side for self-protection. When more troops or gear needed to be moved, the CH-47 Chinook was used. This twin-rotor helicopter resembled a flying boxcar and could haul about three times as many personnel as a Black Hawk.

The marine corps' helicopter force was a generation behind the army's fleet. The marines still used the older UH-1 Hueys, the aircraft the Black Hawk replaced in the army, for light transport duties. For attack they also used the older AH-1 Cobra, an aircraft since replaced in army service by the Apache. The Cobra could still be effective when used properly, but it carried a lighter weapons load and had much less armor to protect against ground fire. The geriatric member of the helicopter force was the CH-46 Sea Knight. This aircraft, which dates from the Vietnam era, displayed its serious reliability and maintenance problems as well as its limited lift capabilities. A badly needed replacement was in the works at the time of the war, but, unfortunately for the marines, that replacement was the problem-plagued V-22 Osprey. The heavyweight of the marine lineup was the CH-53 Sea Stallion. This single-rotor aircraft was big, capable of hauling substantially more than even the army's Chinook to even greater distances. When the marines wanted to go deep with a lot of troops and gear, they used the Sea Stallion.

The Brits fielded a fairly capable helicopter force as well. Their mainstay was the Sea King, which flew both from carriers and from land bases. For attack duties the Brits used the Lynx, another platform that deployed from both sea and land bases. They also fielded an interesting variant of the Sea King that acted like a mini-AWACS, the Sea King AEW (airborne early warning).

NAVAL VESSELS

The primary task of Coalition naval vessels was to attack inland. To do this, the main tools were aircraft and cruise missiles. The secondary task for the naval contingent was to keep the waters of the Persian Gulf open so that supplies for Coalition ground forces, as well as humanitarian aid, could flow into Iraqi ports.

The headlining vessels for the Coalition were the aircraft carriers. These floating airbases expanded the number of runways available outside of crowded Kuwait. The U.S. carriers—four Nimitz class and one Kitty Hawk class—had approximately 70 aircraft (both fixed and rotary-wing) on board, while the British *Ark Royal* carried a helicopter-only air wing. (The *Ark Royal* can carry fixed-wing Harriers but did not for this war.) The aircraft flying on U.S. carriers included the F-14 Tomcat, F/A-18 Hornet, F/A-18E Super Hornet, S-3 Viking, EA-6B Prowler, E-2C Hawkeye, C-2 Greyhound, and SH-60 Seahawk. Lynx, Chinook, and Sea King helicopters flew off the *Ark Royal.*

Aside from aircraft carriers, the U.S. and British navies deployed a range of amphibious assault ships that looked like smaller aircraft carriers. Their role was to provide deck space for helicopters, well decks for various amphibious craft that could carry marines ashore, and berthing space within for large numbers of marines. These amphibious ships could also launch vertical-landing aircraft like the AV-8B and Harrier.

A second general category of vessels in the Iraq War was the surface combatants, which included cruisers, destroyers, and frigates. Their contribution to the fight came in the form of cruise missiles, guns for naval gunfire support, and helicopter landing pads. All of the U.S. cruisers and destroyers had the capability of launching Tomahawk cruise missiles. These missiles were carried and launched from what were called vertical launch cells (VLS). These cells were fitted in clusters and varied in number depending on the ship's class. They could take a variety of munitions aside from the Tomahawk; therefore the actual load of Tomahawks carried per mission could vary. A typical load per ship was probably forty to eighty Tomahawks.

Most of the Coalition surface combatants also had at least one main gun over 100mm. U.S. cruisers had two 127mm guns, U.S. destroyers had one or two 127mm guns (the Spruance class had two 127mm guns while the Burke class had one), U.S. frigates had one 76mm gun, U.K. destroyers and frigates had one 114mm gun, and one of the Australian frigates had a 127mm gun while the other had one 76mm. While the range of these guns was limited to 15–25 kilometers, they had high rates of fire (16–20 rounds per minute for the 127mm, 25 rounds per minute for the 114mm, and 80 rounds per minute for the 76mm). There were a few rare cases when fighting occurred close enough to the waters of the Gulf (in the Al-Faw Peninsula, for example) to allow for some naval gunfire support.

The last category of Coalition vessels was the fast-attack nuclear submarines, referred to by the military as SSNs. While the SSNs had no naval targets to occupy them, both U.S. and British submarines that were deployed to the region had the ability to launch Tomahawks. Some of the American SSNs had specially fitted vertical launch cells just for Tomahawks, while the rest of the submarines could fire them through their torpedo tubes.

The Iraqis had no navy to speak of. What little they had twenty years ago was sent to the bottom of the Gulf in the 1991 war.

MUNITIONS

Between the two Gulf wars, the revolution in munitions was driven by precision. Extremely accurate weapons had become the norm rather than the exception. Of all munitions dropped in the 1991 war, only 7 percent were precision weapons. By 2003, approximately 70 percent of the munitions employed were precision weapons.

Most of the precision munitions in the Iraq War used laser or GPS guidance. In laser guidance, a device that could track laser beams was fitted on the nose of a munition. That laser-seeking device was then hooked to a set of fins that guided the munition. When a laser beam was focused on a target the laser-seeking device and fins steered it in the direction of the beam. That laser beam, or "spot," could be customized with a light pattern so that it would not be confused with some other laser spot.

The actual laser spot can be produced from many sources, including man-portable laser designators used by special forces personnel. The advantage of laser guidance was its precision; the downside was that fog, sandstorms, and clouds could block the laser beam and thus prevent target marking. GPS guidance uses Global Positioning System satellites to both mark targets ("he's at this exact spot") and track where the munition is. The munition's GPS system then can track where it is in flight relative to the aim point and move guidance fins on the munition as needed. While this mode of guidance is not quite as precise as laser guidance, it is immune to bad weather.

Inertial guidance, which basically relies on sensed motion relative to some previously known position, was also used by some munitions. The way it worked was not unlike blindfolding someone in a room and then pushing them to the side five feet. Using what the person saw before he or she was blindfolded, and then adding what felt like five feet of lateral motion, the person would have a pretty good idea of his or her new location. While obviously not as accurate as laser or GPS guidance, inertial guidance could be effective over shorter distances.

One of the higher profile precision munitions was the cruise missile. The Tomahawk could be fired from U.S. cruisers or destroyers or from U.S. and British submarines. The CALCM (Conventional Air Launched Cruise Missile) was a U.S. Air Force munition launched from B-52 bombers. The Tomahawk had greater range, while the CALCM carried a larger warhead. The two could be distinguished by the round cigar-shaped fuselage on the Tomahawk versus the angular fuselage on the CALCM. Another way to tell them apart was their air intake scoop; the Tomahawk's was on the bottom, while the CALCM's was on the top. Unlike the Tomahawk, the CALCM production line had long since been closed at the time of the Iraq War. All of the CALCMs in use since the 1991 Gulf War had been converted over from variants that had been equipped with nuclear warheads during the Cold War—thus, the C for conventional in CALCM. The British also had their own air-launched cruise missile, the Storm Shadow. Making its operational debut in this war, the Storm Shadow launched from Tornado aircraft.

Other missiles of interest included the ATACMS, HARM, Maverick, Hellfire, and TOW. The ATACMS (Army Tactical Missile System) was launched from the MLRS tracked rocket artillery system. These missiles were larger than the standard MLRS rockets, carrying 50 percent more payload, and flew out much farther (160km vs 45km). Extended-range versions of the ATACMS reached out nearly twice as far but carried a warhead only about a third the size.

The HARM (High-speed Anti-Radiation Missile) homed in on enemy radars much like a moth to a flashlight. This forced the Iraqis to shut down their radar—thus losing their ability to track friendly aircraft—or lose it to the HARM. Maverick was a general-purpose missile for attacking enemy vehicles or bunkers out to about 25 kilometers. Hellfire was a small (~100 lbs) munition fired mostly from helicopters. It could engage targets out to 8 kilometers and did especially well against armored vehicles. It came in several variants, one guided by laser homing and the other by radar. The TOW (Tube-launched Optically-tracked Wire-guided missile) was fired from a wide range of helicopters and ground vehicles. It was a short-range (3.7km) munition designed to take out armored vehicles or bunkers. Its primary weakness was a slow flight speed that required about 20 seconds to reach targets at maximum range. A more recent addition to the antitank quiver was the Javelin man-portable system. At about 50 pounds for both the missile and the launcher, it was much more portable than the TOW. While its range was shorter (2500m vs. 3750m), it had the big advantage of being fire-and-forget: unlike the TOW, which required the missile to be guided by the shooter all the way to the target, the Javelin guided itself so the troops could shoot and scoot. Javelin also attacked vehicles through their thinner top armor.

While missiles were very useful, especially when heavy enemy defenses made it advisable to keep aircraft at a distance, they were expensive. Precision-guided bombs, on the other hand, were cheap enough to be used in large numbers. The precision bombs used in Operation Iraqi Freedom included JSOWs, JDAMs, and laser-guided bombs.

JSOW used a GPS guidance package and flip-out wings that allowed it to glide as far as 65 kilometers from the release point, a respectable distance considering it had no motor. JDAM was a simple GPS guidance kit (GPS tracker and fins) strapped onto a range of dumb bombs. While JDAM could fly only about 20 kilometers to a target, it was a very cheap munition, costing about 2 percent that of a Tomahawk. One of the more innovative free-fall munitions used two new technologies. The first was the bomb shell called the Wind Corrected Munitions Dispenser. This bomb shell had an inertial guidance package and fins that directed it accurately to a point on the ground even when dropped from high altitude. Inside the bomb shell was the Sensor Fused Weapon, a smart anti-armor munition used for the first time in combat in this conflict. At a pre-set altitude the bomb shell would burst open and release ten tube-shaped submunition dispensers. Each dispenser was slowed and stabilized by its own small parachute. Once stabilized, each dispenser released four hockey puck shaped discs, each with its own infrared sensor and projectile. These sensors then looked for target vehicles over a 500 × 1200 foot area and fired down on them from above, where armored vehicles have thin armor. So one CBU-97 could fire forty anti-armor projectiles down on vehicles, at the direction of the infrared sensor on each projectile.

Since Iraq had no navy to fire cruise missiles and its air force could not get off the ground, the most noteworthy Iraqi munitions were ballistic missiles. Before the war, Iraq had a history of importing ballistic missiles and modifying their designs for their own particular needs. The Scud-B was a basic Soviet-era missile, while the Al-Hussein was a modified version with greater range and less payload. The Al-Samoud was a shorter-range missile of Iraqi design.

All of these ballistic missiles used fairly crude inertial guidance packages and thus were not very accurate. While many of the Coalition's precision munitions might be expected to hit within 5 to 20 meters of their target on average, a Scud's average miss distance was more like 1,000 meters. This makes these missiles of limited military utility. A large number of missiles equipped with conventional high-explosive warheads would have to be fired at any one point target to have a reasonable chance of destroying it. Given the size and cost of these missiles, that was not feasible.

The Iraqis had two ways to change that equation: either change the target or change the warhead. In the Iran-Iraq war in the mid-1980s, Iraq enlarged the target to include whole cities, with some success. Striking city targets can have political effects by pressuring a government to respond. The other option was to replace high-explosive warheads with chemical, biological, or nuclear payloads—which produced wide-area effects so that their exact point of impact was less critical. In the Iraq War, the Coalition was concerned with both the targeting of cities and the use of WMD warheads (weapons of mass destruction), a capability which many intelligence analysts believed the Iraqis had. No such weapons have been found to date.

1. Armored Vehicles

Name	Type	Fielded by	First fielded	Weight (tons)	Main armament	Troop capacity	Engine (hp)	Notes
M1A1 Abrams	Tank	U.S.	1980	63	120mm	–	1500	1,2
Challenger II	Tank	U.K.	1983	68	120mm	–	1200	1
M2/M3 Bradley	APC	U.S.	1981	37	25mm/ATGM	6	600	5
Warrior	APC	U.K.	1986	28.2	30mm	7	550	
LAV-25	APC	U.S.	1985	14.1	25mm	6	275	6
AAV	APC	U.S.	1971	26.4	40mm	25	400	7
M113	APC	U.S.	1960	15.9	12.7mm	11	275	8
FV432	APC	U.K.	1963	16.8	7.62mm	10	240	
T-72	Tank	Iraq	1971	49	125mm	–	840	3
T-62	Tank	Iraq	1962	44	115mm	–	580	
T-55/Type 69	Tank	Iraq	1949	39.6	100mm	–	520	4
BMP-2	APC	Iraq	1982	15.7	30mm/ATGM	7	300	
BMP-1	APC	Iraq	1967	14.9	73mm/ATGM	8	300	
BTR-60	APC	Iraq	1961	11.3	14.5mm	14	180	6
YW531	APC	Iraq	1969	13.8	12.7mm	13	320	9
BRDM-2	Scout	Iraq	1963	7.7	14.5mm/ATGM	–	140	6

Type: APC: armored personnel carrier, meant to both transport infantry to and across the battlefield and support them with firepower.

Fielded by: The nation that employed this vehicle in this conflict.

First fielded: The year the first version of this vehicle was put into service. The actual version deployed for this conflict may have been substantially upgraded.

Weight: Total weight of this vehicle.

Main armament: Diameter of the main gun. ATGM: anti-tank guided missile. Many vehicles carry these missiles to allow them to engage tanks effectively at long range. Many ATGMs are effective out to 3,000–4,000 meters. Tanks usually have several machine guns in addition to their main gun.

Troop capacity: For those vehicles that carry infantry, this is how many.

Engine: The power generated by this vehicle's engine in horsepower.

Notes:

1. Use British-designed Chobham armor, a classified mix of steel and ceramic layers highly effective against both conventional armor-piercing rounds and HEAT (high-explosive anti-tank) rounds.

2. Uses a turbine engine instead of the diesel engine used in most armored vehicles. Adding to the M1A1's international flavor is its German-designed 120mm gun.

3. Has a smaller 3-man crew because it replaces the usual 4th man with an auto-loader.

4. The Type 69 is a Chinese copy of the T-55.

5. The Bradley's 25mm is highly effective versus other APCs out to 2,500 meters and fires at 200 rounds per minute. But against even an older T-55 it would need to be very close and shooting at the sides or rear of the tank to penetrate its armor. That's where its TOW missile system comes in. The TOW can knock out any Iraqi tank out to 3,750 meters, even from the front. This pairing of rapid fire cannon and a long-range missile system is common on modern APCs.

6. Has wheels instead of tracks. This generally involves trading some off-road mobility for greater on-road efficiency and speed.

7. Fully amphibious. The AAV is often launched from navy amphibious ships several miles offshore; it swims ashore slowly at about 8 mph. The AAV's 40mm gun is a low-velocity grenade launcher. While highly effective versus soft targets it does not do as well as the Bradley's 25mm versus armor.

8. Exists in many versions from command vehicles to ambulances. These figures are generic approximates.

9. Chinese-made.

Sources: The information in these tables is adapted from the following texts: A. D. Baker III, *Combat Fleets of the World 2000–2001* (Annapolis, MD: Naval Institute Press, 2000); Tony Cullen and Christopher Foss, eds., *Jane's Land-based Air Defense* (Surrey, U.K.: Jane's Information Group, 1997); Chris Foss, *Jane's Modern Tanks* (Glasgow, U.K.: Harper Collins; 1995); Mark Lambert, ed., *Jane's All the World's Aircraft 1992–1993* (Surrey, U.K.: Jane's Information Group, 1992); Rene J. Francillon, *The Naval Institute Guide to World Military Aviation 1997–1998* (Annapolis, MD: Naval Institute Press, 1997). Information was also taken from the following websites: www.raf.mod.uk, www.fas.org/man/index.html, www.globalsecurity.org, www.chinfo.navy.mil/navpalib/factfile, www.hqmc.usmc.mil, www.digitalfact.co.jp/missile/missile-data/index-e.htm.

2. Artillery Systems

Name	Type	Self-propelled	Fielded by	First fielded	Caliber	Range (km)	ROF	Weight (tons)	Notes
M270 MLRS	Rocket	Yes	U.S.	1983	227mm	45	12	26.4	9
M109A6 Paladin	Cannon	Yes	U.S.	1963	155mm	30	4	27.5	1
AS-90	Cannon	Yes	U.K.	1993	155mm	40	6	46.4	3
M198	Cannon	No	U.S.	1982	155mm	30	4	7.9	11
M121	Mortar	Yes	U.S.	1991	120mm	7	16	~16	10
M119	Cannon	No	U.S./U.K.	1975	105mm	19	6	2.3	2
Astros II SS-60	Rocket	Yes	Iraq	1983	300mm	60	4	22.1	8,13
Astros II SS-40	Rocket	Yes	Iraq	1983	180mm	35	16	22.1	8,13
G5	Cannon	No	Iraq	1981	155mm	39	3	15.2	7
Type 66	Cannon	No	Iraq	1955	152mm	24	6	6.3	5,12
2S3	Cannon	Yes	Iraq	1973	152mm	24	4	30.4	5
M-46	Cannon	No	Iraq	1954	130mm	34	10	9.3	5
Astros II SS-30	Rocket	Yes	Iraq	1983	127mm	30	32	22.1	8,13
2S1	Cannon	Yes	Iraq	1974	122mm	22	5	17.3	5
D-30	Cannon	No	Iraq	1963	122mm	22	8	3.5	4
BM-21	Rocket	Yes	Iraq	1963	122mm	33	40	15.1	6,13

Type: General type of artillery piece it is. Rocket artillery fires longer rounds with their own propulsion systems. Cannons propel the round via an explosive charge set off in the barrel of the cannon. While cannon rounds themselves can have small propulsion systems on them the preponderance of the movement of the round comes from that initial explosion. Mortars are light cannons that use much higher trajectories to loft their rounds. They have far less range than heavier cannons.

Self-propelled: Is this system mounted on its own vehicle? Those that are can relocate faster, which improves survivability. The advantage of the towed systems is far less weight.

Fielded by: The nation that employed this system in this conflict.

First fielded: The year the first version of this system was put into service. The actual version deployed for this conflict may have been substantially upgraded.

Caliber: Diameter of the munitions used, in millimeters.

Range: Maximum distance at which targets can be engaged, in kilometers.

ROF: Rate of fire in rounds per minute.

Weight: Total weight of the system.

Notes:

1. This ROF is sustainable for only three minutes, then it drops to one round per minute.

2. Can be parachute airdropped or carried by many Coalition helicopters. This ROF is sustainable for only two minutes, then it drops to three round per minute. The M119 is a rare example of a foreign designed and fielded weapon bought by the U.S. military.

3. This ROF is sustainable for only three minutes, then it drops to two rounds per minute. The AS-90 is one of the few major pieces of British equipment that could be called clearly superior to its American equivalent, the M109A6.

4. This ROF is only the burst rate for the first few minutes of firing. The sustained ROF is four rounds per minute.

5. ROF is an initial burst rate. Sustained rate is substantially lower.

6. All 40 rounds can be fired in 20 seconds, but it takes 10 minutes to reload another 40 rounds.

7. Three rounds a minute is sustainable for 15 minutes, then the ROF falls to two rounds per minute. Outstanding towed piece made in South Africa.

8. Once all of the rocket rounds are fired, a considerable reload time is required. Made in Brazil.

9. While all twelve rockets can be fired in one minute, the reload process takes nine minutes. The 45 km range figure relates to the MLRS-ER extended range round that carries a smaller warhead. Standard M26 rounds have a range of 30 km.

10. ROF is for the first minute only. After that it drops to four rounds per minute. Basically an M113 APC adapted to carry a 120mm mortar. Also comes in a mortar-only towed version.

11. ROF is a burst rate only, not sustainable for more than a few minutes. Can be carried by larger helicopters like the CH-53 or CH-47.

12. Chinese-made.

13. A wheeled vehicle that is slightly less mobile off-road but faster and more efficient on-road.

Sources: See Table 1.

3. Air Defense Systems

Name	Type	Guidance type	Self-propelled	Fielded by	First fielded	Range (km)	Maximum altitude (ft)	Notes
Patriot	High-altitude SAM	Radar	No	U.S.	1985	160	74,000	5
Starstreak	Man-portable SAM	IR	No	U.K.	1990	7	–	2
Stinger	Man-portable SAM	IR	No	U.S./U.K.	1981	4.8	11,800	10
HQ-2	High-altitude SAM	Radar	No	Iraq	1967	35	84,000	7
SA-6	Medium-altitude SAM	Radar/Optical	Yes	Iraq	1965	24	43,000	8
SA-3	Medium-altitude SAM	Radar	Yes	Iraq	1961	22	37,000	9
Roland 2	Low-altitude SAM	Radar/Optical	Yes	Iraq	1981	6.3	17,000	
SA-8	Low-altitude SAM	Radar	Yes	Iraq	1973	6.5	15,500	
SA-13	Low-altitude SAM	IR	Yes	Iraq	1975	5	10,800	6
SA-9	Low-altitude SAM	IR	Yes	Iraq	1968	4.2	10,800	
SA-16	Man-portable SAM	IR	No	Iraq	1981	5.2	10,800	
SA-14	Man-portable SAM	IR	No	Iraq	1974	4.5	9,300	11
HN-5	Man-portable SAM	IR	No	Iraq	1986	4.4	7,100	1,2
ZSU-23-4	Gun	Radar/Optical	Yes	Iraq	1966	2.5	7,700	3
ZSU-57-2	Gun	Optical	Yes	Iraq	1957	10	13,000	4
100mm	Gun	Radar/Optical	No	Iraq	1949	21	42,000	4
85mm	Gun	Radar/Optical	No	Iraq	1944	18	31,000	4
57mm	Gun	Radar/Optical	No	Iraq	1950	12	18,000	4

Type: Type of air defense system and general altitude range. SAM: surface-to-air missile. The man-portable SAMs are all low-altitude systems.

Guidance type: Radar: uses radar emissions from a ground emitter or the missile itself to track the target. IR: infrared, tracks the heat emitted by the target. Optical: optical sensor on the missile or on a gun sight tracks the target.

Self-propelled: Is the system mounted on its own vehicle? Systems that can relocate faster than towed systems, thus making them both more survivable and more lethal.

Fielded by: The nation that employed this system in this conflict.

First fielded: The year the first version of this system was put into service. The actual version deployed for this conflict may have been substantially upgraded.

Range: The horizontal distance out to which this system can engage targets.

Maximum altitude: The highest altitude up to which this system can engage targets.

Notes:

1. Chinese-improved copy of the SA-7.

2. Comes in man-portable and vehicle mounted versions.

3. A lightly-armored tracked vehicle that can fire on the move. It has a four-barrel 23mm gun system with a very high ROF. This system proved very lethal to Israeli aircraft in the 1973 Yom Kippur War.

4. Slow rates of fire and/or poor guidance systems make these guns rather ineffective versus most aircraft.

5. With the new PAC-3 missile Patriot is effective versus short-range ballistic missiles.

6. Designed to succeed the SA-9.

7. Proved highly effective versus Israeli aircraft in the 1973 Yom Kippur War downing 64. This SAM also downed a U.S. F-16 over Bosnia in the 1990s.

8. While a rather old system this was the SAM that downed a U.S. F-117 over Serbia in 1998.

9. Fairly sophisticated French system.

10. Chinese copy of the SA-2.

11. Reasonably good man-portable SAM that brought down numerous Coalition aircraft in the 1991 Gulf War.

Sources: See Table 1.

4. Combat Aircraft

Name	Type	Fielded by	First fielded	Typical radius (km)	Maximum payload (lbs)	Mach 1+	Notes
F-16	Multi-role fighter	U.S.	1979	1,370	~15,000	Yes	1
F/A-18C/D	Multi-role fighter	U.S. /Aus.	1980	510	13,700	Yes	2
F/A-18E	Multi-role fighter	U.S.	2002	960	17,750	Yes	
F-15C	Air superiority fighter	U.S.	1974	1,770	23,600	Yes	
F-15E	Multi-role fighter	U.S.	1988	1,770	24,500	Yes	3
F-14	Multi-role fighter	U.S.	1974	1,110	14,500	Yes	4
A-10	Close air support	U.S.	1976	900	16,000	No	12
F-117	Stealth strike fighter	U.S.	1982	1,440	4,000	No	5
AV-8B	Multi-role fighter	U.S.	1971	870	9,200	No	6,14
AC-130	Close air support	U.S.	1967	2,400	42,600	No	7
B-1	Long-range bomber	U.S.	1986	8,650	75,000	Yes	13
B-2	Stealth long-range bomber	U.S.	1992	11,660	50,000	No	5
B-52	Long-range bomber	U.S.	1955	7,720	65,000	No	8
Tornado F3	Multi-role fighter	U.K.	1984	1,850	18,700	Yes	11
Tornado GR4	Strike fighter	U.K.	1980	1,390	18,000	Yes	
Jaguar	Strike fighter	U.K.	1973	1,300	10,500	Yes	
Harrier	Multi-role fighter	U.K.	1969	650	8,200	No	9,14
MiG-29	Multi-role fighter	Iraq	1985	1,050	8,800	Yes	15
MiG-25	Air superiority fighter	Iraq	1972	870	6,500	Yes	
MiG-23	Multi-role fighter	Iraq	1970	970	6,600	Yes	
MiG-21/F-7	Multi-role fighter	Iraq	1960	740	5,800	Yes	10
Mirage F1	Multi-role fighter	Iraq	1973	580	13,900	Yes	16
Su-25	Close air support	Iraq	1981	750	9,700	No	

Type: The role this aircraft plays, defined by both the aircraft's design and how air forces decide to use it. Air superiority aircraft essentially only hunt other aircraft. Multi-role aircraft can both attack ground targets and other aircraft. Close air support (CAS) aircraft specialize in striking ground targets in proximity to friendly ground units. CAS aircraft tend to do poorly if caught in the air by a hostile aircraft. Strike aircraft are focused on attacking ground targets and have limited or no air-to-air capability.

Fielded by: The nation that employed this aircraft in this conflict.

First fielded: The year the first version of this vehicle was put into service. The actual version deployed for this conflict may have been substantially upgraded.

Typical radius: The distance the aircraft can usually reach and still return to base. This figure does not include aerial refueling, something most Coalition aircraft frequently did. These figures are approximations, highly dependent on flight profiles, specific weapons loads, and internal versus external munitions carry.

Maximum payload: Total weight of weapons, sensors, or external fuel that can be carried. This maximum payload figure could probably not be carried out to the distance listed under the typical radius section of the table.

Mach 1+: Can this aircraft go supersonic in level flight?

Notes:

1. Flown by the U.S. Navy, U.S. MC, and Australian Air Force, and based from aircraft carriers or airfields.

2. Known as the Super Hornet. Flown by the U.S. Navy from aircraft carriers.

3. First fielded date refers to this F-15E variant.

4. Two major variants saw service, the F-14A, and the F-14D, the D model having substantially upgraded engines and avionics. Originally, F-14s were only air-to-air, but they were upgraded in the 1990s with a ground-attack capability.

5. Carries its weapons in an internal bomb bay only, to preserve low radar signature.

6. Operated from both ships and airfields. Derived from the British Harrier.

7. Comes in several variants that carry a mix of direct fire cannons (e.g., 20mm, 40mm, 105mm) that fire out of the side of the aircraft as it flies slow banking turns.

8. Can carry dumb bombs, laser-guided and GPS-guided bombs, and the air force's CALCM cruise missile.

9. Can operate from ships but did not in this conflict.

10. The F-7 variant is a Chinese copy of the MiG-21 and has been widely exported to Third World air forces.

11. The recent addition of equipment that allows the F3 to detect enemy radar sites and engage with Alarm anti-radiation missiles has turned this formerly pure air superiority fighter into a multi-role platform.

12. In addition to under-wing munitions it also carries a very powerful 7-barrel 30mm gatling gun. The A-10 is heavily armored against ground fire.

13. Falls in between the B-2 and B-52 on the stealth scale while having a supersonic capability both lack.

14. Can land and take off vertically if needed.

15. The best fighter in the Iraqi inventory. In the 1991 Gulf War five MiG-29s were lost in duels with F-15Cs without any U.S. losses.

16. French-made.

Sources: See Table 1.

5. Reconnaissance and Support Aircraft

Name	Type	Fielded by	First fielded	Typical radius (km)	Maximum payload (lbs)	Endurance (hours)	Notes
U-2	Reconnaissance	U.S.	1956	4,250	–	12	4
RC-135	Reconnaissance	U.S.	1973	3,300	–	11	
Global Hawk	Reconnaissance UAV	U.S.	2002	5,500 w/24hr loiter	–	42	3
Predator	Reconnaissance UAV	U.S.	1996	750 w/14hr loiter	200	29	5
Hunter	Reconnaissance UAV	U.S.	1995	125	–	10	
P-3	Reconnaissance	U.S.	1962	4,400	10,150	17	
EP-3	Reconnaissance	U.S.	1991	4,400	–	17	
S-3	Reconnaissance	U.S.	1975	1,750	7,000	8.5	11
E-2	Reconnaissance/C3	U.S.	1964	770	–	7	12
E-8 JSTARS	Reconnaissance/C3	U.S.	1991	3,300	–	11	13
E-3 AWACS	Reconnaissance/C3	U.S.	1977	3,300	–	11	14
EC-130	Reconnaissance jammer/C3	U.S.	1986	2,590	–	11.5	6
RC-12	Reconnaissance	U.S.	1988	925	–	4	15
EA-6B	Jammer	U.S.	1971	1,770	4,000+	4.5	7
KC-135	Aerial tanker	U.S.	1957	1,850	115,000 of fuel	–	8
KC-10	Aerial tanker	U.S.	1981	3,540	200,000 of fuel	–	8
KC-130	Aerial tanker	U.S.	1962	1,850	66,000 of fuel	–	8
VC-10	Aerial tanker	U.K.	1964	–	154,000 of fuel	–	2
C-5	Heavy lift transport	U.S.	1970	2,740	261,000	–	9
C-17	Heavy lift transport	U.S. /U.K.	1993	2,220	172,000	–	1
C-130	Medium lift transport	U.S. /U.K. /Aus.	1959	1,900	36,000	–	10

Type: The role this aircraft plays, defined by both the aircraft's design and how air forces decide to use it. The reconnaissance aircraft possess a mix of electro-optical, infrared, radar, and signals collection sensors to look for the enemy. UAV refers to unmanned aerial vehicle. Jammers interfere with some form of sensor or communications belonging to the enemy. C3: command, control and communications, think flying air traffic control tower. Several aircraft from Table 4 could be listed here. For example, the F-14 can fly recon missions with the TARPS pod. Table 5 is limited to aircraft more purpose-built and focused on missions listed.

Fielded by: The nation that employed this aircraft in this conflict.

First fielded: The year the first version of this aircraft was put into service. The actual version deployed for this conflict may have been substantially upgraded.

Typical radius: The distance the aircraft can usually reach and still return to the same base. This figure does not include aerial refueling, which most Coalition aircraft frequently did. These figures are highly dependent on flight profiles, specific weapons loads, and internal versus external munitions carry. In some cases the given radius figure includes a loiter time for that distance from a base.

Maximum payload: Total weight of weapons or external fuel that can be carried. This level of weapons loading is not the norm as range considerations are often more important. If an aircraft were actually loaded this heavily, range would be substantially less.

Endurance: How long can this aircraft stay aloft with maximum fuel and while flying at the most fuel-efficient speed? Primarily of interest for reconnaissance, C3, or jammer aircraft.

Notes:

1. Typical radius figure is for 160,000 payload. This aircraft has significant rough airfield capability.

2. The fuel payload for the VC-10 is a maximum total and does not factor in any set distance from its base for this offload to take place.

3. Operates at 60,000+ feet and thus above the reach of many air defense systems.

4. Operates at 80,000+ feet and thus above the reach of many air defense systems.

5. Unlike most UAVs, Predator can be armed with two Hellfire missiles.

6. Jams enemy communications in addition to collecting and analyzing them and acting as a flying command post. The EC-130 designation refers to several specialty aircraft based on the C-130 design.

7. Jams enemy radars and can attack them with HARM missiles.

8. Maximum payload figures are for fuel that can be offloaded at the typical radius distance. These aircraft can certainly fly much further, but greater distance reduces the amount of fuel they can offload to other aircraft.

9. Typical radius figure is for the maximum payload figure.

10. Rough-field capable.

11. Carrier-based aircraft that used to focus on the anti-submarine mission, but has since largely gotten out of that business.

12. Carrier-based propeller-driven aircraft with large external radar dome.

13. Based on the Boeing 707 airframe and carries a large radar housing under the front of the fuselage. Primarily tasked with detected ground targets at long-range.

14. Based on the Boeing 707 airframe and carries a large external radar dome mounted on the back of the aircraft. Primarily tasked with detecting enemy aircraft and coordinating the actions of friendly aircraft.

15. A rare army fixed-wing aircraft.

Sources: See Table 1.

6. Helicopters

Name	Type	Fielded by	First fielded	Typical radius (km)	Maximum payload (lbs)	Notes
AH-64 Apache	Attack	U.S.	1986	200	6,500	1
UH-60 Black Hawk	Medium transport	U.S. /Aus.	1979	300	8,000 or 11 troops	4
AH-1 Cobra	Attack	U.S.	1967	240	1,200	
UH-1 Huey	Light transport	U.S.	1962	160	3,900 or 10 troops	
OH-58	Attack/scout	U.S.	1969	230	2,000	
CH-53	Heavy transport	U.S.	1965	500	32,000 or 55 troops	
CH-46	Medium transport	U.S.	1964	120	4,000 or 14 troops	5
CH-47	Heavy transport	U.S. /U.K. /Aus.	1968	210	26,000 or 44 troops	
AH-6/MH-6	Light attack/transport	U.S.	1966	230	1,200 or 6 troops	2
Lynx	Attack/transport	U.K.	1977	340	1,800 or 12 troops	
Sea King	Medium transport	U.K.	1977	450	8,000 or 19 troops	
Sea King AEW	Airborne Early Warning	U.K.	1983	400	–	3
Mi-8	Medium transport	Iraq	1966	250	8,800 or 24 troops	
Mi-24 Hind	Attack/transport	Iraq	1973	160	5,290 or 8 troops	

Type: The role this helicopter plays, defined by both the helicopter's design and how air forces decide to use it. Many of the helicopters on this table operate from both ships and shore bases.

Fielded by: The nation that employed this helicopter in this conflict.

First fielded: The year the first version of this helicopter was put into service. The actual version deployed for this conflict may have been substantially upgraded.

Typical radius: The distance the helicopter can usually reach out to and still return to base. This figure does not include aerial refueling, which some Coalition helicopters could do. These figures are approximations, highly dependent on flight profiles, specific weapons loads, weather, and overall payload carried.

Maximum payload: Total weight of weapons, external fuel tanks, passengers, or cargo that can be carried. For a helicopter loaded to its maximum, range is usually shorter than that listed under typical radius.

Notes:

1. The AH-64D model deployed is a major upgrade from the A model. The D has a large mushroom-shaped radar mounted above the rotors that allows it to engage targets in adverse weather and in rapid succession. This helicopter is also better protected from ground fire than most.

2. Used by U.S. special forces.

3. Has large external radar dome, that folds down once the helicopter takes off, to detect air targets at long range.

4. Seen in many variants in army, navy, air force, and coast guard service.

5. Getting very old and dangerous for the marines that use them. Badly in need of replacement, as the delayed V-22 Osprey is supposed to do.

Sources: See Table 1.

7. Naval Vessels

Class	Type	Fielded by	First fielded	Displacement (tons)	Crew	Cruising range	Aircraft on board	Notes
Nimitz	Aircraft carrier (nuclear)	U.S.	1975	95,360	6,007	–	70	
Kitty Hawk	Aircraft carrier	U.S.	1961	81,990	5,627	8,000/20	71	1
Ark Royal	Aircraft carrier	U.K.	1980	20,710	1,051	7,000/18	22	
Wasp	Amphibious assault	U.S.	1989	40,530	1,147	9,500/20	38	4
Tarawa	Amphibious assault	U.S.	1976	39,970	1,067	10,000/20	26	3
Ocean	Helicopter carrier	U.K.	1999	21,580	461	8,000/15	18	2
Ticonderoga	Cruiser	U.S.	1983	9,590	387	6,000/20	2	6,7
Arleigh Burke	Destroyer	U.S.	1991	8,320	398	4,400/20	0	5,6,7
Spruance	Destroyer	U.S.	1975	9,250	393	6,000/20	2	7
Type 42	Destroyer	U.K.	1978	4,250	253	4,500/18	1	9
Perry	Frigate	U.S.	1979	3,660	214	5,000/18	2	
Type 23	Frigate	U.K.	1990	4,300	181	7,800/17	1	8
Type 22	Frigate	U.K.	1988	4,850	232	7,000/18	1	
Anzac	Frigate	Aus.	1996	3,600	163	6,000/18	1	
Darwin	Frigate	Aus.	1980	3,960	187	5,000/18	2	
Boutwell	Coast Guard Cutter	U.S.	1967	3,050	177	9,600/19	1	
Los Angeles	Attack submarine (nuclear)	U.S.	1976	7,100	141	–	–	7
Trafalgar	Attack submarine (nuclear)	U.K.	1983	5,200	130	–	–	7
Swiftsure	Attack submarine (nuclear)	U.K.	1974	4,900	120	–	–	7

Class: Refers to a class of vessels and not necessarily a particular vessel's name. For example, four Nimitz class aircraft carriers were involved in Operation Iraqi Freedom, only one of which was called *Nimitz*.

Type: The type of vessel, those with nuclear propulsion systems so noted.

Fielded by: The nation that employed this vessel in this conflict.

First fielded: The year the first version of this vessel was put into service. The actual version deployed for this conflict may have been substantially upgraded.

Displacement: A measure of weight for ships.

Crew: Total number of crew.

Cruising range: The distance this vessel can travel without refueling in nautical miles for a given speed in knots. For nuclear power vessels, no range is listed; limiting factors are crew fatigue and other stores. Nuclear powered vessels replace their nuclear fuel only after several decades in service.

Aircraft on board: The total number of aircraft on board, both fixed-wing and helicopters.

Notes:

1. Can embark up to 960 Royal Marines for short periods of time. Can employ Sea Harriers and Harriers though for this conflict it deployed with just helicopters.

2. Can embark 500 Royal Marines and 26 boat crew.

3. Can embark 1,900 marines, helicopters, and AV-8Bs.

4. Can embark 1,890 marines, helicopters, and AV-8Bs.

5. These numbers reflect the earlier Block I and II class Burkes, not the Block IIA. There were two Block IIAs that served in this conflict. They differ primarily in having +10% displacement and the ability to carry two helicopters on board.

6. Equipped with the very capable Aegis air defense system, which was designed to counter massed air attacks from both aircraft and missiles.

7. Capable of launching Tomahawk cruise missiles.

8. A modern frigate with very capable short-range air defenses but no long-range anti-air capability.

9. These ships provide the Royal Navy with its long-range SAM capability.

Sources: See Table 1.

8. Munitions

Name	Type	Fielded by	First fielded	Guidance type	Range (km)	Overall weight (lbs)	Warhead weight (lbs)	Notes
Tomahawk	Cruise missile	U.S./U.K.	1985	GPS/radar	2,590	3,200	1,000	9
CALCM	Cruise missile	U.S.	1980	GPS	1,100+	~4,000	3,000	3
Storm Shadow	Cruise missile	U.K.	2003	GPS	250+	~2,900	~1,000	6
ATACMS	Tactical ballistic missile	U.S.	1990	GPS/Inertial	160+	3,690	1,200	8
AGM-130	Powered glide bomb	U.S.	1994	GPS/command	65+	2,900	2,000	
HARM	Anti-radiation missile	U.S.	1983	Radar homing	50+	800	45	10
JSOW	Unpowered glide bomb	U.S.	1998	GPS	65	1,500	500	
Maverick	General purpose missile	U.S./U.K.	1983	IR/optical	25	660	300	
CBU-97 WCMD	Anti-armor glide bomb	U.S.	2002	Inertial	19	1,000	~900	6
JDAM	Unpowered glide bomb	U.S.	1998	GPS	15	2,000	2,000	1
LGB	Unpowered glide bomb	U.S./U.K.	1976	Laser	9	2,000	2,000	2
GBU-37	Deep penetrator bomb	U.S.	1991	GPS	8+	5,000	5,000	7
MOAB	Unpowered large glide bomb	U.S.	2003	GPS	–	21,500	18,000	5
BLU-82	Unpowered large bomb	U.S.	1970	Unguided	–	15,000	12,600	4
Hellfire	Antitank missile	U.S.	1986	Radar	8	108	~15	11
TOW	Antitank missile	U.S./U.K.	1970	Optical	3.7	50	7	12
Javelin	Antitank missile	U.S.	1996	IR	2.5	26	~8	13
Al-Hussein	Tactical ballistic missile	Iraq	1988	Inertial	600	15,500	700	
Scud-B	Tactical ballistic missile	Iraq	1962	Inertial	300	14,080	2,200	
Al-Samoud	Tactical ballistic missile	Iraq	1994	Inertial	150	–	–	

Type: Munition type.
Fielded by: The nation that employed this munition in this conflict.

First fielded: The year the first version of this munition was put into service. The actual version deployed for this conflict may have been substantially upgraded.

Guidance type: How this munition is guided, if it is guided at all. GPS: it uses the Global Positioning System of satellites to plot the munition's position relative to where it is trying to go. Radar: it tracks a target or its path to a target by radar illumination. Radar homing: it tracks the emission source of an emitting radar. Laser: a laser designator aims at a target and the munition follows that beam to the target. Command: a human directs the flight of the munition. Optical: an optical sensor on the munition tracks the target. Inertial: the guidance system tracks where the munition started from and where it is supposed to go and tracks its movement relative to gravity and momentum.

Range: Total distance the munition can travel on its own.

Overall weight: Weight of the entire system.

Warhead weight: Weight of the part that explodes.

Notes:

1. Comes in 1,000-lbs and 2,000-lbs versions, both with the same range. These are really just traditional unguided "dumb" bombs with fins and GPS guidance kits strapped on; very cheap (by precision weapon standards) and almost as accurate as a laser-guided bomb.

2. Comes in 500, 1000, and 2000-lbs versions.

3. CALCM: Conventional Air Launched Cruise Missile. Comes in several versions, all of which were converted over from Air Launched Cruise Missiles in the nuclear inventory. The B-52 is the only platform that can launch the CALCM.

4. First used in Vietnam; can only be dropped from a C-130.

5. Reportedly can be dropped from both the B-2 and C-130.

6. Air-launched from British Tornado aircraft.

7. Carried only on the B-2. For destroying deeply buried targets like command bunkers.

8. Fired from the M270 MLRS launcher. Instead of 12 standard rockets, two ATACMS rounds can be loaded. The range and warhead size are for the standard Block I ATACMS. There is an extended range variant (Block IA) that has a smaller warhead of 350 pounds but can reach targets 300km distant.

9. Can be launched from U.S. or U.K. submarines or U.S. surface ships (Burke or Spruance class destroyers, Ticonderoga class cruisers).

10. Homes in on enemy radar emitters.

11. Can be fired from various attack helicopters or Predator UAVs.

12. Can be fired from a range of ground platforms and helicopters.

13. Fired from a man-portable launcher. Unlike the TOW system, Javelin is fire-and-forget, allowing the personnel that fired the missile to move immediately after firing the missile. As the Javelin missile approaches the target it attacks from the top, where a tank's armor is thinnest.

Sources: See Table 1.

NOTES

Prologue: The Gulf War, 1991

1. Norman Cigar, "Iraq's Strategic Mindset and the Gulf War: Blueprint for Disaster," *Journal of Strategic Studies,* 15 (1992): 19.

1. The Origins of War

1. Con Coughlin, *Saddam: King of Terror* (New York, 2002), p. 156.
2. Quoted in Samir al-Khalil (Kanan Makiya), *Republic of Fear: The Politics of Modern Iraq* (Berkeley, 1989), p. 193.
3. Ibid., pp. 74–75.
4. Ibid., pp. 206–207.
5. Quoted in Con Coughlin, *Saddam,* p. 73.
6. Speech by Saddam Hussein, January 2, 1980.
7. Quoted in Stanley Chodorow, MacGregor Knox, and Conrad Schirokauer, *The Mainstream of Civilization,* 5th ed. (New York, 1989), p. 1052.
8. MacGregor Knox, "March-April 2003: The End of the Beginning of the Third World War," paper presented at the Commission on Globalization Conference on "National Sovereignty and Universal Challenges: Choices for the World after Iraq," Brussels, June 19, 2003.

2. The Opposing Sides

1. Colonel Andy Milani, "Pitfalls of Technology: A Case Study of the Battle on Takur Ghar Mountain, Afghanistan," unpublished paper, U.S. Army War College, April 2003, p. 42.

2. Quoted in Anthony H. Cordesman, "The 'Instant Lessons' of the Iraq War, Main Report," Third working draft, April 14, 2003, Center for Strategic and International Studies, p. 11.

3. Quoted by Crystal Carreon, "Plane Takes Heavy Fire, Limps to Safety," *San Jose Mercury News*, April 11, 2003.

4. Quoted in Samir al-Khalil (Kanan Makiya), *Republic of Fear: the Politics of Modern Iraq* (Berkeley, 1989), p. 169.

5. Quoted in Somerset de Chair, *The Golden Carpet* (New York, 1945), p. x.

6. Al-Khalil, *Republic of Fear,* p. 28.

7. Richard Hart Sinnreich, "Relearning Old Battlefield Lessons," *Washington Post,* April 24, 2003, p. A25.

3. The Ground Campaign in Southern Iraq

1. Evan Wright, "The Killer Elite," *Rolling Stone,* pt. 1, June 26, 2003, p. 58.

2. Roger Roy, "Simply Semper Fi," *Orlando Sentinel,* April 27, 2003.

3. Quoted in Robin Gedye, "'Mujahideen' Lead Fierce Fighting," *London Daily Telegraph,* April 11, 2003.

4. Quoted in Gina Cavallaro, "Battle for Nasiriyah: Leathernecks of 1/2 Ran into a Buzz Saw and the Bloodiest Day of the War," *Marine Corps Times,* May 12, 2003.

5. Ibid.

6. Major Jamie Cox, "Callsign 'Deadly'—Snakes in the Attack: A Personal Account of an AH-1W Pilot during the War with Iraq," unpublished manuscript.

7. Wright, "The Killer Elite," part 1, p. 64.

8. *The Daily Telegraph: War on Saddam* (London, 2003), p. 112.

4. The British War in the South

1. Major Jamie Cox, Operations Officer, Marine Light/Attack Helicopter Squadron 269, "Call Sign 'Deadly'—Snakes in the Attack: A Personal Account of an AH-1W Pilot during the War with Iraq," unpublished manuscript.

2. Sgt. W. Morris, "No Bridge Too Far: An Nasiriyah, Iraq 22–25 March 2003," *The Gunner,* June 2003, p. 5.

3. Christopher Hitchins, *Regime Change* (London, 2003), p. 103. As Hitchins notes, Majid was accurate about the international community.

4. Richard Norton-Taylor and Rory McCarthy, "Scots Guards Destroy Fourteen Iraqi Tanks in Confrontation," *Guardian*, March 28, 2003.

5. Martin Bentham, "British Snipers, Baath Stoolies Chip at Basra," *Daily Telegraph*, website, April 4, 2003.

6. Ibid.

7. Quoted in ibid.

8. Keith B. Richburg, "British Use Raids to Wear Down Iraqi Fighters," *Washington Post*, April 3, 2003, p. A25.

5. THE AIR WAR

1. Quoted in David A. Fughum, "New Bag of Tricks," *Aviation Week and Space Technology*, April 2, 2003, p. 22.

2. Ibid.

3. Colonel Andy Milani, "Pitfalls of Technology: A Case Study of the Battle on Takur Ghar Mountain, Afghanistan," unpublished paper, U.S. Army War College, April 2003.

4. Quoted in Stewart Payne, "Tornadoes Lead the Way for Blitz on Saddam Command," *Daily Telegraph*, March 22, 2003.

5. Quoted in Bradley Graham and Vernon Loeb, "An Air War of Might, Coordination, and Risks," *Washington Post*, April 27, 2003, p. A1.

6. Quoted in Anthony Shadid, "In Shift, Air War Targets Communications Facilities," *Washington Post*, April 1, 2003, p. A1.

7. Williamson Murray, *Gulf War Air Power Survey*, vol. 2, *Operations and Effects and Effectiveness* (Washington, DC: Government Printing Office, 1993).

8. Quoted in David A. Fulghum, "B-1 Strike on Saddam: Acting on Intelligence from Baghdad, the U.S. Made Another Attempt to Kill Iraq's Leadership," *Aviation Week and Space Technology*, April 14, 2003, p. 28.

9. Nuha Al-Radi, "Baghdad Diary," *Granta*, 42 (1992): 209–229.

6. THE END OF THE CAMPAIGN

1. Monty Reel, "The Bridge at Samawah," *Washington Post*, April 4, 2003.

2. Quoted in James Kittfield, "Interview with Lieutenant General William Wallace," *National Journal*, May 6, 2003.

3. Quoted in William M. Arkin, "Good News from the Front," *Los Angeles Times,* May 11, 2003.

4. Evan Wright, "The Killer Elite, Part 2: From Hell to Baghdad," *Rolling Stone,* July 10, 2003, p. 59.

5. Robert Debs Heinl, Jr., *Dictionary of Military and Naval Quotations* (Annapolis, 1966), p. 329.

6. Quoted in Ellen Knickmeyer, "Marines within Four Miles of Baghdad," Associated Press Dispatch, April 3, 2003.

7. Jonathan Finer, "For Marines, a Fight with a Foe That Never Arrived: 'Heavy engagement' Becomes No Engagement," *Washington Post,* April 4, 2003, p. A28.

8. Quoted in Wright, "Killer Elite," pt. 2, p. 61.

9. 5th Regimental Combat Team, "Narrative Summary."

10. Peter Maas, "Good Kills," *New York Times Magazine,* April 20, 2003.

11. Jonathan Finer, "Troops Pause after Battle in 'Hell on Earth,'" *Washington Post,* April 8, 2003, p. A01.

7. MILITARY AND POLITICAL IMPLICATIONS

1. Carl von Clausewitz, *On War* (Princeton, 1976; rpt. 1984).

2. Ibid., pp. 108, 113.

3. Admiral William A. Owens, *Lifting the Fog of War* (New York, 2000).

ACKNOWLEDGMENTS
AND SOURCES

We could not possibly have produced this book without the extraordinary cooperation of a host of individuals at the highest levels of the American and British governments and the military organizations of those nations. As trained historians, both of us recognize that we have not written an academic history of the war. While we had considerable access to raw documentary material, the four months available to research and write this book simply did not afford the time to acquire and examine the massive holdings that will eventually become available to historians in the military archives of the United States and the United Kingdom. Instead, we had to rely on our previous knowledge and research in military history, which includes the Gulf War, as a framework for interpreting the interviews, documentary evidence, and reports of embedded journalists who covered the conflict.

The embedding of reporters and photographers may prove more valuable in the future to historians—at least those writing about real people—than all the electronic data collected about this war. The embedded journalists captured the smell and feel of events they were covering, and these descriptions and images convey as much as the cold, dry documents produced by military organizations. When journalists offered a glimpse into the activities of soldiers and marines in combat, we have relied on their work to make our story something more than a dry tale of operational maneuver. We also had access to a considerable number of situation reports (sitreps in military terminology) and after-action reports, but by and large such documents provide single flashes of light in the darkness.

The most useful aids to us in our effort to develop a coherent story line were the numerous interviews we conducted with senior military leaders, staff officers, and combat commanders. Those whom we interviewed made every effort to present their experiences as accurately as humanly possible. In the final analysis, of course, it was our responsibility to put together the many complex pieces we gathered into a narrative that shed light on the whole war.

In particular, we would like to thank General Michael W. Hagee, Commandant of the U.S. Marine Corps, and General Jack Keane, Vice Chief of Staff of the U.S. Army, for their efforts to ensure that their organizations helped us to the greatest extent possible. Lieutenant General Edward Hanlon of the marine corp's Combat Development Command was also enormously supportive from the onset. Partly as a result of their efforts, we had the privilege of interviewing leading military figures in the campaign as well as a number of those who planned the war. Some of these individuals have asked to remain anonymous, and we have honored those requests in both the text and in these acknowledgments.

Among the interviewees who proved particularly helpful we would like to express our gratitude to the following: Major General Jonathan Bailey, the British army's Director General of Doctrine and Development, provided access to a number of British officers who served in military operations in Iraq or were involved in military planning. Lieutenant General William Wallace, U.S. Army, V Corps commander, gave detailed and thorough answers to a number of questions we posed about the campaign on several occasions. Lieutenant General Jim Conway, U.S. Marine Corps, commander of I MEF, took the time during a hurried visit to Quantico to give us an in-depth interview concerning his conduct of MEF's operations. Similarly pressed for time during a flying visit to Quantico, and on another occasion, Major General James Mattis answered our questions thoroughly and in his usual self-deprecatory fashion. Major General Buford Blount, U.S. Army, commander of the 3rd Infantry Division, not only responded to an extensive series of questions but was willing to read sections of the manuscript to help ensure accuracy. Major General David Petraeus, U.S. Army, commander of the 101st Division, generously supplied information and insight about the activities of his division. Finally, Major General David Deptulla of the air force's Air Combat Command offered his usual perceptive views on how the air campaign had gone.

Outside of the combatant commanders, we would especially like to thank Colonel Phil Exner of the marine corps' Studies and Analysis Division for bringing together much of the information on which our description of marine operations is based. In the office of army's Vice Chief of Staff, Ms. Patti Benner was a crucial player in unlocking doors for us. Lieutenant General Paul Van Riper, USMC, retired, used his extensive friendships and contacts within the marine corps to get us the assistance we needed. Two individuals were particularly helpful: Lieutenant Colonel Frank Hoffman, USMCR retired, and Dr. Ken Finlayson from the special operations community. Colonel Greg Fontenot, U.S. Army retired, at the U.S. Army Lessons Learned Office at Fort Leavenworth was also enthusiastic and obliging.

We would like to single out our research assistant, Alec Wahlman, for special praise. Alec provided us with mountains of information from open sources, and that database was essential in telling the story of the Iraq War. He also pulled together the appendix on the weapons used in the war, which provides a framework for understanding the capabilities on the opposing sides. The maps were superbly prepared by Malcolm Swanston and Jeanne Radford of Cartographica Ltd.

Joyce Seltzer, who sponsored our book at Harvard University Press, deserves our deep gratitude for having faith in this project. In the editing and production phase, two individuals stand out. Lesley Mary Smith—with all the perception and intellectual ruthlessness that her Oxford education provided—read many of the chapters, and her criticism of syntax and word choice was always apt and helpful, no matter how painful. And finally, we want to thank Susan Wallace Boehmer, quite simply the best editor with whom we have ever worked. Fair, reasonable, patient, but always tough, Susan herded two sometimes truculent authors toward the goal of producing a readable and intelligent book. To whatever degree this has been achieved, she deserves much of the credit.

INDEX

Page numbers in italic type refer to tables.

helicopters, 271–272, *288–289;* deep
attack plan and, 104–111; drive to
Baghdad and, 200–202
Helmick, Brigadier General Frank,
235
Herr, Michael, 221
Highway 1, 101, 211, 220–222, 223–
227
Highway 7, 101, 220–222, 223–227
Highway 28 ("pipeline road"), 101
Hobart, Captain Karin, 106
Hoehn, Major Mark, 155
Holder, Colonel Donald, 5
Hoon, Geoff, 144
Hornbuckle, Captain Zan, 214–215,
216, 218
Horner, Lieutenant General Chuck, 11,
159, 170
human shields, 103, 147, 205
Hussein, Qusay, 36, 102, 146, 155,
203, 234–235
Hussein, Saddam: actions after Gulf
War, 9–10, 36; as Baath Party activist, 24, 25, 26–27; Bush arguments
for using force against, 41–44; execution of subordinates, 4, 15–16, 79–
80; goals for Iraq, 27–28, 81; Gulf
War and, 4, 8; invasion of Kuwait,
30–32, 54–55; Iran-Iraq war and,
28–30; Iraqi military leadership and,
79; misperceptions of U.S. by, 4,
236; political victory in 1991 and,
8–12; preparation for attack and, 96,
175; promises to fedayeen and, 222;
search for, 255; suppression of opposition by, 96; targeting of, 154–155;
use of chemical warfare and, 145–
146
Hussein, Uday, 36, 102, 155, 189, 203,
234–235

implications, of Iraq War: military,
241–251; political, 251–256
inertial guidance systems, 275
information dominance, 238–241, 244
intelligence: advance on Baghdad and,
203, 207–208; An Nasiriyah and,
125–126; Basra and, 153; ground
truth and, 156, 246; human, 153,
240–241 Iraqi nuclear programs and,
33, 41–42; stealth attack on Saddam
and, 154–156; tactical intelligence
and, 58
intelligence, surveillance, and reconnaissance (ISR) aircraft, 163. *See also*
Joint Surveillance and Target Radar
System; reconnaissance aircraft
interdependence: Goldwater-Nichols
Act and, 51–52; Gulf War and, 11–
12; joint leadership and, 61; modern
battlefields and, 242–243
interservice rivalry, 242–243
Iran: Iraqi invasion of, 28–30, 79–81;
Iraqi politics and, 188–189, 254
Iraqi military forces, 77–85; air defenses
and, 161–163, 170, 171; air strikes
on ground forces of, 181; fedayeen
in, 84–85; 51st Mechanized Division, 117; historical roots of, 77–79;
invasion of Kuwait and, 81–82;
knowledge about, 246; lack of cohesion in, 224, 226; morale in, 172,
174, 225, 230; preparation for war,
82–85; Republican Guard in, 83–84;
U.S. overestimation of, 8–9, 81; war
plan of, 100; war with Iran and, 79–
81; weaknesses of, 81–83, 191, 192.
See also fedayeen; Republican Guard
Iraqi people: assault on Baghdad and,
210; Baath party control and, 240–
241; Coalition assault on Baghdad